OUT OF THE BLUE

OUT OF THE BLUE

CONFESSIONS OF AN UNLIKELY PORN STAR

BY BLUE BLAKE

RUNNING PRESS
PHILADELPHIA • LONDON

© 2008 by Glenn Marsh

All rights reserved under the Pan-American and International Copyright Conventions

Printed in the United States of America

This book may not be reproduced in whole or in part, in any form or by any means, electronic or mechanical, including photocopying, recording, or by any information storage and retrieval system now known or hereafter invented, without written permission from the publisher.

9 8 7 6 5 4 3 2 1

Digit on the right indicates the number of this printing

Library of Congress Control Number: 2008926944

ISBN 978-0-7624-3388-9

Cover design: Scott Idleman

Interior design: Stewart A. Williams

Typography: Futura, Century Schoolbook, and Helvetica

Publishers Note: Some names have been changed at the author's discretion.

Running Press Book Publishers

2300 Chestnut Street

Philadelphia, PA 19103-4371

Visit us on the web!

www.runningpress.com

This book is dedicated to Harold whom without even knowing it made me a better person.

CONTENTS

PROLOGUE 1

CHAPTER ONE 3

CHAPTER TWO 17

CHAPTER THREE 25

CHAPTER FOUR 35

CHAPTER FIVE 61

CHAPTER SIX 97

CHAPTER SEVEN 109

CHAPTER EIGHT 119

CHAPTER NINE 131

CHAPTER TEN 135

CHAPTER ELEVEN 207

CHAPTER TWELVE 243

CHAPTER THIRTEEN 273

CHAPTER FOURTEEN 285

EPILOGUE 299

PROLOGUE

I HAD WANTED TO WRITE THIS BOOK for years, but never knew quite where to start, and more importantly, if I even had a story that people would be interested in reading. Friends and colleagues kept pestering me to get it written, saying what fun it would be to have my name in print so that every time I popped into the local bookstore, I could glow with the knowledge that an autobiography with my name on it was sitting alongside such literary classics as Jenna Jameson's *How to Make Love Like a Porn Star* or Ron Jeremy's *The Hardest (Working) Man in Showbiz.*

    The problem with my book wasn't the title. I had thought of a title years ago: *Confessions of an Unlikely Porn Star*. I liked it, but there was something missing. *Out of the Blue: Confessions of an Unlikely Porn Star.* Much better! It conveyed the surprise I felt about being admitted into the inner sanctum of the porn world. Not only being invited in, but rising rapidly to the upper echelons of porndom, being on first-name terms with such legends as Jeff Stryker, Ryan Idol, Chi Chi LaRue, Gino Colbert, Matthew Rush et al. I had known these people for years through the magic of video. Now they knew me and I let their presences wash over me . . . their foibles, their tantrums. . . . I took it all in, knowing one day, when

OUT OF THE BLUE

I had been cast aside, no longer buff enough to compete with the current crop of superstars, I would write a memoir of the adult industry—an exposé of the pallid underbelly of the Beast.

However, things didn't quite happen that way. They never do. After a successful porn career in which I developed a big, dumb blue-collar persona (I realized this sold movies), I retired after winning Best Actor at the Grabby Awards in Chicago for my work in a movie I wrote and starred in called *Men In Blue*. Of course I didn't retire, never to be seen again. That just didn't seem to be on the agenda. I retired from acting and created my own production company, Big Blue Productions. I decided to write, produce and direct my own projects without anybody's interference.

So here lay my dilemma: I wanted to write a tell-all book about the industry, but I was still smack bang in the middle of it. I have given this a lot of thought. Perhaps I will always be involved in the industry, writing salacious scripts when I'm sixty years old, asking nubile youths to undress in front of me so I can admire their creamy skin, forcing them to perform in front of my camera, giving me their most intimate parts of themselves, laying themselves bare for a piece of celluloid that will be forgotten in a year or two.

So then, when would I even get around to writing my book? Now seemed as good a time as any. If I succeed in capturing only a brief moment in time, it's still a part, from my point of view, that hasn't been captured before. Yes, now is as good a time as any.

CHAPTER ONE

"CAN SOMEBODY STOP that bloody Doberman licking Caesar's balls?" I yelled. Eddie, my makeup man, ran over waving his brushes in the air.

"Shoo! Shoo!" he shouted. The dog ran off with a pack of five others that had been lying in the shade of a large oak tree, a pack including three Labradors, a giant poodle and a mutt of indeterminate breed.

"I thought it was the caterer," shrugged Caesar, who had been in mid-thrust atop his co-star Dane Brando. I threw down my script and yanked at my thinning hair and for the tenth time that day wondered why I had ever even begun to attempt making a movie as epic as *Cowboy*.

I'd written a script about a bodybuilder named Cowboy O'Connor who drifts across America using his charms to survive, the beauty of his physique belying the cruelty in his heart. Then I rented a 400-acre ranch in California, owned by a former porn queen, and we went into pre-production for *Cowboy*.

I cast Caesar in the lead role, having already used him in one of my earlier movies, *Married Cops Do*. That one was about straight cops fucking each other. It made a fortune and launched the career of big, straight bodybuilder Duke Miller. Duke was a 280-pound Italian-American from Rhode Island. The night we met he told me over dinner how much in love with his fiancée he was. Later, in my guesthouse, I pushed every object that wasn't nailed down into his arse while he knelt on the bed watching straight porn—*Gang Bang Girl #13*. Cucumber, champagne bottle, baseball bat, I had them all up there, and I had a bad crush on Duke after that . . . for a week.

Caesar and Duke had been a winning combination.

This was now two years later, and Caesar was a superstar. He was perfect for the role of Cowboy: 6 feet tall, blond, blue-eyed, 230-pounds of pumped-up testosterone-drenched muscle. Caesar was bisexual and lived with a pretty blonde lady. Like so many girls of the new millennium, she got off on the idea of sharing Caesar with another man. I imagine it was better than sharing him with another girl.

Caesar was an icon in the gay industry alongside such names as Ryan Idol, Jeff Stryker and Ken Ryker; all of whom I found to be totally fascinating characters. I'd spent six months Off Broadway starring in the play *Making Porn* with Ryan Idol, and due to our severe differences I swore I would never work with him again onstage.

However, we almost crossed paths again after Ryan jumped out of a five-story window and broke almost every bone in his body the night before he opened in a new Off Broadway comedy. The producers of the show phoned me and asked if I would step into Ryan's role. They sent me the script. God, it was awful. No wonder Ryan jumped out of a window. If I was in the show I'd have been right behind him. Ryan, however, made a miraculous recovery and before I knew it, my cold glacial heart had melted, and we were both off to South Beach

CHAPTER ONE

together to perform *Making Porn* at the Colony Theater on Lincoln Road.

Miami was sensational. It was July and very tropical. Wall-to-wall Cuban men: my favorite. And we were stars, darling! We stayed at a fabulous hotel called South Beach Villas, owned by a very jovial millionaire called Joe Pallant. Ryan and I each had our own villa that backed onto a pool that was always 120 degrees for some reason. It was like queer soup when all the gay boys were splashing around in it. Joe employed a stunning-looking staff to run the place. One employee, Javier, a dark-haired, dark-eyed lothario took a shine to my friend Keith, who played my best friend Jamie in the play. I loved him. He was Italian, and his mother looked like Gina Lollobrigida. She came to see the show one night in a backless dress that exposed the top of the crack of her ass. She was seventy. I fell in love with her too. Meanwhile, Keith and Javier began a sweaty, intense love affair that ended badly when Keith had to return to Manhattan. Keith worked part time in a hair salon there, and Javier flew to New York to be with him. Javier had the choice of South Beach and his own villa or sharing a studio apartment in New York with Keith. Keith was left crying over the Vidal Sassoon shampoo bottles.

Our production of *Making Porn* in South Beach got rave reviews. Ryan's performance didn't. His reviews stank. Mannie, the producer, (a 45-year-old with braces on his teeth) gave us strict instructions not to show Ryan any of the reviews. One night some of the cast got drunk and cut out the reviews and pushed them under Ryan's door. Next thing we knew, Ryan turned into a raving drunk and on the penultimate Saturday night of the show turned up for the performance five minutes before curtain up. The show was sold out—350 seats, two shows—and Mannie raced around like a madman gnashing his braces.

"Where is he? Where is he?" screamed Mannie, as his boyfriend trailed behind looking every bit as skinny and pale as Mannie. They both lived in Detroit and Mannie's boyfriend was a secret transvestite. When Mannie was busy, his boyfriend would put on high heels and a g-string bikini and vogue by the pool to "I Am What I Am" by Gloria Gaynor. Occasionally Mannie would catch him and there would be huge fights between them.

Back at the theatre, just as Mannie was about to implode, Ryan strolled in the stage door from the street looking cool as a cucumber but reeking of liquor.

"Where have you been?" Mannie screamed. Ryan, who had been out drinking all day with friends, simply rolled his eyes.

"I'm here, aren't I?" he snapped.

"How dare you show up so late, disrespecting me, disrespecting your fellow actors. I should fire your late ass!" *Oh no . . .* I thought.

"No need to fire me, I fucking resign!" snarled Ryan.

"You can't resign! You have four more shows to do!"

"Then you fucking better know my lines," snarled Ryan. For a second I envisioned Mannie's naked skinny arse on the stage in South Beach where all those tanned, toned, unforgiving bodies would be horrified by the sight of his parchment-like flesh. I had never seen Mannie in daylight. He was like the living dead. His mother must

CHAPTER ONE

have married Boo Radley. Pushing that thought aside, I realized that Ryan had every intention of not doing the show. He shoved past Mannie and began throwing his costumes into a cardboard box. By this time the audience was getting ugly. They had heard how good the show was. This, coupled with hearing about how Ryan could lose it at the slightest provocation, had filled the theater to the rafters. They weren't going to be disappointed.

Ryan pushed his way through the curtains holding a box full of costumes, and the audience began to clap, thinking the show was beginning. Ryan stepped to the foot of the stage and said, "Ladies and gentlemen, there is no fucking show." With that, he stormed off. Mannie's anguished screams rang out in the theater. The tickets were selling at $50 apiece and we had two sold-out nights: a total of 1,400 seats and $70,000 down the drain. Mannie went nuclear. He phoned the Miami police and tried to have Ryan arrested for stealing theater property. They grabbed him outside the theater where Mannie met them.

"Tell him he has to do the show!" Mannie yelled at the cops.

"What exactly has been stolen?" asked a burly cop with great teeth and a big package. Amazing, even in times of trauma my libido was capable running wild. Of course, Ryan hadn't really stolen anything, so the police had to let him go. Mannie, humiliated, had to refund everybody's money, which must have killed him. I never did the play again with Ryan, which was a shame because by this time he had become rather good in the role and I had grown to appreciate his eccentricities. There definitely was never a dull moment around Ryan Idol.

OUT OF THE BLUE

My film *Cowboy* was shot in the middle of a California summer. The temperature would soar every day to over a hundred degrees and we would be driven mad by the insects and marauding dogs. My cameraman was a sweet, talented guy called Andre Adair. He was skinny and blond and had arrived in porn via the UCLA film school. He was very soothing to be around, which was a good thing because if anything could go wrong on the shoot it did. The first day we arrived we were shooting an oral scene only. This meant there was to be no penetration between the two stars, Caesar and Rhett O'Hara. Rhett was an incredibly good-looking straight boy from Louisiana. A year earlier I had broken my leg in a bicycle accident and Rhett had applied for the job as my chauffeur and cook. At the time Rhett was working for an overweight psychic who raked in $500 an hour doing psychic readings over the phone! The psychic wore a white afro wig, which he insisted was his own hair, and only dressed in turquoise jewelry and different shades of white. I knew he was having sex with Rhett, so I think Rhett was glad to escape the clutches of this crazed swami, even if it meant cooking for and chauffeuring around a temperamental porn producer.

One day I was sitting by the pool, my leg in plaster, and Rhett was bringing me lemonade. It was an incredibly hot day and I said to Rhett, "Why don't you take a swim?"

I couldn't swim because my bloody leg was in plaster, so I needed to live vicariously. Rhett didn't need asking twice. He peeled off his clothes to reveal a tight firm body. He had been in prison once and his chest was covered in prison tattoos. He had the face of an angel but a

CHAPTER ONE

convict's body. When he took his pants off my eyes nearly fell out of my head. His cock was HUGE. Obviously the psychic's wig hadn't been on as tight as I thought. Fuck preparing me chicken casserole; this boy could be a big star. I signed him immediately. Yes he was straight, but so were ninety percent of the bodybuilders I used. It's called "gay for pay."

So Caesar and Rhett were scene partners on the first day of shooting. They both had to suck each other off in bed. There was a minimal amount of dialogue. Easy. The scene went well. They both had no problem cumming, and they handled what little dialogue there was well. The only problem was that Caesar had competed in the California Bodybuilding Championships the week before, and because of all the squats he had done in the gym to build up his huge ass, he had developed hemorrhoids. This prevented us from filming his asshole, which is what fifty percent of my audience wanted to see. He assured me that he was having them treated and that it wouldn't cause a problem for the rest of the movie. Famous last words.

The second day of filming didn't involve Caesar. We were shooting Tom Katt and a guy from Texas named Evan Taylor, who bore a strong resemblance to Richard Gere. Evan was very easygoing and so was Tom, but Tom just wasn't attracted to Evan. They were playing construction workers in the movie and Evan had to fuck Tom on a bulldozer. Tom had also just competed with Caesar in the California Bodybuilding Championship and had placed fourth to Caesar's fifth. Tom really should have won but due to the politics of bodybuilding he didn't.

OUT OF THE BLUE

Judges aren't going to award a star of gay porno a bodybuilding title. Years later Tom realized this and gave up the porno to become a priest. Tom was enormous—5'9" and 230 lbs. ripped—he looked like he'd been carved from granite. Evan had a nice body but nothing like Tom's.

We set up the scene and by midday we were ready to shoot. Because of the heat, we had to keep maneuvering the bulldozer to keep it in the shade. Of course, this made for lousy continuity. Evan could tell from Tom's performance that Tom wasn't really into him and that, coupled with the heat and the fact that Tom's ass was so huge he couldn't find the hole, meant we were heading for big problems. Tom was the bottom in the scene, and after they took their Viagra—thank you, Mr. Pfizer—we started with some ass-eating and dick-sucking. Perfect . . . both cocks hard and Evan licking Tom's muscles. After an hour of oral, we were ready to begin the fucking. That's when the problems began.

We tried every position: doggy, reverse cowgirl, limber showgirl. In porn, all the fuck positions have names. Everyone knows doggy. Reverse cowgirl is when your partner sits down facing the camera and you sit on his cock, also facing the camera. Limber showgirl is when you're both standing up fucking, and the fuckee has one leg high in the air so the penetration can be seen by the camera from underneath. This normally requires a "coochie light," which is a light that's held by the lighting guy underneath to illuminate the asshole. This can be messy, as lube and butt juice can sometimes spill out onto the lighting guy. Always be sure your lighting guy is a piggy so he doesn't mind. It's even better if he actually likes it.

CHAPTER ONE

We finally ended up with Tom lying on the six-foot high wheel of the bulldozer with my crew holding his legs apart out of camera shot. To achieve this effect I gave several Mexican day laborers $20 each to hold Tom's legs up and apart, since I had run out of crew. The Mexicans had been wandering around on the ranch and didn't speak a word of English so God knows what they were excitedly saying to each other. When you shoot porn you develop an attitude where you have no shame. You just want to get the shot. If my granny had been on the set I would have paid her to hold Tom's legs open. God rest her soul.

So here we were, Tom on his back on top of a tire, three Mexicans holding his ass open, a lighting guy holding the coochie light to light his hole, and an assistant keeping the marauding dogs away. We were ready to roll.

"He's too high in the air," stammered Evan.

"Somebody get Evan an orange crate to stand on!" I screamed . . . and I do mean screamed. A crate was hastily produced and Evan stepped onto it.

"I can't find his hole," he said.

"Spread his legs wider!" I shouted at the Mexicans. They looked at me with sunburned faces. "How do you say 'spread his arse cheeks' in Spanish?" I demanded.

"*Separe sus piernas para que su culo queda abierta,*" my makeup artist said. He spoke Spanish! Who knew? The Mexicans spread Tom's legs wider. Each leg must have weighed as much as a baby elephant and the poor Mexicans were sweating and getting a real eyeful of Tom's hole getting stuffed by Evan's cock. I'm sure selling raffia piñatas in Tijuana suddenly seemed most appealing. Tom was a real trouper as he lay there covered in Mexican worker sweat and still managed to remember his dialogue.

"Yeah, man, fuck me with that big Texan cock!" Who wrote this crap? Oh yeah, I did!

"Did we get all of that?" I asked Andre my cameraman.

"I think we're going to have to fake a good half hour of it," Andre replied. Faking it was when the models couldn't get hard so they would pretend to fuck. It happened all the time in the adult gay industry.

"OK, guys, give me some faking, and keep the energy up!" I shouted.

That night I cried myself to sleep. In all my years in porn I had never been involved in such a disastrous project. This movie, as well as costing a fortune, was going to ruin my career. I was directing the Titanic of Porn—not the James Cameron *Titanic* where Kate Winslet pretended she fancied the boyish Leonardo DiCaprio and Billy Zane ran around the deck in a bad wig—the real life 46,000 ton ship that sank with almost everybody on board, including the captain . . . me.

I woke early the next morning filled with trepidation. We couldn't possibly have a worse day than the day before, could we? As it turned out, yes we could. Caesar was bottoming that day for an amateur boxer I had found in a local gym and named Brad Rock. Brad was straight and had two little kids. He had a huge cock and the biggest balls I had ever seen in my life. He had very pale skin, very black hair, very red lips and very blue eyes. He reminded me of a malamute. He was incredible looking.

CHAPTER ONE

Brad had starred in my film *Hard as Rock*, and was quickly becoming a big star. He was supposed to be fucking Caesar. My deal with Caesar was for him to appear in three scenes in the film. One oral with Rhett O'Hara, one fucking Dane Brando and another where he got fucked by Brad Rock. He swore to me his hemorrhoids would be healed in time for him to get fucked by Brad, and I had no choice but to believe him. We all arrived on the ranch and Caesar asked to speak to me.

"Blue, we have a problem." I knew exactly what he was going to say; in fact, as he said it, the words seemed to be coming out in slow motion:

"I caaaan't geeeeet fuuuucked." I could feel the top of my head about to explode.

"WHAT?" I screamed. "Are you trying to ruin my movie!?" My voice echoed around the ranch as the crew and the pack of dogs ran for cover.

"Hey, it's not my fault!" shouted Caesar—and it wasn't his fault of course. Caesar and I stood nose to nose with fists clenched. Andre, my cameraman, told me afterwards he was sure we were going to have a knockdown, drag-out fight.

"OK . . . " I hissed between clenched teeth, "This is what we are going to do. We are going to do the oral, fake the fucking, then when your arse is better in a week we are going to shoot the close-ups of insertion." This was a total fucking pain, but it was the only solution to this nightmare.

Everybody on the set agreed it was the only way around the problem and with the magic of editing it could be done. The only thing that worried me was that porn stars had a high rate of flakiness. In fact, the flakiness factor rivaled that of a piece of cod. And I was worried that either Brad Rock or Caesar would end up in prison or commit suicide before I could finish filming *Cowboy*. I know that it sounds heartless, but by this time my heart was made of granite. I had turned into Cecil B. DeBlake and nothing was going to stand in my way of finishing this movie.

"OK," I barked, "Caesar and Brad, you're down in that gorge and Caesar, you're eating Brad's arse."

"But I think I saw a snake!" said Caesar.

"Did Jennifer Lopez say that when she was filming *Anaconda*?!" I screamed. "EAT HIS ARSE!" The gorge was indeed full of snakes, but we kept them away from the actors by having Eddie, my makeup artist, throw rocks to distract them . . . well, until he passed out due to heat stroke and dehydration. It was 110 degrees.

The oral and arse eating went surprisingly well and we faked all the fucking. Caesar, as if knowing I was at the end of my tether, gave a superb performance and Brad Rock was at the top of his game. There is something extremely sexy about watching two very masculine, straight men kiss. So I made them snog each other's faces off. I always know when a scene will be hot because I get a hard-on, and believe me; I was gigantic in my pants watching these two studs go at it. I might even have had a wank behind the monitor . . . I don't remember.

Finally, after a week we were finished filming at that damn ranch. As we drove away, I noticed the pack of wild dogs fighting over a used condom that had been left behind in the dirt. Bon appetite, Lassie!

The final scene for *Cowboy* was shot the next day in

CHAPTER ONE

my house in Laurel Canyon. I had built a shower that could fit ten people, despite the fact that only two of us lived there. I had seen it in an issue of *Homes and Gardens*. All made of gothic tile it would serve as the set for a three-way between three bodybuilders: Staten McCormack, Ray Stone and Kelly Madison. They had shaved their heads in order to look alike because in the movie they were supposed to portray Caesar's father, cousin and uncle. They were all showering together in their underwear and then two of them would fuck Kelly Madison. Of course it was ridiculous because who showers in their underwear? But it just looked so sexy. They all had the same kind of bodies and apart from the fact that we ran out of hot water half way through the scene and everybody began to turn blue, everything went without a hitch. Perhaps the curse of this damn film had finally been lifted.

Years later we sold the house to the actress Julie Bowen. Before she bought the place she told me she showed her friends how beautiful the shower was by playing *Cowboy* for them and telling them to ignore the naked skinheads and just appreciate the beauty of the Ann Sacks tile inlays.

A week later Caesar and Brad returned so we could shoot the insertion shots. I had completely run out of money to carry on with this film. I couldn't even afford to pay the videographer's day rate, so I snatched up the camera and I shot it myself. As I lay on my back in the dirt and leaves while shooting Caesar's hole in a really tight shot so that it would match the rest of the footage, I prayed to God that anybody who bought the film wouldn't notice my amateurish shaky camera work. Luckily, Caesar's arse had healed and it came off without a hitch.

That night I replayed the entire movie in my head. I had put my heart and soul into the film so it bloody better make some money.

In the January 2003 issue of *Adult Video News* (the porn bible where all the latest gay and straight films are reviewed) Vincent Lambert awarded *Cowboy* a four and a half star rating out of a possible five:

"The much hyped and long discussed Blue Blake's *Cowboy* rides into town this month. And it is well worth the wait. . . . Blue Blake's *Cowboy* is a neat little thriller. It is lovely to look at. Has a meaty story line, good performances and, most important, hot man action. It is nicely edited by Michael Zen. We even like the catchy "Cowboy" theme song by Rock Hard (Maybe because it sounds like it was inspired by Madonna's own dancing-cowboy video, 'Don't Tell Me'. . . . Pre-noms across the board. . . ."

That year *Cowboy* was nominated for numerous Gayvn awards—the porn world's equivalent of the Oscars. I was personally nominated for three of those awards: Best Movie, Best Director, and Best Screenplay. Caesar won Best Actor, he deserved it. . . . I won bloody nothing!

CHAPTER TWO

WHEN I FIRST BECAME A PORN STAR and did interviews for the press, I would always be asked by the interviewer, "Was it your lifelong dream to be a porn star?"

And I would always look at them in astonishment and give the same answer, "Absolutely not."

It had never even crossed my mind. I was born in July, a Cancerian, one of the least appealing signs of the zodiac, at least to look at. I have a sister who's a Leo and I would always read her stars in the paper, pretending they were mine. Leos always get:

"Today is your day, oh beautiful Leo. Blessed child of the shining sun, you will have a day of public worship and everybody will bask in your beauty." A typical Cancerian quote would read: "Poor unfortunate crab . . . try to keep your chin up, trapped in your plain body." Well, I didn't feel like no damned crab, so for years I told people I was a Leo. I even shanghaied my sister's birth date, August 5th, much to the bemusement of my mother and the chagrin of my sister. Looking back at this, it must have been the start of the reinvention of myself from Nottingham-born Glenn Marsh to London-born Blue Blake.

Nottingham in the 1960s was a strange mix of Northern charm and gorgeous-looking people. For some reason, they say that the most beautiful women in England are

OUT OF THE BLUE

born in Nottingham. One of those girls was my mother, Jean. She had the look of Julie Christie but was 250 miles away from Swinging London, where perhaps she could have been discovered by David Bailey and become the next Twiggy. Instead she worked in a betting shop.

A betting shop, one of those foul British institutions where you take your hard earned wage packets and fritter them away on some losing nag at the 3:15 in Doncaster. Horse racing, dog racing . . . they'll take bets on anything. Betting shops always smell of cheap liquor, old men and cigarettes—thousands upon thousands of cigarettes. The walls are yellowed by nicotine and the plastic furniture is screwed down in case some drunk who's lost a week's wages picks up a chair and hurls it at the nearest cashier. They work behind heavy plastic screens, obviously for their own safety.

It was in this romantic environment Jean met Victor, my father. Victor looked like a young Robert Wagner but was as dumb as a box of hair. He was beautiful but cruel and self-absorbed. My mother, of course, fell madly in love with him.

They were married and seven months later I was born. We were incredibly poor or perhaps just very working class. Our first house had no bathroom. The toilet was outside at the bottom of the yard and we didn't use toilet paper but strips of newspaper torn up and hung on a hook. My father's mother would drown kittens when her cat got pregnant in the very same toilet. This lasted until I was four when we moved into a house with indoor plumbing.

My mother was eighteen years old and my father was

CHAPTER TWO

twenty when I was born. My parents' marriage was stormy from the very start. On their wedding day my father chased my maternal grandmother around the garden with a carving knife for not ironing one of his shirts properly. It was the shape of things to come.

When they'd been married for two weeks, Victor, who was perturbed that his tea was cold, threw a twelve-piece tea service through the front room window. The window was closed.

This was the final straw. Jean may have been beautiful, but she certainly wasn't stupid. She crammed as many of her belongings as she could into her mini-van and drove home to Mother. Grandma welcomed her with open arms. After all, she was still recovering from her own Olympic sprint around the rose bushes, with crazy Victor in hot pursuit brandishing sharp dinnerware.

My father was incredibly handsome and my mother was incredibly naïve. So, when he begged her to come home, she did. He promised he would never let his temper get the best of him again . . . until the next time. So began a cycle that would last the next twelve years. My father would have uncontrollable rages and smash things. Once, he smashed six dining room chairs and a dining room table.

From when I was ten to when I was sixteen years old, we lived in a large, detached house at the bottom of a *cul-de-sac*. I even remember the address, Twenty-eight Elm Tree Avenue. My parents had by this time made a little money through owning and running a fish and chip shop. The house was spacious and light and had a great staircase that ran down the center of the hall to the front door.

OUT OF THE BLUE

I'd blow up an airbed and slide down the stairs at what seemed to my adolescent self like fifty miles an hour.

I wasn't an easy child. I weighed nine pounds when born and had a shock of blond hair and blue eyes. Our next-door neighbors called me "killer" because I was always stomping around, getting into trouble. One time, my grandmother left me, foolishly, with her houseguest Lilly, while she went to pay the gas bill. She was only gone ten minutes, but when she returned the house was full of smoke and I was choking under the kitchen table. I had thrown every one of her velour cushions into the fire, along with my favorite teddy bear and all of my argyle cardigans. Strangely, I still to this day don't own a cardigan. I don't even like the sound of the word "cardigan." Any chance I got, I would throw things into her hearth. My grandmother was convinced I was going to be a fireman when I grew up. Personally I think I was just reacting to the madness that surrounded me as a child.

When I was five years old, I found a can of gold spray paint in the garage. And before you could say, "let's spray the living room gold," I had done it, everything: Sofa, chairs, TV screen, wallpaper, even my suede shoes. My mother came home and cried. She took me to a child psychiatrist who told my mother I was just a "free spirit." This was the Sixties; remember. Meanwhile, I had to be watched like a hawk.

Behind our house was an enormous sports field that belonged to the local Catholic boy's school. There was a running track, tennis courts; even a long jump and high jump pit full of sand where we would spend hours building sand castles. The field was about twenty acres, sur-

CHAPTER TWO

rounded by houses that backed onto it. In about ten of these houses lived children my age, and we all grew up together, one enormous gang.

There was Mandy Fob and her brother Grant. Both had some sort of blood disease, which meant they couldn't do physical education at school and didn't have to stand in line for school lunches. We teased them about having yellow skin. Children are cruel.

In the house next door to me lived my best friend Matt Palmer, his younger brother, Clive, and their older sister, Sharon. I remember Sharon was sexy and slutty and she'd let me finger her when we went to the local cinema. She'd pretend to be asleep. I was twelve; she was thirteen. Clive was eleven. He'd let me finger him, too.

In the house opposite lived Jan Rombie, who was an only child. His parents had him late in life, so he was really spoiled. He was given outrageous amounts of pocket money and bragged that he never had to brush his teeth. At the time, I was insanely jealous. I now realize he probably doesn't have a tooth left in his head. His parents were chain smokers and their house always smelled like a dirty ashtray. His father bred budgerigars in sheds in the back garden; very successfully, I might add. Every wall in the house was covered in rosettes which read: "Best in Show," "Best Beak," "Best Feathers," etc.

Jan's mother was a seamstress, so the house was always full of the noise of birds and the constant whir of her Singer sewing machine. Even so, it was a friendly environment, and an escape from the tense atmosphere in my own home.

OUT OF THE BLUE

Further down the road lived Patrick Cox and his brother David. Their parents were divorced and they lived with their mother. In their den, they had the only lava lamp I had ever seen and I would beg Patrick to switch it on when I visited. I asked my mother if we could have one and she looked at me as if I'd gone insane.

Also on the road lived Wanda Fleur, my first girlfriend. She had long, beautiful, shiny brown hair and brown eyes. I was madly in love with her from the age of nine. She also had the best collection of Barbie clothes I'd ever seen. We'd spend hours dressing her dolls in mini skirts and tube tops. It must have been so obvious to her parents that I was gay.

Further down the road lived Jennie Warmsley. We all called her Jennie "Wormsley." She never looked clean and their house smelled of Wendy, their pregnant bulldog, and the cigars her mother would smoke. My mother forbade me to play with Jennie, saying I would catch something. Jennie looked like Sissy Spacek in *Carrie*, sadly bovine. I realize, looking back on it, all my best childhood friends were cute. Even then I was drawn to the cute ones.

We were all about the same age, except my sister, Victoria, who was eight years younger. My mother would make me take her out with us, so she just automatically became part of our gang. We would pretend to make movies and I would direct and orchestrate the action. We always made action films. My best friend, Matt Palmer, played the hero because he was fearless and was constantly risking his life with the most foolhardy stunts. One day, I had him swing from a tree, holding on to a

CHAPTER TWO

burning rope, twenty feet in the air while we pretended to film it. We had no cameras. We were just wild kids.

MY FOUR-YEAR OLD SISTER would insist on playing the vamp . . . at four years old! At the time, it seemed very innocent. It now seems like kiddy porn, without the porn.

It goes without saying; we were obsessed with films. I went to the movies as often as I could. My local cinema was called The Futurist, and every Saturday morning all the children would run down to watch such classics as *Dr. Who and the Daleks* and *Herbie Rides Again*. I lived in the cinema. I was fascinated by the huge drapes which were all lit up to hide the screen in hues of blue and gold and red. I loved the coming attractions, especially if it was summer and a James Bond movie was on its way. In the movie *Diamonds Are Forever* there is a scene where Sean Connery is naked from the waist up, but it's shot to suggest that he's totally naked. He was so buff and furry-chested. I went home and jerked off every night for two weeks thinking about him.

The first grownup movie I saw was *Saturday Night Fever*. You had to be eighteen to get in and I was twelve. I went with a group of friends from school and when we snuck in it was like a religious experience. The following night, emboldened by my previous night's success, I went to see Joan Collins in *The Stud*; a soft-core potboiler full of women with slipper tits. This was definitely pre breast implants. After that, I was addicted to movies with an X certificate. In England "X" meant over eighteen only. Slowly the movies we pretended to make grew darker and darker until my mother caught us dressing

OUT OF THE BLUE

my sister in a polythene mini dress made from a bin liner. She forbade Victoria to play with us anymore saying she was too impressionable. The seeds in me, however, had been planted. I wanted to be a world-famous star. Whatever it would take, I was willing to do.

CHAPTER THREE

THE YEARS ON ELMTREE AVENUE FLEW BY. Typical teen years of studying, parties and long hot English summers. I was attending a local high school called West Bridgford Comprehensive, which had an amazing drama department and the teachers there encouraged my budding thespian talent. Before I knew it I had turned sixteen and left West Bridgford "High." In England, to work in the theater or on television, you need an Equity card, which allows you to belong to the entertainment union. You can't work without one, but they are incredibly difficult to get. However, once you have one the world is supposedly your oyster, and the easiest way to get one is by dancing in cheesy cabaret venues throughout the world. I was sixteen years old and ready to take the acting world by storm. The only problem was I needed that damn Equity card, but I knew just how to go about getting one.

    I started attending Clarendon College where I was taking 'A' levels in English literature and Theater Arts. My parents were divorced and I was living with my mother and sister. It was the time of the "New Romantics," after the punk era; and I drifted around dressed like Adam Ant, or in various costumes ranging from mad clown to pirate king. My hair was various shades of blue, green, purple and maroon.

OUT OF THE BLUE

To get my Equity card I had taken a job dancing at the local straight workingmen's club, The Musters Hotel, which was owned by two friends of my mother's, Sally and Rex Harvey. They had a cabaret room and every night along with the other resident acts we would perform with touring performers, bands with saccharine names like "Summer Rain," or female singers called "Brandy Delight." The female singers always closed their acts with Gloria Gaynor's "I Will Survive." It still makes me smile when I hear that song, and I've heard it sung a million different ways, mostly badly.

I danced on stage for three pounds every night wearing fake leopard skin trousers and a black silk kimono. I got a perm and was convinced I was the second coming of Christ. The audience was made up of truck drivers who would watch me dumbfounded as I turned cartwheels sometimes in satin shorts wearing no underwear. Each night I slept with a different straight trucker. It was paradise.

After a few months, Rex Harvey insisted I find a girl to dance with so that my act wasn't so homoerotic. Word had spread and the Musters Hotel cabaret room was now full of truckers and chicken hawks lured by my boyish figure. The atmosphere was unusual to say the least. I was at college with a girl called Angela Kelly. She was blonde and had 36D breasts so I asked her to join my act. She would dance in stockings and high heels and a matching mini black silk kimono. She would be perfect.

We rehearsed together to "Super Nature" by Cerrone. We had decided to make our act a little edgy. The lights would go up on stage and I would be gyrating on the floor in a silver Lycra body stocking. Angela would stride on

CHAPTER THREE

and proceed to grind her stilettos into my crotch, yanking at my perm. I would pretend to slap her face (we were learning stunt fighting at college at the time) and then we would simulate sex on stage, fully clothed. We called ourselves "Touché—The Touch Dancers."

The night approached when we were to make our stage debut. I had told my mother and she was bringing one of her best friends; a bricklayers' wife named Bernice, who always struck me as needing a drastic makeover. She looked like she combed her hair with a towel and had never heard of lipstick.

We had publicity photos taken with both Angela and I growling in faux leopard skin outfits, and they were posted for weeks beforehand on the coming attractions board at the cabaret.

We arrived that night to perform and to our astonishment the place was standing room only. It was wall-to-wall men. Surely, they hadn't come to see, "Fernando and his Performing Parrots." It slowly dawned on us that they had come to see us!

The evening started well. Rodica, one of the resident singers, started the show with, "I Will Survive." What a surprise. After that the band played a collection of show tunes. But the crowd was getting restless and various cries of "BRING ON THE STRIPPERS!" were being yelled. Strippers!? We weren't strippers. We were both sixteen, I weighed 160 pounds at six feet tall. My body was milk white and I had never even heard the words "bench press."

Kevin, the *compere*, raced into our dressing room and announced, "You're going on early. It's getting nasty out there." Angela was fastening up her stockings and we just stared at each other. "Oh, we'll be fine," I said. "What's the worst that could happen?"

To get on the stage we had to enter from a flight of stairs behind the bandstand that led to our dressing rooms. The lights dimmed and I went on first to take my position at the foot of the stage. I would be onstage on my own for the first thirty seconds of the song. The lights went up and the music started and I began to writhe around on the floor. The air was heavy with cigarette smoke and testosterone and the pounding beat. Suddenly Angela made her entrance and it was as if all the oxygen had been sucked out of the room. There was a stunned silence, and then the men were screaming, standing on chairs, and grabbing their cocks. The shouting was so loud we couldn't hear the music, so our carefully rehearsed routine went out the window. Luckily, we were both used to dancing with each other so we improvised. Unluckily, the atmosphere sent us a little crazy and I ended up biting off Angela's stockings as she spanked me onstage.

The Musters Hotel had never seen anything like it. We ended the number and took our bows and that's when all hell broke loose. Guys were stomping on the floor shouting, "More, more, more, more!" but we had no more to give them. We ran off up the stairs, passing a scared looking Fernando grasping two of his parrots. That was when we heard the first crash. Someone had thrown a beer bottle at Fernando and his feathered performers. Then the whole place erupted. Chairs were thrown over the bars, fighting broke out, the air was full of parrot

CHAPTER THREE

feathers and cursing and Angela and I had to barricade ourselves inside our dressing room as the crowd rampaged throughout the club.

We were fired the next day.

My mother was pretty upset by the show after her friend Bernice said it was the most obscene stage show she'd ever seen. What did she know? She didn't even wear eye makeup. She didn't speak to my mother for years after that.

I, however—after getting over the shock of nearly being gang-raped by hundreds of truckers—realized I had hit upon an idea that could be lucrative as well as sate my desire to perform and to be involved in something where straight men would view me sexually. We could take "Touché—The Touch Dancers" on the road! But where could we perform such a risqué act, which was only really suitable for sexed-up men?

Of course . . . the troops in Northern Ireland.

Our act was perfect for the troops. We found ourselves an agent who specialized in booking cabaret acts for the army bases and we blew them away. They had never seen an act like ours. We added Sarah Brightman's song "I Lost My Heart to a Starship Trooper" to our act and, I swear, I would wear a gold lame one-armed cat suit and Angela would wear a gold toga and gold Lurex body stocking. The troops loved it! We were totally out there. Every time we did a show Angela fell in love with someone new. She was a sultry blonde and could have any man she wanted. Her breasts were like creamy pillows and she had a hypnotic effect on all guys within ten feet of her. I always thought she'd become a huge star. Instead, a few years later, she got pregnant, had a baby she named Joe and moved back in with her Mum and Dad.

The troops were very appreciative. They were risking their lives practically every day fighting against the I.R.A. For entertainment, various cabaret acts would come over from England and perform for them, though none as sexually charged as Angela and me. Also, the soldiers were gorgeous! Really handsome, healthy guys who were incredibly grateful and friendly. I had sex with as many as I could persuade . . . which wasn't very many. So did Angela.

Touché broke up when Angela got a job singing in a Nottingham nightclub called "The Palais de Dance." She had a great voice, and she wanted to be a singer, so she got a job with the Michael Miller Band covering chart hits of the day. This left me with no income and I was still attending college. Angela owed me one. I had helped her get her Equity card and that was a big deal. So she got me an audition to be a dancer with the Michael Miller Band, the first dancer they had ever had. Michael was a really nice guy—in his forties, going bald with lousy teeth, but a really great guy. I auditioned to a song called "Dance Yourself Dizzy." It was a number I knew his band covered. He gave me a job three nights a week: Wednesday (grab a granny night), Friday and Saturday. I was now a member of the Michael Miller Band.

The Palais was really famous in Nottingham . . . for being a dive. There were fights every night and they employed a dozen bouncers to keep the trouble down. It was full of women dancing around their handbags, with white stilettos and legs the color of Spam. They wore no

CHAPTER THREE

stockings. In those days, the guys didn't dance. It was considered too "queer." Instead, they stood around the dance floor, getting drunk on pints of lager and eyeing up the talent. Occasionally, a fight would break out and from my vantage point on the stage I would see bouncers materialize from nowhere to drag off and eject the rowdy youths.

The bouncers were so sexy. Especially one named Mike. He was a huge bodybuilder, and I had never met a real bodybuilder before. I was seventeen and had been dating a local butcher named John Glover. He was forty-four. My mother was freaking out. She didn't approve of me dating men let alone a middle-aged butcher. John treated me terribly, and he was shagging every gay boy in Nottingham under the age of twenty-one. He was handsome, blond, bearded, drove a Jeep and smoked Gauloises cigarettes. He was building a house and living in a caravan in his garage. I thought that was romantic. I was, of course, incredibly stupid. My mother, in a fit of panic, called the police one day and they warned John to stay away from me or he'd go to prison. The legal age of consent in England to be gay at that time was twenty-one. I was four years away from that.

That night at seven o'clock I waited for John to take me to dinner. Seven came and went and I thought he must have said eight o'clock. Eight came and went and vainly I struggled with the idea that perhaps he had said nine o'clock. I stood in the freezing cold but he never came. In fact, I never heard from him again. Years later he died of a heart attack in bed with his eighteen-year-old Chinese lover. It makes my skin crawl to think of what would have happened to me if I had given up my life to live with John Glover. And although I hated my mother for phoning the police at the time, I now understand completely. I was horribly young and John was trying to fuck me all the time. It hurt too much and I would make him stop. I thought I would never enjoy the feeling. As I write this I can smell his cigarettes and see his blue eyes. It makes me remember again that I was once in love with him. He must have been my first love.

To get over John Glover, I set about seducing Mike, the bodybuilder bouncer. Mike was totally straight and when he bent over I could see he wore briefs. I was madly in lust with him. I would sit on his knee between songs when the Michael Miller Band played something too slow for me to dance to. I would stroke his beard and tell him he was the biggest guy I had ever seen. This always works on bodybuilders. They want to hear how huge they are. Mike was twice my weight and I think if he had been capable of sleeping with me he would have done it. He was really straight unfortunately!

He gave me a ride home from a party one night. It was Christmas. We stopped outside my house and my heart was beating so hard I could hear it in my head and I could barely swallow. "Why don't you let me suck you off?" I ventured. Mike smiled, folded his hands behind his head and leaned back in his seat.

"I'm straight," he said.

"I know . . . that's why I want you so badly." This was a great revelation to me, and would be a recurring theme for the rest of my life. That he was straight made me want him even more. It was the thrill of the chase, try-

CHAPTER THREE

ing to get a straight man into bed, a straight bodybuilder bouncer no less. I had always been sexually forward. I think it came from growing up poor and, in the absence of toys, having only my own genitalia to play with.

"You don't want me," Mike teased. "I'm a fat old man." As he said this, he stroked his eight-pack abs through his shirt.

"Mike, I'm serious," I said putting my hand on his enormous thigh. "I won't tell anybody. I promise. I just want to suck your dick." He looked at me for what seemed like hours and then said gently but firmly, "Go to bed kid. I've got to get home and get some sleep." I never did end up having sex with bodybuilder Mike: the one that got away. Perhaps that's why I still think about him and how sexy he looked in his bouncer's tuxedo.

That year I found out I had been accepted to study drama for three years in London. A drama school called Mountview Theatre School. I applied for a grant from the local council and one day a letter arrived. I had a grant. I was off to live in London. I was eighteen years old. My journey had begun.

CHAPTER FOUR

COMPARED TO LIVING IN NOTTINGHAM, London was like living on the moon. It was still the time of the New Romantics and streets like the Kings Road were ablaze with new trends. Bands such as Duran Duran exploded on the music scene and my best friend Keith Burns and I would emulate their pretty boy looks. It's incredible to think back now and realize that every day we went out wearing eyeliner and lipstick. We were by no means transvestites; just totally in the center of the Eighties fashion explosion. We were good-looking young guys out to have a good time. The fact that we were enrolled at a drama school that encouraged such individualism made us all the more wild.

Mountview Theatre School is situated in a cozy area of North London known as Crouch End. It sits on a little hill and the residents of Crouch End are incredibly bohemian. I think because many are ex-Mountview students. We permeated the area with permissiveness. I was sharing a three-bedroom apartment with two girls, Sam and Jax, who were both fantastically blonde and sexy. Another recurring theme in my life would be my love for the company of glamorous blonde women.

Sam's real name was Melissa and her father was a wealthy eye surgeon. She was six feet tall and bleached

OUT OF THE BLUE

her hair suicide blonde. She had pouting lips, spoke with an upper crust accent and dated every beautiful guy in the school. To this day she is one of the sexiest women I have ever met in my life. Years later she fell in love with a wealthy stockbroker, married, and now has two handsome blond sons.

Jax's real name was Jacqueline. We had known each other in Nottingham from the nightclubs and I was mad about her looks and infectious personality. I never saw Jax wear anything but mini-skirts. She highlighted her strawberry-blonde hair until it was white. She had been dating a Pakistani called Ashiq. He was a bit of a villain and scared me at the time. He went to prison. Jax went to drama school—amazingly the same one as me. So of course we ended up as flat mates. Jax was a brilliantly talented actress.

One show we performed together at Mountview was the musical *Marat/Sade*. It's a hideous show. Set in a mental asylum, the Marquis de Sade gets the crazy inmates of the Clinique de Charenton to perform the murder of Jean-Paul Marat by Charlotte Corday. Sam played Charlotte, much to everyone's dismay, as all the girls wanted the role and another student, Jolyon Baker, played the Marquis. Considering Glenda Jackson played Charlotte Corday in the movie, Sam had a tough act to follow. She certainly looked better than Miss Jackson but the combination of the length of the play and the summer heat left the audience catatonic. It was mid-summer, the play was three hours long, and I was wearing a powdered wig and horsehair dress under the stage lights. I was one of the singers. A great role but it was too hot for

CHAPTER FOUR

me to concentrate. Jax had landed the grotesque role of the daughter of the owner of the clinic. Every night she would have to sit on the stage in wig and gown and watch the play performed. Unfortunately, at the end of the play the inmates would supposedly freak out from too much excitement and grab the owner's daughter and rip off her clothes and fornicate with her on the stage. We had to sing a song called "What's the Point of a Revolution without General Copulation." As we sang it we were expected to pretend to copulate. It was insanely bad.

One night while doing the show, we reached the climax when the owner's daughter would have her clothes ripped off and would be raped. Jax started crying and screaming, "No . . . no . . . I'm pregnant for God's sake!" *Excellent acting,* I thought, as we tore at her petticoats.

"She's very good, isn't she?" whispered another actor playing a lunatic with no ears.

"Tremendous," murmured another. "I especially like the bit about her being pregnant. Very moving."

Jax was in fact pregnant, by her Pakistani lover who by now had served his jail time. Who knew?

I remember Mountview Theatre School so vividly because I spent two and a half great years there. The first year was spent split into three classes: One-One, the intellectual group, all very serious, regarding themselves as the most talented; One-Two, the musical theatre group, wild and wacky, they regarded themselves as the ones who would become famous; and One-Three, students who didn't seem to fit into the other two classes. I was in class One-Two. So was Sam. Jax was in One-One.

Mountview's main school was based in a huge

Victorian building that had once been a private home. Over the years sections had been added on and when the school became too big to accommodate all the students, annexes were rented. Hence, every day Crouch End residents would be treated to a procession of young drama students traipsing through the town center, doing what they do best—being dramatic. I always thought we must have resembled a cartoon drawing of a cloud of dust with various arms and legs flying out as we whizzed by. The movie *Fame* had just opened at the cinemas and we were possessed. The school played it one night to a sold out audience and for weeks we would try to stop cars in the street to dance on them.

We not only had acting classes but various studies in historical dance, mime, circus performance and the class I hated most—fencing. Don't get me wrong. I hated historical dance too, all that whirling around in tights and a cape. But the saving grace was that the historical dance teacher had an enormous cock. You could totally see it through his tights. It was obscene, and I loved it. He wasn't hot looking, but he was my teacher and here I was staring at his huge cock as he danced a minuet around the room. I would have blown him if I'd had the chance.

Fencing, on the other hand, was taught by a grizzled teacher who looked like he smoked a hundred cigarettes a day. His claim to fame was that he had taught the sword fighting to the actors in the movie *The Three Musketeers*. I didn't give a shit, as I said, I hated fencing.

We had to wear white fencing masks and white jackets to prevent the foils from hurting us. They always hurt, no matter what. The straight guys in class were

CHAPTER FOUR

great at it . . . and the lesbians. It was strange. Half the guys in my class were gay or bi, but none of the girls. Then I found out years later there were several dykes lurking in the closet—all the girls who didn't dye their hair, wore sweatshirts and training shoes, and invariably got thrown out of school end of year for not being "colorful" enough.

All the staff was certainly colorful though. There was Babs, a fifty-something who taught voice and elocution. She was like some fabulous school madam who always wore tweed skirts, pearls and cameo brooches. She took us for vocal warm-up every morning. We would stagger into the 9 a.m. class, covered in last night's makeup (and that was just the guys). We were drunk every night but Babs never seemed to notice.

Dougie taught voice and acting. It was 1981, but Dougie wore skin-tight bell-bottom pants, flowered shirts and a purple paper-boy cap made of crushed velvet. He was *very* gay. The gayest person I'd ever met. He had never met a color he didn't like. He was also in his fifties and as bald as a coot. He wore clogs and platform shoes. I had wanted platform shoes when I was ten years old. My mother bought me a pair one Christmas. They were tan and orange. I could hardly walk in them. That didn't matter; I was ecstatic. They looked slightly girlish. My mother was always trying to cross-dress me. She once bought me a cheesecloth blouse and tried to convince me it was a boy's shirt. For years I had a pageboy haircut. Only girls have pageboy haircuts. I bet Dougie had a pageboy haircut growing up. He certainly still had the fucking shoes. I really liked Dougie.

OUT OF THE BLUE

But I really fancied Alan, our movement teacher. He was a hunk in his late thirties who wore a mustache and rode a motorbike. He was an unorthodox teacher. Once while demonstrating his non-skills in chiropractics, he cracked a student's neck, rendering him immobile for five weeks. The student had to walk with a cane for months. Alan wore tights and a white t-shirt and he had really beefy legs and a meaty arse. I wanted him to fuck me so badly, but he only had eyes for my roommate Sam. She flirted with him constantly. Sometimes the teachers had flings with the students. I know this for a fact because *I* had a fling with one of the acting coaches, Terry. He was married to a woman, so of course he was like catnip to a Siamese to me. Thinking back, he wasn't physically my type at all: skinny, in his fifties, going bald. He wore thick bifocals that blew his eyes up. We would meet at my apartment and I would cook spaghetti Bolognese for us after classes. I couldn't afford wine because my student grant meant I was living on 15 pounds a week. He would bring cheap wine and we would drink by candlelight and then we would fall into bed.

Jill Megiddo taught jazz dance. She taught me to dance and I loved her. She always wore her thin blonde hair scraped back and she was five feet tall. She had the body of a stocky boy and was married to a choreographer named Ivor Megiddo. Sadly she died of cancer at a young age.

I had natural rhythm but I was a club dancer. I had entered the World Disco Dancing championships in Nottingham and I came in last. They wanted us to dance to "Born to Be Alive," by Patrick Hernandez and I was so nervous and drunk on rum and blackcurrant that I fell

CHAPTER FOUR

off the stage while doing a cartwheel. I was wearing black rubber pants and a tiger skin shirt. I was a FREAK.

So Jill taught me to dance. I wasn't great. I was good. Good enough to get a job in any musical in London's West End if only I could have carried a tune. I couldn't sing a note. Nevertheless after *Marat/Sade* we mounted the musical *Grease* and I got the highly coveted role of Kenickie, the rough tough who knocks up the school slut Rizzo. I had a big number, "Greased Lightning," and I had barely begun to learn the song when the casting director realized what a mistake he had made. They took it off me and gave it to one of the chorus but let me stay in the role. "You can't have everything," said Keith, one of my best friends. That was rich coming from Keith, who *did* have everything and went on to star in *Les Miserables, Miss Saigon, Cats,* and *Blood Brothers.*

Despite my lack of vocal ability *Grease* was a hit, and the thrill of performing in front of a live audience made it very difficult to go back to school and start rehearsals for a play that was less entertaining . . . *Troilus and Cressida.* I played Troilus and Jax played Cressida. Pregnant. Every time I had to kiss her I could feel her ballooning stomach. She had to wear a long white nightgown that covered her blossoming figure throughout the production. Worse than feeling Jax's baby kick was that every night I had to break down and cry on stage. Another student asked me how the tears came so freely. I had no idea; perhaps it was just that the entire situation was very, very depressing.

I was broke. I had spent my grant too quickly on unnecessary luxuries . . . like soap. I was stuck doing the

OUT OF THE BLUE

lousy *Troilus and Cressida* and kissing the face off of my pregnant friend on stage. I needed a job badly. All I had in my pantry was a bag of sugar and a potato. Everybody was in the same boat at drama school. I was down to my last 20p when the phone rang in my flat.

"Hello . . . " I said flatly.

"Darling, are you still looking for work?" It was Tricia, a girlfriend of mine.

"Yep."

"I've gotten you a job!" she squealed. "Doing stripping telegrams! Dressed as Tarzan!" I could have passed out on the floor of my apartment either from shock or lack of vital nutrients.

I fell right into the work and all of a sudden I was loaded. I spent the summer break running all over London dressed in nylon leopard skin leg warmers and a leopard skin headband with matching loincloth. My body was a toothpick, but I had no shame. I would run into offices and scream and beat my flat bony chest. I would throw women onto tables and French kiss them to celebrate their birthdays, anniversaries and weddings with my arse hanging out the whole time. I got 30 pounds a booking, half of which I gave to my agency. I was ecstatic to make that much money. However, I still wasn't about to give up my acting hopes for singing happy birthday in a loincloth.

One day, while Keith and I were browsing through the jobs-offered section of *The Stage Newspaper,* the entertainment bible of every theatre person in England, I saw an advert for professional dancers to join the Olivier Briac Ballet. They performed all over the world.

CHAPTER FOUR

This was show dancing: topless girls with huge feathers strapped on their backs, sequins, g-strings and two pairs of false eyelashes.

"Let's audition for a laugh," I said. We did. The audition was held at the dance center in London's Covent Garden. Keith and I were the only two guys with forty girls, all over six feet tall and impossibly beautiful. They all wore high heels and had hair down to their waists. The showgirls taught us a routine that seemed to include every bone-breaking contortion known to man. It was difficult, very difficult. The routine ended in the box splits, which I couldn't do, so instead I did a cartwheel. For some reason they liked it. I got the job. Keith didn't.

I was in a dilemma. I was six months away from graduating from Mountview, but I was ready to leave and see the world. My third year was just a succession of rehearsals and performances, so what did it matter if I left and began performing professionally? I had been offered a three-month contract in Damascus with two weeks rehearsal in Paris. I had never lived outside of England so I was thrilled. I also loved Arabic men (this could have been the deciding factor). I went to see Terry Meech, my sometimes lover/acting coach. I told him I wanted to leave Mountview and perform with the Olivier Briac Ballet in the Middle East. He didn't try to dissuade me. He told me he thought I was ready to start my professional career and wished me luck. I left Mountview that day, never to return. Two days later I arrived in Paris to begin rehearsals.

My fantasies about romantic Paris were quickly dispelled. The place we were put up in was a fucking dump. We were staying in a small town outside of Paris called

OUT OF THE BLUE

Barbais in a huge fortress. The dance troupe was held prisoner while we learned one ridiculous dance routine after another. We were two boys and twelve girls. In no time we were taught "the song." It had no name but had been composed as a joke by some former disgruntled dancer and passed down from one generation of Barbais dancers to the next. It described the atrocious living conditions we endured in Barbais and it went like this:

Welcome to Barbais
It's a holiday . . .
If your life is too much fun
There's no telephone
No way to get home
You will never see the sun
Coffee takes an hour
Dare I take a shower?
Have some vinegar
Freeze in bed
There's a great big key
That can set you free
But you'll lost your mind
Instead
Eating shitty pâté
Everybody's ratty.

The first verse is self-explanatory. We had no telephone to contact the outside world. Our parents didn't know if we were alive or dead or sold into white slavery. We were never allowed outside because of the hectic rehearsal schedule and so our bodies grew pale and pal-

CHAPTER FOUR

lid from lack of sunlight. We had to boil water in saucepans for coffee but the gas ring threw off only enough heat to boil the water after an hour. The showers were filthy: full of old dancer hair and tampons. If you didn't drink coffee the only other alternative was horrible red wine that tasted exactly like vinegar. So after a hard day's rehearsal you had the choice of waiting an hour for hot coffee or a quenching glass of warm red wine. The dancers had constant headaches and dehydration. The blankets on the beds were threadbare and every night we shivered in our little cots. We were given a blanket and a sheet each. There was no heat. If this sounds like Hell, it was!

Every day, the choreographer, Guy Etrange, would arrive to bring us wine and pâté. We would hear the outside gate being unlocked by a giant key that hung on his belt. We ate the pâté from the fridge until one day we noticed an unusual sticker on the delicacy: a panting dog. Surely, we reasoned, they didn't make pâté for dogs. The pâté couldn't have been made out of dogs. So . . . OH MY GOD . . . we had been eating dog food that was meant for Guy's stringy looking cocker spaniels. We were ill for days.

I liked the fact that I was working with twelve girls and only one other guy. Kevin was red-haired . . . speaking of stringy spaniels! We didn't get on. I thought he was older than dust. I was twenty and he said he was thirty, but he was forty if he was a day. He had a French boyfriend who came to stay for a few days. We heard them fucking through the paper-thin walls. If Kevin hadn't been so skinny, it would have been sexy.

On the other hand, I loved the dozen girls. They were

all incredibly pretty and fun to be with. They had trained since birth to be dancers, whereas I had just auditioned for a laugh and had been thrown into the deep end. I cried a lot because I couldn't learn the difficult routines. They all had a theme and a costume to go with them. Of course the costumes were topless; it was that sort of show. We started with "The Parisienne." In it I wore a yellow crimpolene jacket and pumpkin crimpolene trousers. The jacket was covered with sequins and it matched the girls g-strings. We had to mime to a French song called "Ce Soir a Casino (Gala Night)." I never had a clue what the song meant as I never learned the words. One of the girls told me to just sing "Mickey Mickey Mickey Mouse" over and over again onstage, because at least my lips would be moving. I did until the assistant choreographer noticed and asked me if I'd gone insane.

The second number was called "L'Africaine." We wore—incredibly enough—monkey skins and nylon afro wigs. I refused to wear my wig after the first dress rehearsal.

The girls had a number called "Le Panthere (The Panther)," and all they wore were cat's tails, ears, and claws. They would sit on the stage and claw the air. I would run behind the stage, and as a prank, reach through the curtain and grip their tails so they couldn't stand up. I was reprimanded severely. We did the Can-Can, but most bizarre of all we would lip synch to "I Love Paris in the Spring Time," while we escorted the girls around the stage. I wore a Victorian suit, top hat, and tails in powder blue; the girls had on powder blue hoop skirts and carried lace umbrellas. Topless!

CHAPTER FOUR

Eventually, I learned all the routines and we received our first dance contract abroad in Damascus. At the time Damascus was at war, so we arrived in a war zone with every male under thirty mobilized and in uniform. I was in heaven!

The girls told me that all Arabs were bisexual and liked nothing more than to buy pretty girls (and boys) jewelry. I had no qualms about collecting some expensive baubles for myself. I liked older guys too, and Damascus seemed full of wealthy, older Arab men. The two girls who were the best at getting diamonds were Bouty and Kate. Bouty was very upper class and all big red lips, processed platinum blonde hair and cleavage. When she strutted down the staircase with the cutout of the Eiffel Tower twinkling with fairy lights behind her, grown men swooned. Kate resembled Barbra Streisand, but at show time wearing three pairs of false eyelashes, her hair in a ponytail down to her waist and 36DD breasts, she looked magnificent.

I hung out with these two and so was invited out for dinner after the show every night. The girls wouldn't sleep with the guys on the first night . . . but I would. I was given rings, bracelets, necklaces, suits, and I had a great time eating at the best restaurants in Damascus.

One time we were out with a guy who owned a huge clothing chain, Mohammed Massid. After dinner, Bouty and Kate went to freshen up their makeup.

"Glenn, do you know what wealthy men would do after eating a good meal, hundreds of years ago?"

"No, Mohammed, what would they do?"

"They would call for a hubbly bubbly and a young boy."

"Why the young boy?" I asked.

"The boy would crawl under the table and pleasure the gentleman with his mouth." Mohammed was married with children and the combination of him telling me this dirty story and him having a wife made my dick rock hard. He placed my hand on his penis and I could feel through his robes how huge it was.

"Would you like to pleasure me with your mouth, Glenn?"

Did he need to even ask? *YES! YES! YES!* My little mind screamed.

"Do you have anywhere we can go?" I mumbled. He smiled a big broad grin. Later I received the most beautiful suit, shirt, tie and shoes.

The contract in Damascus was for three months. After eight weeks I was becoming restless. I was sick of cavorting around in a monkey skin loincloth. The girls were sick of the Arab men, but I wasn't.

The laws in Damascus were strict about what you could or couldn't show of your body in public. No arms, no legs. This was difficult for the troupe to abide by as we were all young dancers and we were used to wearing minimal clothing both on and off the stage. The poverty outside the five star hotel where we performed was horrendous. The streets smelled terrible. Parents would leave children with no arms or legs on blankets to beg. The more glaring the deformity, the more money would be given; I suppose was the logic. On our day off we would wander around the gold stalls in the market. The most desirable currency in Damascus, husbands would buy their wives all the gold their hearts' desired because it

CHAPTER FOUR

was considered a great financial investment, a strategy to ward off the bleak poverty around them.

But more than gold was for sale. We were stared at wherever we went and men would constantly try to buy whichever girl I was with that day. We were blonde and blue-eyed in a country where that was exotic.

Meanwhile the work was stressful. The troupe's dance captain, Sharon Wagstaff, and I didn't like each other. She wasn't talented so everyone was convinced she had shagged her way to the top. The first time I met her was in Barbais. She was shorter than the other girls and had carrot-red hair and a runny nose.

"'Scuse me, I've got a sodding cold," she honked. "Fucking hell!" she said, eying me up and down. "You're skinny! Are you going to be able to lift me?"

"Not in this lifetime," I thought.

"And the other girls told me you're queer. Why do we never get any straight guys?" Sharon hated me. I had no idea how to do all the dramatic lifts that were demanded for a routine called "Les Musketeres," so she had to do the routine with Kevin. He was built like a stick insect and so she was constantly being dropped. He would spin her into scenery, banging her head on backdrops, all the while dressed in a velvet musketeer's outfit with feathered hat. She was topless, except for a lace collar around her neck.

I thought we looked ridiculous. The costumes seen close up were shabby and threadbare from being danced and sweated in for so many shows, ranging from Katmandu to Nepal. The audience loved us nonetheless, and we were sold out every night. The show was called "Paris à Sham" and it was situated in a huge brand new theater in a hotel called the El Sham Palace, the most expensive hotel in Damascus.

I started having an affair with one of the bartenders, Karim. He was a very handsome twenty-five-year-old with jet-black hair—very hairy, almost like a monkey. I would watch him pour cocktails before the show started. He had the fattest, hairiest arse and he wore Jockey underwear in straight-man colors like moss green and maroon. All the time we were dating he treated me like a star . . . he was sadly misguided. He fell in love. I didn't. I can still see his face and the look of shock the night I told him I'd been fired.

What happened was this. The show was divided into two acts. The second act opened with all the dancers doing a number called "Carnivalle," in which we were all dressed in carnival attire. I wore an enormous red sombrero covered with mirrors, a yellow satin shirt tied under my nonexistent chest, red chaps and a g-string. As we waited for the curtain to go up, we noticed that Sharon, Kevin and one of the other dancers were missing.

"Sharon says they're having a cigarette, hold the curtain," shouted Michelle, a northern girl with thick ankles and a bad perm. I loved her. I had to throw her over my head in the Can-Can. I always thought she fancied me, and if I had been straight I would have shagged her. If I had been straight I would have shagged all of them.

"How long are we supposed to wait?" asked my roommate Karen. "I've got a date after with Shireef."

"Shall I tell them to start the show?" I said.

"Glenn!!! You wouldn't dare," they all shot back, scandalized but hoping like hell that I would.

CHAPTER FOUR

"Curtain up!" I shouted. The music started and from our places in the wings we saw Sharon, Kevin, and Nicky running from the dressing rooms at breakneck speed, a trail of Benson & Hedges left in their wake. Sharon was in costume but still wearing a Marks & Spencer's bra. She couldn't get if off in time and so had to dance the first segment in a dirty gray nylon bra. I was laughing so hard I couldn't breathe. I spun off the stage into the wings and into the claws of Sharon.

"The girls said you ordered the show to start!" she screeched over the music.

"I'm sorry," I laughed, "It was just a joke." She slapped my face so hard I saw stars. I was in such shock that when I heard my cue in the music my feet carried me back onto the stage to finish the rest of the number. I cried throughout the rest of it. But they were tears of anger. I should have wrung her fat little neck. I felt humiliated. This was the first time I'd been slapped in the face. The rest of the show was a blur. I don't even remember finishing it. Sharon left immediately and was found later drunk in the rooftop bar.

"Nobody likes me," she cried. God, was that an understatement!

I was fired the next day. Sharon had phoned Guy Etrange and told him I was a disruptive influence in the troupe. I went to watch the show that night, if only to glare at Sharon. But I was spotted by the management and asked to leave. The day I left all the girls cried. They all hated Damascus and said they wished they could get fired too. Karim came to the airport with me and before I climbed on the plane he gave me a gold ring. He told me he would come to London. I wasn't sure if I wanted that but just smiled and kissed him goodbye. Six of the girls had also come to see me off. They cried and kissed me and gave me little mementos. We had become so close in such a short period of time. This was something I would grow to love about performing . . . community.

I arrived back in London with no job, no prospects and 50,000 francs in my wallet. I felt like the world was my oyster.

I had been back from Damascus for a week and was frittering away my francs on bread and cheese. I needed a job. I was also looking for somewhere to live. I had been renting a room in the apartment of a guy who was a headmaster. Every Friday night he would dress in leather and prowl the sordid leather world of gay London. He would wear a dog collar and skintight leather pants that laced up the sides of his bony legs. I had never lived in such close proximity to a leather guy before. His drawers were full of dildos and butt plugs and leather paddles. I know this because when he was at school I would forage through his things, just out of curiosity— kinky underwear and porno movies, fascinating for a twenty-one-year-old with an overactive libido.

He also had piles of porno magazines. Not the good American kind, but the badly shot British ones. All brick laborers with their trousers around their ankles, showing off their uncut wet looking knobs for the camera. I couldn't stop jerking off and looking at them. My favorite was called *Zipper*— lots of meaty guys with the occasional bodybuilder thrown in for good measure. They reminded me of the bouncers at The Palais in Nottingham.

CHAPTER FOUR

In one of these magazines, I found an ad for strippers in a male-only club in Soho. I tore the ad out and reached for the phone.

"Hello. Is this Boys-a-Go-Go?" I asked.

"It is," replied a voice that definitely wasn't boyish . . . more reptilian. I explained I was looking for a job and that I was a trained dancer.

"You gotta get naked," said Snake Lips.

"I could do that."

"Come for an audition . . . 2 p.m. sharp. Sixty-five Dean Street. Be clean." Be clean . . . what the hell did that mean? Did they employ strippers who weren't clean? I rifled through the drawers in the headmaster's bedroom and selected a leather jockstrap and biker's cap, very Village People. I threw them into a bag and ran down to the local tube station, Highbury & Islington, and caught a train to Piccadilly Circus.

In the mid-eighties, Soho was full of sex shops and seedy bars. All the shop windows contained blow-up dolls with yellow nylon hair and gaping, painted plastic mouths. Trotting through Soho I ignored the whistles of the East End Barrow Boys selling tangerines and suddenly I stumbled upon the rat hole that was to showcase my stripping talents . . . Boys-a-Go-Go. What a bleeding dump. Surely this couldn't be the right place. A grotty shop front with dusty string beads hanging in the window.

"Are you going to be a stripper?" I turned to face a skinny kid with shoulder-length greasy hair and a lazy eye standing in the doorway.

"Hmmm . . . I was thinking about it," I muttered, wondering if it wasn't too late to back out.

"Oooh, you'd be fab. I've been doing it for six months now . . . well, not counting the month I had to take off to get rid of my anal warts." He grabbed me by my arm. "My name's Gavin, but I changed it to Rock. Ya' know, like Rock Hudson. People tell me I look like him." I thought Gavin looked as much like Rock Hudson as the undertakers' dog, but I kept quiet and smiled.

"Oooh, you've got a gorgeous smile. Wilbert's gonna love you," he said.

"Who's Wilbert?" I asked, suddenly realizing that "Rock's" fingers on my arm were sticky.

"Oh, he runs the place. Come on, I'll introduce you, you'll get the job if you let him eat your arse in the basement."

Well . . . I thought perhaps Wilbert would look like one of the Barrow Boys selling tangerines, in which case I wouldn't mind a good rimming in the basement to relax me.

Rock dragged me through heavy, dusty curtains that must have given the old age pensioners asthma. As my eyes adjusted to the gloom, I heard a voice say, "Well, well, well, what have we got here?" I stifled the scream in my throat. Who would have thought an Orc from *Lord of the Rings* would be running a strip joint in Soho?

"He's here to be a stripper," said Rock.

"Yeah?" asked Wilbert the Ork. "Lucky for him Gustav phoned in sick. Syphilis again. You're on in five minutes. Do you have a g-string or do you wanna wear one of Gustav's old ones? It's not clean, but you could run it under the tap in the back."

"I brought my own," I stammered, holding up my borrowed leather thong.

CHAPTER FOUR

"Oooh, fancy! The queens love a bit of leather," said Wilbert, licking his cracked lips.

"Don't you want to know if I can dance?" I asked. Rock and Wilbert looked at each other and broke into laughter.

"Who fucking cares? You've got a knob, haven't you? Now get on that fucking stage, we've got a full house. Show him where to go, Rock."

Rock grabbed me with his sticky fingers and led me through more dusty curtains to a tiny room decorated with pictures of girls ripped out of various porno magazines.

"The other strippers use these to get hard," he said. "'Course if you're having a problem getting hard, I could blow you."

The thought of greasy-head getting his halitosis all over my pristine cock made Mr. Winky go from nine inches to three in a microsecond.

"I'll be fine," I said.

"Well please yourself," hissed Rock. "You're not that special. Get your leather on and when the music starts up, go through these drapes and you're on."

I quickly undressed and got into costume. I use the term costume very loosely.

"Gentlemen, do we have a treat for you this afternoon! For the first time Boys-a-Go-Go proudly presents . . . Hunter!"

Hunter? Who the hell was Hunter?

Rock poked his head through the asthma drape and hissed.

"That's you, cuntface! You're on!" All of a sudden, I heard the strains of Tom Jones singing, "What's New

OUT OF THE BLUE

Pussycat." I opened the lurex backdrop and walked onto a stage that was four foot square and covered in lumpy shag pile. The audience consisted of six rows of cinema seats full of old men in raincoats with their cocks out, jerking off in anticipation. I once read someplace that the walrus has the ugliest penis on the planet . . . they got it wrong.

I started to gyrate and the more I gyrated, the more the ghouls beat off. Now here's the strangest thing. I actually started to get into it and before I knew it, I was doing the splits up the side of the wall, bending over backwards and catching pound notes in my teeth as they were thrown on the stage. Wilbert had come to have a letch at me, presumably to see if I had a knob after all. I could see him through the gloom madly applying Chap-Stick with one hand and jerking off with the other. My thirty-minute set came to an end and I bowed deeply to scattered, very scattered, applause.

I exited the stage and Rock pushed past me to do his thirty minutes, wearing underwear that I noticed had a HUGE skid mark.

"You got the job," said Wilbert. "Four sets a day, five pounds a set and you keep your tips." I was thrilled. I would be making fifty pounds a day I reckoned. I whistled all the way home. I found the pervy headmaster waiting for me. He had discovered his leather thong was missing. I was caught red-handed. He told me I had a week to find somewhere else to live. I didn't care. I was going to be the next Gypsy Rose Lee and everything was coming up roses.

After a month however, I was totally sick of stripping.

CHAPTER FOUR

The club was a dump and strippers came and went by the day. Someone was always being fired for arriving late or too drugged up to perform. In those days I didn't even smoke pot, but I was a Bacardi and Coke fiend. I would drink it by the gallon and must have constantly smelled of rum. I had fled the headmaster's apartment and was now living in the East End of London, with a group of guys: "Dirty" Bob, David, and the two Chrises. We all shared a huge house with an Alsatian called Zeppelin that we hardly ever walked. When you *did* walk him, he was so ecstatic to be outside he would giddily bite people, willy-nilly, to show his enthusiasm. Needless to say, I started prowling around with him, scaring all the East End lads. I would eye up some rough piece of trade in Doc Martins and when he started calling me a "fucking queer" Zeppelin would growl and show off his big white gnashers. Sometimes I'd eye up an East End lad and Zeppelin would end up tied outside the local public toilet for an hour.

The house was owned by Dirty Bob and his ex-boyfriend "Camp" David, a huge queen. Bob lived in the basement with a sling, his poppers, and a tub of Crisco. He never smiled because all of his teeth had fallen out from taking speed for decades. David would go to the local leather bar, the Market Tavern, wearing chaps and a butt plug. They hadn't had sex with each other for years. Instead, they bought an enormous house in the East End and took in lodgers. The two Chrises and I were the latest batch of innocents.

Blond Chris had been educated at Eton. He was twenty-one and dating Geoff Posner, who produced all the Victoria Wood specials. Victoria Wood is an extremely successful British comedienne who made a fortune by commenting on the eccentric way British people live their lives. Geoff was short, fat and hairy but I wanted him because of his position of power at the BBC. I always fancied hanging out with Victoria Wood and listening to her opine on whether crimpolene was a more durable fabric than corduroy and the pleasure of draft excluders. In fact, years later I would date Paul Cianni who directed and produced the BBC show *Top of the Pops* and who bore more than a passing resemblance to Geoff Posner. Then of course, I got to stick it to Chris who was hanging out with Victoria Wood while I was being wined and dined by Whitney Houston and Jelly Bean Benitez.

Brunette Chris was a stunner and ran the weekly gay night every Sunday at Legend's on Piccadilly Circus. He had meticulous hair and knew more about hair products than John Frieda. I still can't apply hair wax without thinking of him. So the five of us were living in a five-bedroom house in the East End and I was boyfriendless until one night into the strip club wandered Godfrey Rayner. Godfrey was short, stocky, Jewish and Vice President of Guerlain Perfumes. The moment I noticed him standing there in his cashmere raincoat watching me dance, I fell in lust. Godfrey was forty; I was twenty. He took me to Marbella, Spain for a week and when I came back to the ratty strip hole I had been fired because Gustav the Syphilitic had returned to claim his job. I cried on Godfrey's cashmere shoulder, and then he said the magic words: "I'm moving to New York City, come and live with me in America." He didn't have to ask twice.

CHAPTER FOUR

I said goodbye to the seedy strip club and the crappy East End. The only one who was sad to see me go was Zeppelin the dog, who I heard after I left went crazy and bit off Dirty Bob's nose after Bob tried to make him sniff poppers.

CHAPTER FIVE

I HAD NEVER BEEN TO AMERICA, let alone NYC, and was bursting with excitement the moment I stepped off the plane. While I had seen NYC depicted in many film and TV shows I wasn't prepared for what a huge sexy city Manhattan was. Driving into Manhattan from JFK Airport my breath was literally taken away by the bold skyline that seemed to claw its way into the night sky. I felt deep down this was going to be the city of my dreams and I had an overwhelming sense that finally I had come home.

Godfrey had given up his job at Guerlain and was going into partnership with an old friend of his who owned a florist business on the Lower West Side. He had rented us an amazing two-bedroom apartment on Gramercy Park. In spite of the excitement of this new beginning, things were hard for me. I had no work permit and Godfrey didn't want me to go back to stripping, so money was tight. Every day I scoured the local newspaper for jobs that a twenty-year-old British boy could do that wouldn't offend Godfrey. That didn't leave me with many options. All was not lost, however, as we had great sex and played house. While Godfrey was at work I baked cherry pies, his favorite. But I needed to make my own money. I had started working at an early age and perhaps it was my lower class northern upbringing but I had a strong work ethic and I needed a bloody job.

One morning I saw an ad in the local paper for selling your blood for medical experiments. I called up the company, which was based just outside Manhattan, and went for an interview. I was told I would be living in a facility with twenty other guys from Monday to Friday. We were allowed home every weekend. We would be given a drug daily and once a week we would have blood drawn to see how it affected us physiologically. At the end of the six-week trial we would be free to go and paid 3,000 dollars. I decided to do it. I said goodbye to Godfrey and moved into the facility. Me and nineteen black guys. They considered me a rare exotic creature: British and white. There were five rooms with four of us in a room. Every morning they would inject us with a chemical and we would then spend the rest of the day eating and watching television. We weren't allowed outside. I watched *The Facts of Life* twice a day for six weeks. I became addicted. Was Joe a lesbian? Would Natalie ever get a date?

In the medical clinic we wore regulation blue hospital pajamas, like prison inmates. Thank God blue was a good color for me; it could have been tangerine, which looks great on black flesh but not on pale, skinny me. You were allowed to use the phone for an hour a day, and I would chat with Godfrey about how bored I was and how I missed him and a bottle of cheap wine, and not necessarily in that order.

My first weekend back, Godfrey bought me a gallon of chardonnay and all the ingredients to bake a cherry

CHAPTER FIVE

pie and tried to have sex with me. Immediately I drank the wine, threw the fruit down the garbage disposal and headed for "The Mineshaft." I should have guessed that this was the beginning of the end for Godfrey and me. The Mineshaft was an infamous sex club in Manhattan in the early '80s. Situated in Manhattan's meatpacking district, it was a warren of tunnels and rooms where every deviant act known to man occurred. You could get fisted, pissed on, or just plain fucked while the music pounded. The place smelled of Crisco and poppers and assholes . . . a little like Dirty Bob's bedroom back in the East End of London. I was a kid and curious but more interested in watching than getting involved.

"Do you like what you see?" a rough voice said to me in the darkness.

"Yes," I whispered.

"Suck my cock," Rough Voice said. He pushed me to my knees and I heard him unzip his leather pants. He held a bottle of poppers under my nose and I breathed in heavily. The world spun round as I took his enormous cock into my mouth. It dripped with pre-cum while he held the back of my head and slowly fucked my mouth. I felt his dick swell up and suddenly he was flooding my mouth with man-goo. He pulled away, zipped up his pants and was gone. I was left kneeling on the floor, choking, with a belly full of cum and an empty feeling in the pit of my stomach.

When I got home at 5 a.m. Godfrey was asleep on the couch. It was definitely over for us. I hated him for making me sell my blood and he hated me for being a financial burden on him. I returned to the clinic for the next

OUT OF THE BLUE

five weeks, picked up my check for 3,000 dollars and caught an Air India flight back to London.

While standing in line for my economy ticket boarding card, surrounded by turbans and the pungent scent of Indian spices, I reflected on my brief stay in Manhattan. Apart from flogging my blood and breaking up with Godfrey I knew in my heart of hearts I would return to the city that had held so much promise upon my arrival. The film on the plane was *The Man with the Golden Gun* dubbed into Hindi. I wept into my chicken vindaloo, missing Manhattan already.

I arrived back in London wearing a cheap leather suit that I had bought in the garment district of Manhattan. My only other possessions were what I could fit into a suitcase and a gallon of Bacardi from duty-free. I went to see my best friend Paul Shipley who was living in a house on Muswell Hill. Well, a squat really. He shared it with a variety of sordid characters but he had his own room with no heating. I had met Paul when I had been living with Dirty Bob and Zeppelin. We had bonded one night over a Marks & Spencer's frozen lasagna and a quarter tab of acid. Paul's dark features were the perfect counterpart to my blonde hair and blue eyes and I sensed from the moment we met we would be lifelong friends. I was right.

Paul loved Bacardi and Coke more than I did and that night whilst we warmed our cockles over a small candle in his cramped room he said to me, "So what are you going to do now?"

"I need a job . . . and somewhere to live."

"Well, you can stay here until you find somewhere."

CHAPTER FIVE

I looked around the tiny room and for the second time since I'd left Godfrey, I started to cry, only this time there was no plate of curry to catch my tears.

The next morning when we woke up I couldn't believe what a wreck I looked. The combination of the long harsh flight and the even harsher white rum had made me look haggard and ancient but I was only twenty-one, in fact that day happened to be my birthday.

"Come on, Paul, I've got $3,000, let's go and get a spa."

"Ooh, there's that new sauna that's opened in Camden Town called the Camden Tiger. It has a fifty man Jacuzzi, the largest in Europe. I read all about it in the back of "*Gay Times*."

"Perfect . . . let's go."

The Camden Tiger was situated in an old railway station on Kentish Town Road . . . five minutes from central Camden Town. It was owned by a woman called Alice and run by her two daughters and her three sons. They were Irish and crazy as loons, we would soon discover. Paul and I descended a flight of stairs, past murals of Bengal tigers peering at us through the long grass. It was very exotic in a vulgar way, and I immediately liked it. At the desk sat a good-looking red-haired guy who you could tell immediately wasn't gay. You just felt it. He had one blue eye and one brown eye. I took this as a good omen.

He smiled, "Hello, you two. Have you come for the job of masseurs? I'm afraid we only need one."

"Oh, no . . . " said Paul, "We're just here. . . ."

"That's exactly why I'm here," I cut in.

"Well, you're good looking, but are you qualified?"

"Am I qualified?" I laughed, "Ashtanga, Winky

Wonky, deep fondle, I do it all."

"Hmm . . . ashtanga sounds familiar but I've never heard of winky wonky and deep fondle. Do you have massage certificates?" he asked.

"Burned in a fire, unfortunately," I said. "When do I start?"

Paul, being my best friend, was by now used to my penchant for compulsive lies and remained silent.

"Well, we pay 30 pounds an hour and you have your own private massage room next to the sauna and we provide a uniform. . . . Could you start now? There's already three guys waiting. I'll show you around the facilities."

Fuck the facilities . . . three guys waiting!!! That was ninety pounds and if I gave them a blowjob perhaps a HUNDRED POUNDS . . . show me the money.

I had a blast at the Camden Tiger. I made more money than God, thanks to Victor and Jean's great genetics. After a month I was booked constantly. Being blonde and blue-eyed in Camden Town really paid off. I would let my clients eat my arse on the massage table and soon I got Paul a job as the handyman there. That was a disaster. Paul was way too good looking to focus on scrubbing toilet floors. One of his jobs was to take all the filthy, cum-stained rags—I mean, towels—to the local launderette three doors away. This was a disgusting job and I'm sure if we still had child labor in England it would have been given to some snot nosed seven-year-old. As it was, there was no more sticking kids up chimney pots, so Paul got to play "Orphan Annie."

Twice a day he dragged the dirty towels down to the launderette in sacks. He begged me to help but I was too

CHAPTER FIVE

busy eating bacon sandwiches next door at the "Strangled Swan" public house. The owner's daughter fancied me, and although she only had eight fingers due to an unfortunate birth defect, I would sometimes French kiss her, as I had an obscene craving for free pork products and beer, which eventually led to two appalling outcomes. The first was that I gained forty pounds and the second was that Paul didn't keep a sharp eye on our towels in the launderette because soon he was too busy drinking

Bacardi and Cokes with me at the "Swan" and the local gypsies from the encampment down the road nicked the towels out of the dryers. So the Camden Tiger ended up towel-less.

The reason I remember this so vividly is that the same day that the gypsies were running off with our fine cotton, I was massaging a 500-pound Member of Parliament. After doing a Captain Ahab on Moby, I went to get him a towel but the cupboard was bare. I ran to the front desk, "Alice," I said, "we have no clean towels left. I can't find one anywhere."

"Love . . . I know they were all stolen from the launderette by the local gypsies," she said. "Search around and give him whatever you can find."

The only thing I could find was a filthy hand towel straight off the bathroom floor that we had been using to soak up a leak in the plumbing system.

"It smells of piss," whined Moby.

"Oh it does?" I replied acting shocked. "Well, that will be ten pounds extra." He handed me the ten pounds and split, gripping the washcloth . . . dirty bastard.

"What am I going to do, Alice will kill me!" said Paul

when I discovered him five minutes later, hiding behind the sauna.

"Come on," I said, "I'll sort this out." I pulled on a pair of sweat pants over my massage outfit (a jockstrap) and Paul and I strode down the road to the gypsy encampment. Of course I thought it was going to be all girls with big tits having catfights in colorful gypsy scarves like in *Dr. No*. Needless to say, there wasn't a crystal ball in sight, just scruffy gypsies with no teeth and three-legged dogs fighting over empty potato chip bags. Why the hell did they need towels? They obviously looked as though they have never heard of water. As we strode into the encampment, a fat guy wandered over. He had brass teeth and was wearing a wife beater and a pair of old suit pants with the fly wide open and no underwear. I could see his pubic hair, which for some bizarre reason I found strangely exciting, considering how repulsive he was.

"What do you queers want?" he snarled.

How did he know we were gay? Looking back on it, Duran Duran was still big at the time and I believed, in my mind, I bore more than a passing resemblance to Simon Le Bon. Were the blond highlights and backcombed hair a giveaway? Paul also had big hair. *Dallas* and *Dynasty* were huge hits and Paul used a can of Light & Lovely lacquer each day on his hair, which he teased up until he looked remarkably like Dominique Devereaux.

Years later I was at a party for Liza Minnelli's 50th birthday—she had invited fifty of her closest friends to celebrate with her, so God knows what I was doing there. I was telling John Voight how much I enjoyed his performance in *Midnight Cowboy* when Diahann Carroll

CHAPTER FIVE

wandered over—Dominique Devereaux herself. The days of The Camden Tiger came rushing back.

"Miss Carroll," I gushed, "you look stunning! I have a friend who used to style their hair exactly like yours when you starred in *Dynasty*."

"Is she quite, quite beautiful?" Diahann asked.

"Well, actually, she's a he . . . but yeah, he's good looking."

Diahann flounced off and the rest of the evening was a blur. Red Buttons' wife Alicia Buttons came up to me and pressed a card into my hand.

"I breed stallions . . . if you know what I mean," she breathed.

I had no idea what she meant. Red Buttons glared at me from across the room.

After wandering around for an hour or two without even a sniff of "Sally Bowles," Burt Reynolds grabbed a microphone from off the stage and announced,

"Ladies and gentlemen, unfortunately Liza is feeling ill and won't be able to attend the party, but she sends her love to all her dearest friends." I didn't know Liza from Adam, but I nodded understandingly. As Burt walked past me, he said to Joan Collins, "I'm leaving . . . now!!" Joan Collins nodded her astonishingly young looking face and shimmied out the door with some thirty-year-old antique dealer she was shagging. I heard she later married him because although he appeared dim there was rumor that he had an enormous cock. He must have because she's still married to him. . . .

Back at the gypsy encampment, things were going from bad to worse.

OUT OF THE BLUE

"We want our towels back!" I demanded.

"We ain't got your fucking towels!" Brass Fang yelled.

"Then what is your wife drying those ferrets with?" I screamed back.

A huge woman with pigtails had appeared as if from nowhere, clutching two wet ferrets wrapped in one of our towels.

"Don't make me do something I won't regret!" He threatened. I knew this was one battle I wasn't going to win. I grabbed Paul and we flounced off in a cloud of Light & Lovely hair lacquer. The next day the gypsies fled with their ferrets wrapped in our damn towels.

It was at the Camden Tiger that I met my next boyfriend. Patrick was a real estate agent from Scotland. I arrived for work one day and Alice said to me, "There's a customer sitting in the sauna waiting for you."

Oh damn, I thought. He'll be in a bad mood because although this was a spa, the sauna hadn't worked properly since ten leather guys had a gangbang in there and the roof fell in on their heads. Luckily they were all OK apart from one guy with a mild concussion. But now using the sauna was like sitting in Uncle Jack's potting shed for all the heat it gave off. And why were ten leather guys having a gangbang in the sauna, I hear you ask? Because once a month at the Camden Tiger we threw an all night party called "The Sauna Club." Ten pounds to get in and once you checked your clothes in and got a free bottle of wine at the door it was an absolute ORGY! Paul and I handed out the wine but of course always drank so much that we constantly lost everybody's clothing tickets so no one ever went home with the right clothing. We

CHAPTER FIVE

were always cramming guys into taxis wrapped in toilet paper and linoleum matting. We had no towels to give people as the damn gypsies had stolen them and frugal Alice refused to replace them.

We had a Jacuzzi that seated fifty people. After the first party we drained it and found an inch of pubic hair and a turd—somebody had shit in the Jacuzzi . . . filthy swine.

So I opened the sauna door and there sat a handsome brunette with rugged features. He shagged me on my massage table and we fell immediately in love. As Christmas was approaching we agreed to spend it together.

Patrick told me he lived on his own in a flat in South London, having just broken up with his air steward boyfriend, a "trolley dolly" named John. I had never seen Patrick's flat, as I was working 10 a.m.-10 p.m. at the Camden Tiger and would stagger home alone exhausted to soak my raw fingers. However, Patrick came to the Tiger at 6 p.m. each night, and we would fuck on the massage table

"Oooh, he's gorgeous!" cackled Alice. "I'd fuck him myself!"

I was making a ton of money doing massages and I was booked solid. I was massaging ten guys a day in an underground sex den masquerading as a high-class sauna.

"Why don't you buy your own flat? Patrick suggested one night. He knew how busy I was so he figured I must have stashed the cash away.

"I wouldn't know how," I said.

"I'll show you, it's a piece of cake."

My own place!!! In London!!! Could I really do that? I started looking at suitable areas that would be fun to live in and finally decided on Earl's Court. Patrick proposed that I rent a place there first to see if I'd like it.

That Monday I took the day off with the excuse that I had to escort Sharon, the eight-fingered barmaid, to the local dog track as her pet whippet was running in the 12:30 and she needed moral support. She usually went with her butch lesbian sister Janice, who always wore men's shoes and trousers, but Janice had gotten into a knife fight at the local gay bar "The Black Cap" with a 6-foot-3-inch drag queen from Ethiopia called Skinny Winnie.

Alice grudgingly gave me the day off saying that Andrew, the assistant manager, could fill in for me. I went next door to the Strangled Swan and begged off taking Sharon to the dog track by telling Sharon I was allergic to canine fur.

"But I saw you feeding a Spam fritter to that three-legged gypsy dog before they fucked off with your towels," Sharon whined.

"He was hungry," I justified, "and desperately in need of nutrition."

She was right. I had felt terrible for the poor starved creature the day we had visited the gypsy encampment. So I bought a Spam fritter from the pub and fed it to the dog the same day.

"OK . . . OK . . . look, I'm going to look at flats in Earl's Court, I'm thinking of buying one. I can't live in that tiny room anymore with Paul. I adore Paul but all the other squatters are vegans and practically weave their own clothes . . . and Patrick said he would drive me around."

"Patrick, Patrick, Patrick . . . go on then, fuck off," she sulked.

CHAPTER FIVE

Earl's Court was known in the '80s in London as Kangaroo Valley due to the enormous number of Australians who lived there. The place was full of hard drinking, hard-partying Aussies and gay people.

I found a flat on Kenway Road above the Khal-Al meat shop and rented it immediately. Every time I flushed the toilet, my bathroom somehow smelled of meat. The flat had one small bedroom, living room, kitchen, bathroom and closet; but it was all mine. To get in you had to walk down a little alley and turn left, through a black gate, which was also the back yard of the meat company. Up a rickety iron staircase there were two flats. I had the lower one 16-A Kenway Road. I painted it white and bought furniture from Ikea.

I never did spend Christmas Eve with Patrick. He didn't show up on Christmas day either so I went crying to Andrew's house, clutching a bottle of sherry with Paul. Andrew spent the evening burning the turkey and telling me all men were bastards. I drank the whole bottle of sherry and passed out on the fake fur rug in front of the electric fire. I never heard from Patrick until years later when I bumped into him at the gay nightclub Heaven. "Sorry about that Christmas," he said. "The truth is, I had a boyfriend living with me, the air steward. I was seeing both of you at the same time and it just got out of hand. I didn't mean to hurt your feelings." Patrick's looks had dimmed and he had put on weight. It was difficult to believe he had once been so handsome.

I celebrated New Year's Eve that year with Alice, Andrew and Paul. Drunk on Pernod and black currant, Alice leaned across the table and said to me:

OUT OF THE BLUE

"Oooh, love, forget that bleedin' Patrick. I've got a great idea for the New Year.... I've been looking in *Gay Times* for business ideas and I've come up with 'Tiger Boys,' I'm going to open up an escort agency."

"Do you know anything about running an escort agency?" I asked incredulously.

"NO," laughed mad Alice.

"But who is going to run it?"

"You are!" she grinned.

In London in 1985, there were three gay escort agencies and five individual escort ads. Twenty-three years later there are three times as many agencies and about five hundred escort ads, not counting what is posted online. Back in the day the agencies and the gay escorts all advertised in *Gay Times*. One of the agencies was called "Number One."

A few days had passed and Alice and I were sitting eating cheese and onion sandwiches at the front desk of the Tiger.

"Alice, I have no idea how to run an escort agency," I said.

"Well, you wank plenty of men off in that massage room ... how difficult can it be?"

"What does that have to do with running an escort service?"

"Listen, I've got it all planned. You'll go for an interview with one of the agencies pretending you want to be a hooker ... I mean escort. You'll find out how much they charge per booking, how many bookings you can expect a day, and we are up and running!"

"Hmm ... I would feel nervous calling them."

CHAPTER FIVE

"I did that already. You've got an interview in Kings Cross in an hour."

"You called them?"

"Yes. I said I was your crippled mother and needed cash as I was bedridden. Try to do an Irish accent like mine."

"But I have massages booked. . . ."

"Ooh, love, Andrew said he would cover for you. The agency's called Number One and you're to meet someone called Jonathan. Here's the address."

The interview went amazingly well. Jonathan was a nice guy and told me bookings were 25 pounds for an incall and sky's the limit for an outcall. I could keep all my tips. Out of the 25 pounds, the agency got £7.50. So I would earn 17.50 pounds an hour—with tip probably 30 pounds. Jonathan told me I could do up to ten bookings a day and make a fortune. Hotel bookings could bring in as much as 100 pounds per hour.

"Are you top, bottom or versatile?" He asked.

"Hmm . . . versatile, I suppose, but I don't want to get fucked or fuck anybody without seeing them first."

"You can't be picky, you'll get used to it. Most of them want to suck your dick and, because you're young, eat your arse."

"Do you own the agency?" I asked.

"No, that's Andy. You'll never meet him. He's very secretive. An escort tried to stab him once after drinking methylated spirits, so now Andy doesn't meet anybody. You're not handy with a blade are you?" asked Jonathan almost suspiciously.

"No . . . of course not."

Jonathan looked me up and down then grinned.

OUT OF THE BLUE

"I think you're going to do really well."

I went back to the Tiger and reported back to Alice. She cackled with glee about how much money could be made and set off to the Black Cap public house to recruit escorts. Skinny Winnie had already told Alice he/she wouldn't mind turning tricks for the new agency but I severely doubted we would be retiring on the money made from an over-the-hill Ethiopian drag queen. Every time I went into the Black Cap it seemed to be full of speed freaks offering me "whiz" or drag queens. Good luck I thought, as Alice disappeared up the stairs.

Alice returned the Black Cap that night empty handed but drunk. She and I were at the front desk when the phone rang.

"Camden Tiger, Ben speaking," I said. Ben was the name I used for massage work.

"Hello, Ben . . . this is Andy," a business-like voice said. "I've got a 200 pound booking for you at the Savoy Hotel in half an hour . . . can you do it? I think he's an Arab."

I stood up, kissed Alice on the cheek and without a second thought walked out of the Tiger and into a whole new life.

Once home, I took a shower and searched through my meager wardrobe for something that would be suitable to wear to a fancy hotel. I had nothing!!! By this time I had stopped wearing all the new Romantic/Punk outfits I used to run around in and all I had were T-shirts and jeans.

I slung on a T-shirt and clean pair of jeans and prayed the security guards wouldn't think I looked like a rent boy at the hotel. I jumped in a cab and ten minutes later

CHAPTER FIVE

stepped out at the Savoy Hotel. My heart was beating a mile a minute. What if the guy didn't like me and sent me away and Andy never gave me a booking again and I had to go back to massaging hippos at the Tiger? All these thoughts flooded my head as I made my way to the suite on the 16th floor. I'd had no problem with the hotel security. I just swanned in like I belonged there.

I stood nervously at the client's door and knocked. Someone in the room could be heard approaching the door and I could tell he was now looking at me through the peephole. The door opened and there stood one of the most gorgeous Arabs I had ever seen in my life.

"I think I might be at the wrong room . . . I'm sorry," I said.

"No, no, you're Ben, correct? Please come on in, this is the right room," said Sexy Arab. "My name's Omar. You are extremely beautiful."

Well, this was going to be a piece of cake as the feeling was mutual.

"Did Andrew from the agency tell you of my problem?" asked Omar. FUCK, HE HAS A PROBLEM!!!

"No," I answered.

"Well, the problem is my penis is incredibly large and no woman can take it which is why I hire boys . . . but it seems most boys can't even get it in their mouths let alone allow me the honor of making love to them."

Was he joking? I was being paid 200 pounds to try and cram a monster cock into my mouth and he was apologizing! I had a massive hard-on.

"Hmm . . . oh dear, I hope I'll be to your satisfaction," I breathed, trying to sound seductive.

"Andrew told me you were a virgin." I burst out laughing and then realized he was serious. Quickly I tried to cover my mistake.

"Virgin . . . oh, yes, this is my first time," I stammered, trying to sound coy. "Be gentle with me, Omar."

Saying this, I ripped off his underwear like I was a wolverine and he was smuggling a baby lamb in his knickers. And boy, it WAS the size of a baby lamb! His cock was huge! I fell to my knees, stretched my jaws like one of those snakes you see on the Discovery Channel swallowing a pet poodle, and Omar fell back on the bed moaning with pleasure. He kept saying not to stop.

"Don't you want to fuck me?" I gasped.

"I'm afraid it will hurt you, especially since you are a virgin."

"Virgin? Oh, yes, well let's try. I think I can manage," I squealed as I did the splits on his cock like Olga Korbut on the balance beam. He felt huge inside of me and luckily he came immediately. I wasn't sure how much of that punishment I could have taken.

When I left that night Omar pushed five hundred pounds into my hand. FIVE HUNDRED POUNDS!!! I floated out of the Savoy on a cloud of cash. I had discovered my dream career. Andy phoned almost the minute I walked in the door.

"Omar loved you, he wants to see you again tomorrow night. And I've got another call for you in Shepherd's Bush. Can you be there in forty-five minutes?"

And that was how it all began. Andy would call me at least five times a day with bookings, and being so young and incredibly horny, I did them all. Of course, I

CHAPTER FIVE

soon realized that not every client was going to look like Omar or be as much fun, but I fell into the swing of things pretty quickly. If some ugly is sucking your cock, just close your eyes and think of that new sofa and voila! Ugly Gob turns into Mister Gorgeous.

After a couple of months of working, I still hadn't met the mysterious Andy. We talked frequently on the phone and he began to confide in me. He didn't have many friends, it seemed, and those he had were hookers that worked for him, many of whom had ripped him off by running away without paying him. I was young but I wasn't stupid. I always made sure he got his cut on time and I reported the exact amount the client gave me.

What I found so fascinating about the job was that I would meet all sorts of interesting men from all over the world. Invariably, they were successful businessmen who were married with children, exactly the type of men who turned me on most.

An interesting aspect about escorting is that a lot of the clients confide in you as if you were their psychiatrist. They would explain to me that they were secretly gay but had gotten married due to society's pressures and because it was expected of them. I learned over the years that there are tons of gay men trapped in marriages with wives who never know about their husbands' secret longings and desires.

Over the two years I worked for Andy I built up an enormous list of regular clients. Andy gave me a lot of work because I was extremely honest and didn't mind getting up at two and three o'clock in the morning to turn a trick. This, of course, got really old, really quickly. Andy was the type of guy that would call you up and say, "Ben, I have a booking for you. You have to be Italian."

"But, Andy, I have blonde hair."

"Well, can't you run down to the supermarket and buy a black dye and run it through your hair? He'll be at your place in thirty minutes."

If you refused, Andy would cut off further work until you apologized for not being more agreeable. He would toss you a few severely overweight clients as punishment, then you would return to the full time work until you refused again, then the whole cycle would start all over. So, yep, I was loaded, but I had no life of my own, being at the constant beck and call of Andy.

One day Andy phoned with a real surprise.

"Listen, do you fancy going to Brazil? To Rio?" he asked.

"With a client?" I gasped.

"No," a long pause. "With me, I was supposed to go with a college friend, but they let me down. So I thought maybe we could go together."

Now remember, I had no idea what Andy looked like and he only had a description of me from various clients. I felt put on the spot. Would declining hurt my chances of getting the better clients?

"Well, I've been buying a lot of clothes and furniture, so I don't know if I have enough cash."

"Don't worry about that," he replied, "I'll give you more work. So you'll have plenty of money to pay your expenses."

Hmm, Brazil. I'd never been, but it sounded fabulous and exotic and I loved Brazilians.

CHAPTER FIVE

"OK, let's do it, it will be sensational, we'll have a blast together," I gushed, hoping for the best in spite of my fears.

"Oh, there's one more thing. Skinhead Michael will be there with a client of his. The client's a paraplegic."

Skinhead Michael was another boy who worked for Andy. I had met Michael when he and I did a threesome with a client who wanted us to bathe him, powder him then put him in a diaper. It's a form of sex called infantilism and seemed to be very popular with straight, powerful businessmen. I was always popping down to Mothercare to buy diapers. I told the girl behind the counter I had an aged father who had bladder control issues so I needed XXXL and she gave me a discount.

Michael lived in a freezing cold apartment in South Kensington. By day he was a skinhead, and by night he was a drag queen called Maria Malapasta. He worshipped Maria Callas and his sole aim in life was to meet some ninety-year-old millionaire who would drop dead and leave him everything.

I thought even if I didn't like Andy I would have a laugh capering on the sands of Ipanema with Skinhead Michael, so I accepted Andy's offer to go to Rio de Janeiro.

"Darling, you must be simply insane! Do you have any idea what Andy looks like?" I was sitting in Harry's Bar in London with my friend Shakira, a thousand-pound-an-hour hooker. I had met her when Andy had called me and asked if I could fuck a girl while a client watched. I had fucked girls before but very rarely. Most of the time I had pretended to be drunk, which justified why I couldn't get a hard-on when I made out with them.

I explained this to Andy, but he told me Shakira was exceptional, a stunning Indian goddess whom clients paid a fortune to fuck.

The first time I met her outside the Dorchester Hotel, she climbed out of a black Porsche wearing a tangerine suede miniskirt, thigh-high suede Manolo Blahnik boots of the same color and matching lipstick.

"Darling, you're gorgeous," she shrieked. "Now don't stand there with your mouth open, let's take this bastard for every penny he has."

"But I don't know if I'll be able to fuck you."

"You're hilarious!" she laughed "Of course you'll be able to." She looked at me with Persian kitten eyes and stroked her waist-length black hair and I knew right there I'd have no problem.

She dragged me up to the client's suite.

"Cocaine?" he offered.

"No, darling, I never touch the stuff, but Ben will have some." Cocaine!!! I had never done coke before in my life!

"Thanks," I stammered. The client, who bore a striking resemblance to Mahatma Gandhi, offered me an enormous platter and a straw. There must have been ten grams on it.

"Help yourself, I'm going to freshen up," said the old man. He went into the bathroom. I reached for the straw.

"Are you crazy?" whispered Shakira, grabbing the straw from my hand. Saying this, she opened up her purse, took out a jiffy bag and poured in the whole plate. "We can sell it to a friend of mine," she laughed, "I'll give you half the cash." She rubbed some onto her teeth as the bathroom door opened.

CHAPTER FIVE

"What happened to the coke?" gasped Mahatma.

"Poor Ben . . . he has a dreadful habit . . . shall we start with you licking my pussy, and has anybody ever told you look remarkably like Omar Sharif?"

Shakira was a star and I adored her. Every Friday lunch we would eat at the most expensive restaurants in London and I gladly worshipped at her shrine.

"Darling, you simply can't go to Rio with Andy. He's frightening looking." She leaned over and whispered conspiratorially in my ear. "When he was a baby, the midwife delivered him with fire tongs after he got stuck mid-birth and now he has a head the shape of a monkey nut, very E.T."

"Shakira," I gasped, "that can't be true."

"Fine. See for your self," she pouted. "But don't say I didn't warn you. Waiter, more champagne." The waiter jumped to attention and I suddenly realized Shakira, who was wearing no panties, had been flashing the waiters. No wonder we always got amazing service!

Shakira hadn't been lying. Andy did look like E.T., but who said I couldn't enjoy a fabulous holiday in South America with an extraterrestrial.

I met Andy at Heathrow Airport and we caught the Varig flight to Brazil. During the entire twelve-hour flight I marveled at Andy's resemblance to the Steven Spielberg puppet. Quite remarkable. He told me on the flight that he had started off in hotel management but had fallen upon escorting quite by accident and had eventually opened his own agency.

We were to stay at the Rio Othon Palace Hotel on Copacabana Beach. Skinhead Michael and his client Pat, the paraplegic, would be also at the same hotel. Pat had broken his neck showing off in the surf years before and could now move only his head around. Despite his affliction he turned out to be an incredibly sweet guy. He had taken Skinhead Michael to Rio for three weeks and I was blown away by how Michael cared for him. Michael was his nurse, friend and sexual playmate. For kicks Michael would pick up stunning Brazilian hookers and they would have sex with Michael in front of Pat.

If Michael could be such a saint, I figured I could put up with "Phone Home" for two weeks. Wrong. In no time I had a blazing row with Andy. The months of resentment for putting up with his crap, "Can you be Swedish? Can you pretend you had a sex change? Can you shag a granny trannie?" came boiling out. The four of us had been out drinking Mojitos at a steak restaurant on Ipanema Beach. I had met the Brazilian Ambassador to England in Rio, and I had been having dinner with him every night. I was developing a taste for rich food and even richer men. Andy was pissed off I wasn't spending more time with him, but he had such an unpleasant personality and I wasn't getting any younger. I was twenty-four for God's sake!

In addition to drinking we had been taking Pat's Valium, so we were all pretty fucked up. Pat and Michael went to bed early because Michael had to rub him with aloe balm. Michael and I had gotten drunk on the beach that day and we had left Pat in the sun by mistake. He was a crispy cripple and Michael felt terrible . . . me too. Left alone, I looked at Andy through a blur of Valium and rum and for the second time that day wished I was shar-

CHAPTER FIVE

ing a room with anybody but him.

"Andy, I have something to tell you," I huffed. "I'm leaving the agency. I'm going to put my own advert in and work for myself."

Andy went thermonuclear. How dare I betray him like this? He was the reason I was the most successful escort in London. Without him, I would be nothing! He told me I was the most ungrateful son of a bitch on the planet despite the fact I was making him a fortune.

"Let me tell you something, you're just some skinny blonde, and you're ten a penny! I can buy and sell you a million times over!" he yelled loud enough for guests at the neighboring tables to hear.

"Yeah, well when that midwife pulled you out of your mother's vagina with fire tongs she must have squeezed your brain too tight!" I shouted.

"What midwife? I was born at the Chelsea and Westminster Hospital," he spluttered.

Shakira, you lying cow!

Andy leaped up and stormed out of the restaurant. After he left the table I reflected on his cruel words. He was right . . . I was too skinny. I was six feet tall but still only weighed 160 pounds. Perhaps I should think about going to the gym. I knew just the place to start hitting the weights . . . Earl's Court Gym.

Andy caught a plane back home the following day. I never spoke to him again apart from when some lunatic threw a hatchet through his office window. He called up and accused me of wielding the deadly weapon. I told him it must have been some other disgruntled employee of his. Rio was a dream without him, and Skinhead Michael

OUT OF THE BLUE

and I became fast friends. I returned to London and wrote my own ad to put in the *Gay Times*:

BEN (24) HOT BLONDE BEACHBOY TYPE. BLUE EYES, GREAT TAN LINE AND PRIVATE CENTRAL LUXURIOUS APARTMENT . . . IF I'M NOT WHAT I SAY, YOU DON'T PAY.

I never looked back. My phone rang off the hook twenty-four hours a day. It got so bad that I had to switch the ringer off at night. Even so, Andy's words still haunted me. I was skinny, but everybody I knew was skinny. I plucked up the courage and finally went to Earl's Court Gym.

The guy on the desk was a fucking GOD. Sean Garret. He had a thick Liverpudlian accent and a flat top and I thought I would melt just by looking at him. He was a huge bodybuilder and totally straight. Oh dear, this reeked of trouble. Everybody in the gym fancied him, it turned out. He lived with his punk rocker girlfriend Kaz in a basement apartment on Gloucester Road. They had both just moved to London from Liverpool. I joined the gym immediately.

Much to my surprise I took to working out like a duck to water. The gym became the hub of my social life. Gyms weren't as popular back then as they are today, but Earl's Court Gym was state of the art. Of course, at first what kept me going back was sexy Sean Garret and his Liverpudlian charm, not to mention his humongous glutes and pecs. Escort clients would hire me and I would close my eyes, pretending I was fucking Sean instead of some old billy goat. God help the client if he was half decent

CHAPTER FIVE

looking; I would french kiss his face off, imagining I was snogging my Liverpool warrior. I jerked off constantly, thinking about Sean. When my muscles started to grow I was blown away. I would ask Sean's advice about my body all the time. He patiently explained to me how I needed to eat a gram of protein for every pound I weighed, and he taught me to cut out the alcohol I imbibed liberally. I started buying all the bodybuilding magazines I could get my hands on: *Flex*, *Muscle & Fitness* and *Musclemag*. They were full of impossibly beautiful men wearing posing trunks. Two bodybuilders I was especially crazy over were Chris Dickerson, who had won the Mr. Olympia title in 1982, and Chris Duffy, who went on to win the Mr. America championship. I would always buy magazines if those two behemoths graced the covers.

Having been a dancer, I had a very fast metabolism, and I didn't feel my body was growing quickly enough. I told Sean my concerns. I wanted to be Popeye, not Olive Oyl.

"I told you, mate, more protein."

"But I'm already eating a cow a day," I whined. Sean stared at me with his big brown eyes and said, "OK, what are you doing on Sunday?"

"Nothing," I stammered. This wasn't strictly true. I had a client who had flown in from America to see me—Thomas Morrison. Thomas was incredibly wealthy and was somehow related to the Vanderbilt family. He had a wife and four children, but for some reason he had fallen madly in love with me. He would send me gifts and pages and pages of handwritten love letters. He was a nice guy, but I felt nothing for him. I was in love with straight Sean.

"I'm doing nothing on Sunday," I repeated.

OUT OF THE BLUE

"Well, Kaz, my girlfriend is out for the night, do you wanna go to a movie and play some pool in Camden?"

"Sure, I love pool," I lied. Pool? The nearest I had come to a pool stick was when I stuck one up a client's ass when he was too gruesome to fuck one rainy day in Weston Super Mare. I had traveled down by train early to find the guy was an albino, so I fucked him on his pool table with a cue. I still remember his pink, grateful eyes and white, white skin against the green baize of the table. I never ate rabbit again.

I wasn't quite sure how playing pool and watching *Blade Runner* was going to improve my physique, but hey, I would be hanging out with Sean and I could pretend he was my boyfriend, at least for the day. Sunday rolled around and Sean told me he would be at my place at noon sharp. The night before I had had dinner with Thomas Morrison then gave him a blowjob while I listened to the Muslims shout at each other in the meat shop below. I sucked his dick, imagining it was Sean's. I nearly let him cum in my mouth.

I didn't sleep that night, and I was up at the crack of dawn on Sunday trying on different outfits. I settled on a pair of ripped jeans which you could see my arse through and a mesh vest that showed off my nipples. I had seen Sean's girlfriend in a very similar outfit. She was a punk rocker, and I believed naively this outfit might confuse Sean enough to let me blow him. I had arranged to meet Thomas Morrison at 9 p.m. for supper. He had whined and sulked about having to wait all day, but when I told him he could stay the night I felt him smile down the phone.

CHAPTER FIVE

At noon, sharp, there was a knock on the door. There stood Sean wearing jeans, t-shirt and a beanie cap.

"Fucking hell, everybody's gonna think I'm queer with you dressed like that," he laughed. My heart sank.

"Should I change?" I asked.

"Nah . . . fuck 'em. I know I'm not a poofter and that's all that matters, isn't it?" he said. I suddenly realized how stupid I was. Of course I wasn't going to have sex with Sean. He was a big, straight, Liverpudlian guy who just wanted to help me out with my bodybuilding. He handed me a plastic bag.

"What's this?" I asked.

"Present for you," he winked. We walked into the living room where I poured the contents of the bag onto my table. Little glass bottles the size of my thumb bounced all over the surface of the coffee table followed by a dozen syringes and surgical needles.

"What are they?" I asked. Sean laughed out loud, "What the fuck do you think they are? They're steroids!"

"Steroids!" I gasped.

"Yeah, you wanna get bigger, don't you?"

"Well, yes, but I was thinking perhaps an extra serving of Weight Gain 2000 and a bag of chicken breasts, but steroids?"

"Everybody's doing them who's serious about being a bodybuilder. Course if you're not serious. . . . " He began to scoop up the vials.

"No, no, wait . . . I mean, will I get much bigger?"

"As big as me," he grinned. I knew nothing about steroids. Wouldn't my hair fall out and my face end up covered in acne? More importantly, wouldn't my dick shrink? How could I be super hooker if I had no dick? I shared my fears with Sean who threw back his head and laughed again.

"Does this look like I have no dick?" Saying this, he unzipped his pants and took out his cock. I could have passed out. Here was the man of my dreams showing me his cock above the Khal-Al meat store. And boy, this was the finest piece of meat I'd ever seen in my life. Then he very nonchalantly stuffed it back in his jeans and I realized I hadn't breathed for ten seconds.

"What do I have to do?" I asked.

"Drop your pants," he replied. I had a massive hard-on that wasn't going away so long as he was in sight. Think of something gruesome, I thought. I caught sight of my closet door behind Sean. A month before I had received a strange phone call.

"Is that Ben?" asked the voice.

"Yes," I replied.

"I'd like to hire you for the weekend. There's no sex involved . . . I just have certain needs."

"Certain needs?" I asked. Well, turns out one of his certain needs was being locked in a broom closet, dressed as a school girl, and gagged and blindfolded with only a bowl of Kit-e-Kat to eat once a day. For that he paid me the cost of staying at a fancy Park Lane hotel, plus I got the extra bonus of having my friends come round that weekend, and when I would tell them to hang their coats in the closet they would open the door and scream in sheer terror.

Anyway, the memory of "Felix" got rid of my hard-on right away so I dropped my jeans for Sean. He didn't pay any attention to my dick. He was busy sucking out the

CHAPTER FIVE

contents of one of the vials into a syringe. The needle seemed enormous.

"This is Sustanon 250. The best steroid on the market, guaranteed to make you huge. Turn 'round." I turned around and felt Sean's big meaty hand on my arse.

"Now relax your arse," instructed Sean, "This won't hurt a bit." Saying this, he plunged the needle into my behind and emptied its entire contents. Surprisingly, it didn't hurt. In fact, I felt no different. Just a small prick and it was over.

"Get ready to get huge," he said. "Now pull your jeans up and let's go play some pool." I spent the afternoon playing pool with Sean at the Strangled Swan pub in Camden. The Camden Tiger had closed down. Alice the owner had employed a straight guy to run the place after I had left and he had spent all the takings on Guinness and pork scratchings. Alice had gotten her three ginger-haired sons to beat him up, and she returned to the plumbing business from whence she had come.

In the Swan as Sean leaned over the pool table, Sharon eyed up his meaty arse.

"Fucking lovely . . . are ya shagging him?" she asked.

"I wish," I replied. "He's straight."

"Well, he's better looking than that cunt Patrick you used to hang around with. I never could stand him, and he smoked like a fucking chimney," she said, lighting her third woodbine in less than half an hour.

"Yeah, horrible habit," I said. Saying goodbye to Sharon, I hugged her close, knowing I would never return to the Strangled Swan again.

Sean and I caught the underground to Leicester Square

OUT OF THE BLUE

where *Blade Runner* was playing. I was drunk from all the lager shandies that Sharon had poured down my neck. I think Sean felt the same way. The movie began and I marveled at the talent of Ridley Scott, a superb director who had started off directing British TV commercials. One of my regular clients was the British director John Schlesinger who had made the movie *Darling*. He lived in a huge mansion off Kensington High Street. His boyfriend, the famous photographer Michael Childers, introduced me to him. I used to see them both. There was no jealousy; they had been together twenty years or more. A few years later Michael Childers ran off with my boyfriend "Tall Steve" to California. Tall Steve had been narrowed down to the last thirty actors to play the new James Bond but didn't stand a chance because, although he definitely looked like he could play James Bond, his strong Cockney accent knocked him out of the running. He didn't even get a screen test. So Michael whisked him off to Los Angeles. Michael was really apologetic, but I didn't care. I was glad to get rid of Tall Steve because all he wanted to do was watch Match of the Day on the television and get rimmed, preferably at the same time. So I spent all my time listening to Liverpool beat Nottingham Forest with my tongue up Steve's arse.

In L.A., Steve tortured Michael to death with his neediness until Michael sent him back to London. Back home Steve begged my forgiveness. I didn't give a shit. Steve was no Sean . . . who was suddenly pressing his leg against mine!!! In the dark cinema!!! We kept our legs glued together throughout the entire movie. When the credits rolled, Sean turned to me and said, "I had a fight with my girlfriend Kaz this morning. I don't suppose I could sleep

CHAPTER FIVE

at your place tonight?" My heart was in my mouth but I tried to appear nonchalant. "Sean, you don't even have to ask." Then it hit me. Fuck, what about Thomas Morrison? Oh, well, didn't I deserve a little happiness?

My mind made up, I threw Sean into a cab and raced back to my love shack above the butchers.

"Have ya got any porno? No queer stuff," said Sean.

"*Tasty Clits*," I said. A closeted client had left the movie behind in my flat along with a pair of rusty nipple clamps. I threw the nipple clamps out the window. I saw Mohammed and Taffik trying them on the next morning while they chopped chickens' heads off in the yard below.

"Yeah, that sounds hot." We sat through ninety minutes of bad pornography . . . and neither of us moved a muscle.

When the movie finished, we sat there in the dark until finally Sean said to me, "My cock's hard." I didn't need to hear that twice. I began swiftly pulling off his clothing. I bent him over and ate his arse for an hour then sucked his dick. Sean lay there moaning in pleasure but didn't reciprocate. That didn't matter to me. I was in ecstasy about making love to him. He began to thrash around on my couch and suddenly he shouted out loud grabbed my shoulders hard and spunked in my gob.

"Why did we just do that?" I asked.

"I really like you," Sean confessed. "You're my mate . . . I've never done this before. I'm straight. I've never done this before." I drew him to me, and we kissed deeply. I was in love, I was. . . . Sean stiffened and shoved me away, shouting, "Aaaah! Fuck, there's some skeleton peering through the window!" Through the window? I was on the second floor! I turned to see Thomas Morrison with his nose pressed against the windowpane! I'd forgotten I was supposed to meet him! He had tried to phone me but I'd switched the phone off. I didn't want any interruptions in my seduction of Sean. So instead Thomas came round to my flat, found the gate locked, but must have seen the light on from the street. Borrowing a ladder from the restaurant's yard next door, he shimmied up the rungs with the excuse he thought I was being murdered by a naked thug in a beanie hat. Sean left, I shouted at Thomas, he cried, then I made him buy me tandoori chicken and let him lick my balls till he came . . . he gave me a hundred quid and I moodily snatched it out of his hand.

I started having an affair with Sean. It was tumultuous constant sex . . . for two weeks. We would hang out with each other every night and train together in the gym every day. We became best friends and secret lovers. Nobody in the gym ever suspected that we were sleeping together and that suited Sean fine. Of course I wanted everybody to know but I kept my mouth shut. I didn't want to scare Sean away. Then he dumped me for a Vietnamese girl named Minh. She had no neck and her parents owned a Vietnamese restaurant where they served a chicken dish made from stray cats . . . at least that was the vicious rumor that I . . . that someone . . . spread around Earl's Court.

In spite of our "break up" Sean introduced me to the serious bodybuilding world: steroids, villains, drugs . . . straight competitive bodybuilders who wanted to get rimmed, fucked and blown. I started going to bodybuilding

CHAPTER FIVE

competitions and my close circle of friends suddenly became a crowd of straight muscle men. The almost "twilight" world of bodybuilding in those days was like another dimension. All we talked about was who had won which contest, our diets, and what different kinds of steroids were on the market. It was an incredibly narcissistic lifestyle that at the time felt great but perhaps was mentally stupefying. My mother visited and apart from the shock of seeing how much bigger I had become couldn't understand why I was living this lifestyle. It all started to seem relatively normal to me. We all thought people who weren't bodybuilders were strange. Even a lot of the girls I knew took steroids, had muscles and competed in bodybuilding contests. The steroids, as well as packing forty pounds of muscle on me, made me sex crazed. I was doing five clients a day. One every hour and still I was picking up guys everywhere. My life seemed to be revolving around turning tricks, working out and pining for Sean so when one day a friend of mine, Conn, told me he was going to New Orleans for a two-week holiday I jumped at the chance to go with him. I figured it would take my mind off of Sean and I had always wanted to visit New Orleans.

I had met Conn at the gym. He was a good-looking stocky blond bodybuilder in his thirties. Although he was Irish, he had gone to university in New Orleans for some reason. His ex-boyfriend owned a guesthouse in the French Quarter, so accommodation would be provided, all I had to do was get the airfare together. I missed America, and the thought of traveling to somewhere as exotic as New Orleans filled me with wild excitement. I got on really well with Conn so I knew we would have a good time. We had had bad sex with each other once or twice so I knew there wouldn't be any weird sexual tension between us. We booked our tickets and caught a plane to the Big Easy.

CHAPTER SIX

I LOVED EVERYTHING ABOUT NEW ORLEANS from the moment we arrived. The French Quarter is a mile square with one main street, Bourbon Street, running down the middle of it. As the taxi drove us to our accommodations on Burgundy Street, I hung out of the window and let my senses be assailed by the sights and sounds of the city "that care forgot." Conn's ex-boyfriend was full of southern hospitality and welcomed us warmly. He lived in the heart of the Quarter with his new boyfriend and they made us feel right at home. In the centre of their guesthouse was a swimming pool that none of the other guests seemed to use, so Conn and I would tan for hours in the thick humid air drinking iced tea. Because Conn worked in a bank in London he wanted to spend the two weeks doing nothing but relaxing by the pool. I, on the other hand wanted to explore the French Quarter from one end to the other and sleep with as many Southern rednecks as possible.

The French Quarter is built on a grid system a little like Manhattan so it was impossible to get lost, plus the bars were open twenty-three hours a day so there was always some place to go. I would prowl the streets and sit on strangers' stoops soaking up the decadent atmosphere. I soon learned two things: one was that the legal drinking age in New Orleans was eighteen, so there was an enormous number of young kids running around drunk; secondly there wasn't even a sniff of a bodybuilder in the Quarter . . . there wasn't a proper gym either.

I complained about this to Conn one evening. He shrugged his shoulders and said to me,

"Now you know why I didn't stay here when I graduated school."

Having resigned myself to the fact that I wasn't going to meet the bodybuilder of my dreams, I simply enjoyed the good old-fashioned Southern cuisine and going dancing every night at one of the local gay bars, the Bourbon Pub.

The two weeks flew by and I realized I wasn't particularly looking forward to going back to London. My final night in the Big Easy arrived and I took one last walk down Bourbon Street enjoying the wild revelry of the other tourists and marveling how the city seemed to be caught in a time that no longer existed in any other part of the country . . . or world.

Heading back to the guesthouse down a small backstreet, I suddenly noticed a pickup truck following me. I have never been the type to assume that I'm going to get mugged so I guessed the driver was looking for some action. I settled down on the step outside my guesthouse and the truck pulled to a stop. The passenger window rolled down and I fell instantly in lust. There sat an incredibly hot man with cropped short hair, deep brown eyes, and wearing a World Gym muscle t-shirt.

"What's the story?" I said very forwardly. I hadn't had sex in two weeks because of the lack of muscle dick, and I was in no mood to beat around the bush. The guy in the

CHAPTER SIX

truck looked a little taken aback.

"What's your name?" he asked.

"Glenn," I replied.

"I'm Dale . . . do you have anywhere we can go?"

Well he was definitely getting with the program.

"I'm staying with a friend and he's in our room now packing . . . so no . . . " I said sadly.

"Fuck . . . what about in your garden?"

"Don't you have somewhere we can go?"

"I'm . . . married," he said sheepishly.

I knew it, but what did I care? It was my last night in New Orleans and I would never see him again, so what the hell?

Perhaps it was the fact that I hadn't had sex for two weeks or the fact that I was madly attracted to this sexy Southern stud, but I knew there and then I was going to take him by the pool and make mad, passionate filthy love to him.

"OK . . . " I said. "Park your truck and come on in."

When Dale climbed out of the truck my knees went weak. He was exactly my type—built like a bulldog and reeking of masculinity and Old Spice.

"You should know now, I'm only a top," said Dale, "I'm just interested in your ass, not your dick."

I didn't care because I just wanted his dick. We kissed passionately and then I sank to my knees and pulled out his cock. He began talking dirty to me, really filthy stuff that was a total turn-on. He made me call him Daddy and he fucked the living daylights out of me in a dark corner of the pool area.

As impossible as this seems I fell in love with Dale

OUT OF THE BLUE

that night. I had never met a man like him before. He made me feel wild and wanton and when we had finished, he took out his wallet and handed me his business card. It read Dale Shaw.

"I know you said you were leaving tomorrow but perhaps you'll call me one day if you ever come back to New Orleans."

Fuck that, I thought. I'll be calling you from London, mate.

I walked slowly upstairs to our room where Conn was busy packing. He looked at me strangely.

"What the hell is wrong with you?"

I sat on the corner of the bed and looked Conn squarely in the eyes, "I just met a guy called Dale . . . and I'm madly in love with him."

Conn rolled his eyes and carried on packing his fruit of the looms.

All I could think about on the long flight home was Dale Shaw. When I arrived back in London I raced back to my apartment and without even unpacking phoned Dale.

Over the next couple of weeks I had a crazy, tempestuous long-distance affair with Dale. We spoke dirty to each other every day for hours. I found out he had a boyfriend named Kenny, who he had been with for twenty years. They lived in the Ninth Ward, an area that would be obliterated by Hurricane Katrina years later. He told me he was a florist. I wasn't expecting that as I had imagined he worked in construction but I pushed that thought to the back of my mind. Surely I had met many macho florists over the years . . . hmmmm . . . actually no, I hadn't. In fact the only other florist I knew well

CHAPTER SIX

was Godfrey's old business partner back in NYC and he was as camp as Christmas. Anyway after one particularly filthy phone conversation with Dale over the phone I knew what I had to do. I called up Conn and told him I was moving to New Orleans to be with Dale.

"Have you lost your mind?" he spluttered. "That guy you met on the last night who shagged you by the pool?"

"I'm in love!" I simpered "You don't understand, Dale is my soul mate."

"Listen, its coming up to summer and its going to be hotter than hell in New Orleans, you have nowhere to live, you have no job, you're doing really well here. . . . "

"I'M IN LOOOOOOOOOVE!" I wailed down the phone.

"Do what you want," scoffed Conn, "but don't come crying to me when it's all over and he's broken your heart. . . . You only met him once."

Of course I knew Conn was insanely jealous otherwise why would he try to keep me from my one true love? It didn't occur to me that I was absolutely INSANE. So I locked up my London apartment drew my savings out of the bank, kissed my friends goodbye and informed them all they could contact me in New Orleans.

"You're bloody mad," said my girlfriend Karen, "Where ya gonna live?"

Karen was a personal trainer at Earl's Court Gym, a pretty blonde girl from Middlesbrough who spoke her mind. We would go out dancing every Friday night and get wasted on wine spritzers and flirt with all the local doormen on the doors of the pubs in Earl's Court. Her boyfriend Danny sold hashish so we were constantly stoned.

"Dale will help me find somewhere to live," I assured Karen.

"What are you going to do for a job?" Karen raged.

"I'll escort like I do here."

"YOU'RE BLOODY MAD!" screamed Karen again, her thick northern accent suddenly growing twice as thick out of concern for me.

I smiled at her beatifically, as if she were the mad one, and kissed her on the cheek.

"I'll call you from New Orleans," I said and off I went to the airport. "Tell everybody in the gym goodbye."

New Orleans turned out to be a nightmare. Who in their right mind moves to America to be with a married florist who gave them one good shag under a magnolia bush whilst drunk on mint juleps?

It started out great. Dale picked me up from New Orleans airport and he looked just as sexy as ever. He drove me around to his friend's house where I would be staying. We knocked but no one was home. Dale had a key. Once inside we made mad passionate love. It was just as fabulous as I remembered it. He then dressed and left for work. With nowhere to be I got up dressed and wandered around the French Quarter. I didn't know anybody but soon the bars were jumping and I was sure there would be no problem getting work as an escort . . . WRONG!!! . . . . I soon found out that New Orleans wasn't London. There were no escort agencies for guys and nobody ran ads. Everybody seemed shocked at the thought that I would even attempt to do something like that, so I didn't.

After two weeks his friend could no longer stand the sight of me sleeping on his pullout couch in his den so he

CHAPTER SIX

told Dale I had to move out. I packed my bags and waited for Dale to pick me up.

"Dale," I whined. "Where am I going to live?"

"Don't worry, I think Kenny will let you stay with us."

I still hadn't met Kenny but I imagined he didn't have a very high opinion of me. I was, after all, having an affair with his boyfriend. We drove to Dale's house. Everybody in the neighborhood was black, absolutely everybody. I felt like I was in Mozambique. The house was small and cozy. Dale led me up stairs through the first bedroom and into the second. There in bed lay Kenny. He wasn't bad looking, sort of an older, hairy Bruce Springsteen look-a-like.

Dale had told me that if Kenny liked me I could stay with them. I knew what he was implying. Kenny looked at me with big dark sorrowful eyes and all of a sudden it was as if the Universe shifted. I understood immediately that Kenny was and always would be madly in love with Dale and that he would do anything to make Dale happy including letting me share Dale's bed. Knowing this I took off my clothes and climbed into bed with Kenny. After our sad three-way Dale told me that I could sleep in the bedroom next door.

Over the next couple of days I learned much more than I needed to know about Dale Shaw from his friends who would drop by "unexpectedly" to gawk at the crazy British kid who had moved to New Orleans.

Dale had been born in a poor New Orleans family. When Dale's father left his mother, she got remarried to a strict religious man. Dale's stepfather ruled with a rod of iron and was so worried that Dale would grow up gay that he wouldn't even allow him to shampoo his hair. Instead he made Dale wash his scalp with soap, all the time making him give him blowjobs while his mother slept. Dale was exceptionally good looking and soon began hanging out in the French Quarter. He was courted by everybody; including the playwright Tennessee Williams himself.

Kenny came along when Dale was twenty and immediately moved Dale in with him. They began a daddy/boy relationship with Kenny effectively providing everything for Dale. It turned out Dale had ADD and found it impossible to hold down a normal job. He drifted from one thing to another until he finally got a job working for a florist who decorated the houses of the wealthy in the Garden District, the posh part of town. Kenny gave Dale an allowance and took care of all the finances. Over the years they had become like an old married couple. Dale ran around New Orleans and Kenny was content to let him as long as he returned home every night. I discovered that Dale had originally been the boy/bottom in the relationship but as he had grown older he had turned into a top. Dale and Kenny no longer had sex with each other unless Dale bought home some young kid home for a three-way. Despite all of this I could tell that Kenny still loved Dale with a fierce intensity that would never die. It was a true love that burned brightly and I was a fool if I ever thought I could extinguish that flame.

The three of us began living together in this little house in the middle of nowhere. I didn't drive so I had to be taken around everywhere by Dale unless I caught a cab. On top of that I had no job and I was very quickly

CHAPTER SIX

running out of money. Dale wasn't rich, so when we went out I invariably ended up paying for the two of us. The city was flooded with the drug Ecstasy from neighboring Texas. A tab cost twenty dollars and sometimes I would buy five tabs a night to share with Dale. It blissed us out, and I suppose kept the foolishness of what I had done with my life in the back of my mind . . . until mornings came around.

In no time I realized I couldn't stay in New Orleans, as there was no work there for me. But I didn't want to leave Dale, as I stupidly believed I was still madly in love with him. So together we conceived a plan. Dale and I would move to NYC, leaving poor Kenny behind. I would work as an escort and Dale would get a job doing . . . well, I am not quite sure what we thought Dale would do. I discovered that he had never been out of New Orleans in his life, but I figured I had earning potential for the two of us. And after all, I was MADLY . . . madly being the operative word . . . in love.

We covertly planned our departure for Manhattan. Dale didn't want to tell Kenny he was leaving him until the very last moment. He was worried about what Kenny might try to do to stop him. I found it impossible to be around Kenny. I had started to really like him as a person and I could no longer even look him in the eyes knowing I was planning to "elope" with Dale, his boyfriend of many years.

A week before we were due to leave New Orleans Dale woke me up in a particularly horny mood. Kenny had gone to work and we fucked for an hour until the phone rang. It was one of Dale's friends who knew we were leav-

OUT OF THE BLUE

ing New Orleans. Dale began a long conversation on the phone—explaining all the details of how and when we were leaving—when suddenly the wardrobe door at the foot of the bed was kicked off its hinges from the inside and out sprang KENNY. He hadn't gone to work, he had been hiding in the wardrobe for hours listening to Dale and I fuck. I knew Kenny was a voyeur and loved to watch and listen to others fuck, but I had not expected this. I was astonished he hadn't suffocated in that stuffy wardrobe amongst all those flannel shirts. More importantly he had heard Dale on the phone telling his friend he was moving to New York with me. Kenny burst into tears, huge convulsing sobs, and he cried and cried. I looked at Dale then I looked at myself in the mirror hanging on the bedroom wall then turned to Kenny crying on the bed and suddenly I was furious. Not at poor Kenny who hadn't hurt anybody in his life, not even for stupid, selfish Dale who cared only about himself, but at me. I was full of self-loathing. What the hell was I doing in New Orleans trying to split up this couple?

I was ashamed of myself. I walked downstairs and called Karen in London. I told her what had happened over the past couple of months.

She said, "Come home love . . . everybody misses you here."

I packed my suitcases and walked out of that little house in the Ninth Ward and climbed into the cab.

"Where to?" Asked the driver.

"The airport." I replied, "I'm going home."

As the cab drove me to the airport in the early morning heat, I took out of my bag the two tickets I had pur-

CHAPTER SIX

chased for Dale and I to go to New York. I wound down the window and threw them out into the street. I never saw Dale again.

CHAPTER SEVEN

I CAME HOME TO LONDON FULL OF TALES of New Orleans and recipes for Gumbo. It was summer and everybody was in a good mood because London was our playground. Every night I was on Hampstead Heath wandering through the undergrowth looking for illicit sexual encounters.

One particularly balmy night, after an evening of wild abandon running from bush to bush, I came home to notice all my lights were on. My heart in my mouth, I ran up the stairs to discover my front door was wide open. My flat had been broken into and I had been robbed! Not just robbed, every single thing I owned had been stolen! The thief had even taken all of my clothes out of the wardrobes and wrapped them up in my quilt and carried them off. I felt like falling on the floor and wailing like a baby. I had recently been dating a guy named Kenneth. He was Hardy Amies's design partner. Hardy had a store on Saville Row and was employed by Queen Elizabeth to design dresses.

Ken had met Princess Diana while he was making a dress for her, and being young, all Diana could talk about was meeting Simon Le Bon. Ken, bless him, had hardly even heard of Duran Duran, so he passed on following meetings with Diana to one of his twenty-year-old assistants. Years later Diana trained at Earl's Court Gym. She trained for a while with a friend of mine who was possibly the best looking personal trainer on the planet. It's strange now looking back that I worked out next to HRH Diana Spencer and yet at the time I never appreciated the fact that I was in the presence of one of the most beloved royals of my generation. Many years have passed and even after all the stars I have met she burnt the brightest. Even in a leotard she was absolutely luminescent. Was it her fame that made her shine so brightly or was it simply an inner radiance? Whatever the answer, she was spectacular.

After Ken was told about Duran Duran, he felt he was perhaps falling behind the times so he looked into pop culture for his next dress for the Queen. England at the time was obsessed with the television show "Dynasty." Joan Collins was the queen of network television and whatever Nolan Miller could create Ken could top . . . for a real Queen no less. He set to work on a "Dynasty" inspired frock but when she finally saw it she took one look at the insanely huge shoulder pads and sniffed, "Ken . . . give it to Margaret . . . she will love it."

I had met Ken years before through "Number One," Andy's escort agency. I was impressed that: he lived in a very grand flat just off High Street Kensington, always opened a bottle of champagne when I visited, and had a big cock. He was fifty, grey and distinguished. We flew around the world and he constantly gave me beautiful handmade suits that must've cost thousands of pounds. When my apartment got robbed the thief snatched them all. Stole my TV, my VCR . . . completely cleaned me out.

CHAPTER SEVEN

All I had left were the clothes on my back and my dirty laundry. The police came round but proved useless. They told me that there was no sign of forced entry and I may have been robbed by someone I knew. I phoned a friend of mine, Melaine, an Israeli Madame who came round and picked me up and took me back to her place to stay the night with her sexy bi boyfriend. She gave me tea and sympathy.

"It's time you moved out of that rat hole," she said. "There isn't even any furniture."

"That's because it was all stolen," I sobbed.

"Have another jaffa cake," she said. "And wipe your tears. This is a message from God. It's time to buy your own place. You can afford it." Melaine had an idea of how much money I made because she would book me when a client of hers wanted a girl and a guy. I had met her when we shared a client who wanted me to fuck him with a bottle of Heinz ketchup while Melaine pissed on him. We had been great friends ever since.

"I passed a place today on Penywern Road. It's a studio basement flat, brand new conversion." Melaine was right. Now was the perfect time to move. Suddenly I had no belongings. A new start would be good for me.

I went to see the apartment the next day. It really was perfect, a big studio with a sleeping platform. It was brand new, had a separate kitchen and bathroom, and a large hall that would serve as a dining area. It was just around the corner from the gym; in fact, I could see into the gym from my kitchen window. I moved right in. I went out and bought all new furniture, fixing up the place like a single guy living the high life. I even bought

OUT OF THE BLUE

a bench press and weights and put them in the window of the apartment. I filled the place with big trees and put framed posters by Skrebneski on the walls. Lots of semi-naked people in black-and-white looking bisexual: Cindy Crawford, Iman, Dolph Lundgren . . . a friend of mine knew Dolph when he was dating Grace Jones. Grace said he had the biggest dick she had ever seen.

After furnishing my new home, I was broke and needed to make some big money quickly. I had a great idea. I knew a lot of competitive bodybuilders who all needed money, so I opened up my own escort agency, Musclemen Masseurs. If Andy could do it and Alice thought she could do it why couldn't I? My agency specialized in jocks, sportsmen and pro bodybuilders. It was a smash hit immediately. I received phone calls non-stop. A normal call went like this:

"Hello, Musclemen Masseurs."

"I need a massage. I'm in the Dorchester Hotel."

"Certainly sir. What sort of guy were you looking for?"

"Do you have any pro rugby players?"

"We certainly do," I would lie.

"Well, I'd like a blonde pro rugby player. Hairy, please."

"I'll have him right over. His name's Gareth."

"Please be discreet, I'm married."

"Oh, we're very discreet, sir. That will be a hundred pounds and ten for the cabs. That includes the agency fees."

"How long will he take to get here?"

"He'll be there in half an hour, sir."

(Click).

CHAPTER SEVEN

I would look at the bodybuilders I had on my books and see who fit the description most closely. I had learned from Andrew at Number One Agency that you didn't have to get the description a hundred percent right. Fuck, you didn't have to get it twenty percent right. Sex is all in the mind. As long as you look vaguely like what they want, you're in the door.

By this time I was in my mid-twenties, had light brown hair, no tattoos, and 200 pounds of tanned muscle (thank you, steroids). I would have been totally generic looking if I had lived in Southern California, but in grey old London I was rocking. So a call from a client like this would come in and half an hour later I was Gareth the Welsh ex-rugby pro who had given up the game due to the fact my father had died in a mining disaster in Llandudno. Lies just spilled out of my mouth when there was a whiff of a straight client dick to be had.

Musclemen Masseurs became so successful that visiting bodybuilders from all over the world would call me wanting to escort. In a very short time the agency became one of the hottest agencies in Europe. Plus I was having sex with all the guys . . . but only when they came for an interview . . . and only more than once if they were exceptionally huge and stupid. I only employed the hugest. By now my steroid intake had increased to two shots a week: 1 ml of Sustanon 250 and 1 ml of Deca-Durabolin. I would get the stuff off of various bodybuilders I was shagging. Friends, who saw the astonishing difference in my physique, started buying steroids from me as well. Before I knew it, I was the main steroid dealer in Earl's Court Gym. How the hell did that happen?

OUT OF THE BLUE

So there I was; owner of a bodybuilding escort agency, selling steroids to the whole of South West London. Then I met Bill Christian, who turned my life upside down.

The hottest gay bar in Earl's Court was the Coleherne. It was the oldest gay leather bar in London and a fucking dump. It was as if "Troll Kingdom" had thrown open its doors and all the trolls had danced down to the Coleherne where they were handed a pair of chaps and a body harness. Remember the hideous headmaster whose leather g-string I nicked to strip in at Boys-a-Go-Go? This was his favorite haunt. Everybody in the Coleherne knew I was a hooker. But what made them treat me with respect was that I was a good-looking, successful hooker with a 50-inch chest.

It was at the Coleherne on a Friday night that I met Bill. He had the thickest head of black hair I had ever seen, a dimple in his chin and dreamy brown eyes. I spotted Bill from across the bar while I was knocking back my fifth pint of lager and lime. He grinned at me and I smiled back and then he pushed his way through the crowd towards me.

"Hello, mate."

"Hello." God, he was gorgeous.

"Do you live around here?"

"About five minutes away," I said.

"Well, fancy a shag?"

Thank God he said that because I had the strangest feeling he was straight and had wandered into the Coleherne by mistake. He was the best looking guy I had ever seen in the place and I couldn't help noticing he had huge muscled thighs that were crammed into his jeans. I think

CHAPTER SEVEN

I fell in love with him the moment I saw him and speaking to him just sealed the deal. As we walked back to my flat he told me he was from New Zealand and he hadn't been living in London long and that he didn't have a boyfriend. I was amazed that a guy this sexy didn't have a boyfriend. He came back to 3 Penywern Road that night and we had amazing sex. He was a total top and fucked the living daylights out of me for hours. When we woke up in the morning he told me that he was leaving on a one-week vacation to New York City but he said he would call me. As we kissed goodbye and I looked into his big brown eyes I knew I was in love, and I think he knew he was in love with me too.

When he returned a week later we took up where we had left off.

Bill was living in a rented room in St. Johns Wood. It was small but he was very tidy and neat so it never looked messy. He worked as a carpenter on a construction site and every night he would come to my place covered in sawdust and we would make mad passionate love. He had a solid body from working out for years. As I got to know him better he told me he had only ever had one other boyfriend but lots of girlfriends . . . he was bi . . . YUM.

It didn't seem to bother him that I was escorting or that I owned my own escort agency. He would never let me spend any money on him and even insisted he pay whenever we went out. I knew he didn't earn a lot of money so one day I got an idea.

"Listen, I get a lot of calls asking for guys who look like you." Bill had a ten-inch cock and the biggest arse I had ever seen . . . and he was a genuine carpenter. "Why don't you do a booking or two every week . . . just to supplement your income."

"Nah . . . that's not for me."

"But it's really easy. I'll only give you the jobs where you have to sit back and get your dick sucked. You'll make a fortune."

"Honestly mate . . . I don't want to do it."

Of course I couldn't leave it alone. I whined and begged and pleaded and cajoled him until finally he agreed to try it. He made an enormous amount of money straight away. I don't think Bill ever actually enjoyed doing the work but perhaps he did it to please me. A few weeks later we moved in together in my small flat on Penywern Road. Bill joined Earl's Court Gym and I filled him up with steroids. We constantly fucked like rabbits and were blissfully happy in our tiny little warren.

It was during this time that I met Harry Giesler. Harry had been born in Germany and had been one of the world's top male models. He was one of those guys that you saw advertising cigarettes and Pierre Cardin suits on billboards all over the world. He was incredibly, ruggedly handsome, but at forty years old he had fallen on hard times. As he was a bodybuilder with a nine-inch cock, Skinhead Michael had suggested he work for my escort agency. He and Skinhead Michael had met in "Heaven." They had become lovers until a week later when they had realized they were both bottoms. Harry came for an interview and the week I put him to work he made two thousand pounds. He was ecstatic.

Bill and Harry weren't crazy about each other. Bill was

CHAPTER SEVEN

jealous of anybody who took up a lot of my time, and Harry and I started running around London together much to Bill's chagrin. Bill didn't like clubbing so every Saturday night Harry and I would go dancing at Heaven and drop acid. We fell into a pattern. Harry would come to my flat and we would head off to the Coleherne for a few pints of beer before going dancing. Bill would stay at home and build cupboards and wardrobes, and then I would come home and let him fuck the hell out of me till dawn.

One day I gave Harry a booking that ended up changing his life. The guy was a regular of my agency though I didn't know much about him. I never pried into my client's personal lives, so all I knew was that his name was Matthew and that he had a lot of money because he never quibbled over price. He liked blond bodybuilders so when he called one day I figured Harry would be perfect. Harry was more than perfect. It turned out Matthew had been in love with Harry ever since he had seen him in a commercial for tobacco years ago. He couldn't believe it when Harry showed up at his door and Harry couldn't believe it when he saw Matthew's luxury penthouse behind Harrods department store. Matthew fell fast and hard for Harry and eventually bought him a Bentley and an amazing two bedroom flat in South Kensington. Harry and I were the only bodybuilding fags in London who rode to Heaven in a Bentley. Matthew unfortunately died a few years later but not before I expect Harry had made him the happiest he had ever been. In turn Matthew left Harry enough money to live on for the rest of his life.

Harry eventually sold the apartment in South

OUT OF THE BLUE

Kensington along with all the furniture and art Michael had bought and purchased a beautiful two-bedroom cottage south of the river Thames. I think the South Kensington apartment held too many sad memories for Harry who was approaching fifty and had given up the "glamorous" life of hooking years before. Harry had experienced what a lot of successful escorts experience. He had met a rich client who fell in love with him and gave him everything. As much as Matthew loved Harry, Harry in his own way had grown to love Matthew. I'm sure Harry will remember him fondly forever.

I was definitely burning the candle at both ends. It was the days of ecstasy and dance music in London. I had first tried ecstasy in New Orleans and now it had become the in drug in London. The biggest club of the month was called "Kinky Gerlinky" run by hostess supreme Gerlinda. She was the "sister" of NYC party goddess Suzannne Barsch and Kinky Gerlinky was the place to see and be seen.

Gerlinda asked Sean and I if we would get some bodybuilders together and put on a dance act at Kinky. We soon became the kinky boys and our infamy only grew. It was a wild time to be young and wealthy and handsome in London. We ruled the school.

CHAPTER EIGHT

I HAD DEVELOPED AN UNNATURAL TASTE for beauty pageants. The summer of 1989 I went to Key West for four weeks on my own. Bill had flown home to visit his family in New Zealand, so I let a friend of mine, Richard, run the agency while I was away.

Key West was amazing. In those days it was still a sleepy little hamlet overrun by gay people and five-toed cats, a supposed legacy of Ernest Hemmingway. Now it's all t-shirt shops and cruise ships pulling in all the time, but in 1989 it was sublime. There were an enormous number of gay bed and breakfasts serving fresh muffins and fruit juice every morning. Later people would head to the local pier where there was a bar and everybody tanned like seals while sipping banana daquiris. At night the entire gay population of the Island would go dancing at the big gay club Copacabana.

One night they held the annual "Mr. Key West" contest. Drunk on tequila, I slipped into a Speedo and paraded myself around the stage at the "The Copa." Amazingly, I won and tottered down the runway, misty-eyed and clutching a bouquet of roses to my ample pecs. For the next month I was a star and I liberally imbibed all the libations sent my way in various gay bars as well as all the free tabs of ecstasy I could gobble down. Upon returning to freezing cold London, I found my friend Richard asleep on my carpet, all my plants dead and a bin full of empty Guinness bottles . . . reality was harsh.

A few months later I was working out at the gym when I spied a flyer somebody had posted on the notice board:

MR. DRUMMER 1990
BRITISH FINAL

WINNER MUST COMPETE IN FULL LEATHER DAY WEAR, EVENING WEAR AND ACT OUT A 3 MINUTE SEXUAL FANTASY OF ONE'S CHOOSING. ALSO GIVE A SPEECH ON THE VALUE OF THE LEATHER COMMUNITY TO SOCIETY AND HOW LIVING AS A LEATHERMAN HAS BENEFITTED YOUR OWN LIFE.

FIRST PRIZE: AN ALL EXPENSES PAID TRIP TO SAN FRANCISCO TO COMPETE IN THE MR DRUMMER WORLD FINAL REPRESENTING THE UNITED KINGDOM.

"Oh my God," I thought. "It will be just like Miss World . . . only with leather men."

I filled out the entry form that afternoon.

Drummer Magazine was the leather men's bible and each year they held the Mr. Drummer Leather Contest in San Francisco to see who would be the world's ultimate leather man. This year there would be contestants from all over the world including one from the UK . . . me, I decided. If I could be Mr. Key West, I sure as hell could slip into a body harness and fool everybody into thinking I wore processed animal skins twenty-four hours a day.

CHAPTER EIGHT

I trotted down to the local fetish store in Soho and persuaded the guy behind the counter to create me various body harnesses for daywear and latex wrestling suits for evening wear. The guy was known as "Black Beauty" because he looked like the horse from Anna Sewell's famous novel, all big gums and thick black hair down to his waist. I let him suck my toes in the changing room for a free pair of army boots. Done up in leather I actually didn't look too bad! I had a regular client who always wanted me to wear leather but I stopped seeing him because he had enormous foreskin that he always wanted me to chew on like a bullmastiff with a rubber chew toy. He had the stretchiest foreskin I'd ever munched. It was unnatural. He told me he was married to a famous super model and she didn't like to chew his foreskin either. Who knew foreskin had so many calories?

The night of the contest we all made our way to the club in Shepherd's Bush. I had all of Earl's Court Gym there supporting me. Walking in my head-to-toe body harness was very difficult and every time I walked past somebody I would get hooked on them for the next five minutes because of all the buckles and straps I was wearing. Leather body harnesses are extremely uncomfortable, and I was wearing a jockstrap made of barbed wire and knee-length leather jackboots. Thank you Black Beauty, Anna Sewell would have been horrified.

There were twelve contestants in the contest, every single one ashen-faced and smelling of stale amyl nitrate. None had ever seen the inside of a gym in their lives. I knocked it out of the ballpark.

"The winner of Mr. Drummer UK 1990 is . . . " ME. I

was handed a leather sash, a check for 500 pounds and a round trip plane ticket to San Francisco for the world final.

Things had been going badly between Bill and me. It was all my fault. I had fallen in love with Bill but we seemed to be moving in different directions. I wasn't as attentive to him as I should have been. I was surrounded by straight bodybuilders who all wanted a bit on the side, behind their wives and girlfriend's backs. I wanted to oblige them. It wasn't fair to Bill who was a really good-looking sexy guy. He could have had anybody he wanted. We broke up and I later regretted the fact for years. Bill moved on really quickly with his life, but I pined for him for a long time.

The Mr. Drummer Contest in San Francisco was huge. Leather men from all over the world attended. Half of San Francisco was gay but the gayest part of all was the Castro District. It was packed with leather daddies and their slaves for Mr. Drummer Week. At first I thought it was rather freakish, but after a couple of days I started to really enjoy the company of the leather fraternity. They were all actually rather sweet, and I learned so much about how to house and care for your slave. I was told about a book called *The Leatherman's Handbook,* which I devoured in one sitting since I was about to be grilled at the pre-judging of the contest. The pre-judging consisted of a panel of about twelve older leather men asking me questions about my leather life style. Questions were thrown at me. "When you go to a bar, do you allow your slave to drink out of a glass or must he always drink from a dog bowl at your feet?"

"When your slave has been rude to you, do you with-

CHAPTER EIGHT

hold from him the pleasure of drinking your piss?" I tried to take all of this as seriously as possible but true to my evil nature I would sometimes find the devil in me overtaking and I gave replies such as,

"Not only do I withhold the taste of my nutritious piss, but I refuse to shit in his mouth for a month."

I knew there was no way in hell I was going to win this contest, but I was already being celebrated for being Mr. Drummer UK so things could have been much, much worse. I became really good friends with Mr. Drummer Australia, a guy my own age who lived in Sydney. He told me over Mimosas he liked being strangled until he passed out during sex.

"Me too," I lied.

All week there were parties every night. One night we were all auctioned off for dinners that had been donated by various local restaurants. The event was held at the world famous leather bar, the Eagle.

We all drew straws to see who would be auctioned off first. I had drawn the shortest straw, which meant I would be auctioned off last. One by one we were paraded onto the stage. An enormous lesbian in the audience had taken a shine to me and was determined to buy me. She was dressed in a leather policeman's motorcycle uniform and was standing with a stunning blonde girl who was wearing a bra, chaps, leather knickers and nothing else. The bidding for me went up to $250 before the lesbian dropped out and I was "acquired" by a leather man at the front of the stage. The contestant before me had sold for $7.50, so I was happy. I think the fact that he was wearing just a leather diaper and boots had scared the potential bidders.

OUT OF THE BLUE

As I walked off the stage I was grabbed by the enormous lezzy. "I'm Officer Betty of the Safe Sex Police and this is my girlfriend Gabriella, she's Miss Cheeks in Chaps 1989."

"What a pleasure to meet you," I said. "And thank you for driving the bidding so high."

"You're hot," said Gabriella. "Have you ever thought of doing porn?" Gabriella spoke all of her words with a heavy Hungarian accent, which brought about images of Zsa Zsa Gabor.

"No," I laughed. "I don't think I'd be very good at it."

"You'd be divine," said Gabriella. "I shoot for *Penthouse* all the time and I'm always looking for guys to do *Penthouse Couples* with me. Would you like me to arrange it?"

"Well, let me have a think about it," I said, feeling incredibly flattered. People in San Francisco were so friendly, I thought for the hundredth time that week.

"Have you done magazines before?" asked Officer Betty.

"Well, all the contestants have to shoot a centerfold for *Drummer Magazine*. I'm doing mine with Mister Germany Drummer."

Betty and Gabriella looked at each other.

"Good God," said Gabriella. "*Drummer Magazine* employs awful photographers. You would be far better off in *Penthouse Couples* with me."

"Or you should be a COLT model," said Officer Betty.

COLT model!!! Yeah, in my wildest dreams. COLT was a company owned by a photographer called Jim French. He produced magazines and calendars with bodybuilders who were the epitome of masculinity. He

CHAPTER EIGHT

worked with the hottest men in the world. No way did I look like a COLT model.

I spent the whole night drinking with Betty and Gabriella. They knew everybody and I was slowly drawn into their world of fetish and friendliness. Betty was the daddy and Gabriella was her lipstick lesbian girlfriend. Betty worked as a plumber and Gabriella owned a leather store in the Castro by day and was a stripper by night.

"I had better be getting back to my hotel," I said.

"We'll give you a ride."

My hotel was a dump, and when we pulled up outside in Betty's truck, Gabriella said, "This place is a fucking rat hole."

"It's where they put all the contestants," I said.

"I have a great idea!" squealed Gabriella. "You have to stay at our apartment. We live on the hill above the Castro, and Betty can drive you around. If you let me take pictures of you wearing leather from my store to put on posters in the window, you can keep the outfits."

"Are you sure?" I laughed.

"No arguments," said Officer Betty. "I'll pick you up tomorrow at noon, so go and pack."

I thanked them profusely and strode into the grubby lobby of the hotel.

"There's a message for you," said the one-eyed desk clerk.

"For me?" I asked. "Who from?"

"Al Parker," he whispered.

"I don't know anybody called Al Parker. Only the porn star."

"That's who the message is from," cackled one-eye.

OUT OF THE BLUE

Al Parker was an enormously famous porn star. He was extremely good looking with a humongous dick. He was hairy with a big moustache and owned his own porn company in San Francisco called "Surge Studios." I had all of his films back in London and couldn't believe he had contacted me. I opened the note: "Saw you tonight on stage at the Eagle. Call me. Al." There must be some mistake, I thought as I walked up to my room. What could Al Parker want with me? I dialed his number.

"This is Al," a really sexy voice said, a voice I recognized immediately from the movies.

"Mr. Parker," I stammered, "this is. . . ."

"Glenn Marsh. I recognize your voice from the contest tonight. Mr. Drummer UK."

"Yeah, that's me."

"I was thinking, perhaps we might get together tonight. I could be there in twenty minutes."

"Sure," I said.

The phone clicked off. My head was spinning. Al Parker. He was so famous. I jumped into the bath and twenty minutes later there was a knock on my hotel door. There stood Al Parker, all 5-foot-5 of him. He looked exactly as he did in the movies, only much shorter. I was to learn that very few porn stars are larger than life when you meet them in the flesh. One thing, however, that was just as big in the flesh was his cock. He was great in bed and while we were fucking I felt him grease up his balls and stick them up my arse alongside his dick, a definite first for me but it felt perverted and great. To achieve this act takes a great deal of patience and a genius in bed. Al was definitely a sexual maestro.

CHAPTER EIGHT

As the sun rose and he was getting dressed a thought struck me.

"Al, you're a COLT model, aren't you?"

"Yep," he said.

"Do you think I could be one too?"

"Sure, why not?" he said. "Listen, do you wanna have dinner tonight?"

"I can't, somebody bought me in an auction and I have to have dinner with them."

"Poor you," he laughed. "How about tomorrow night?"

"I can't, I've got to attend the Leather and Lace Ball. It's part of Drummer Week."

"I'll be there too, how about we go together?"

Me and Al Parker on a date! And it couldn't hurt my credibility in the eyes of the judges.

"Sure, why not?" I said nonchalantly but inside I was screaming with wild glee.

At noon Officer Betty arrived and loaded my suitcases into the back of her truck. I had a rehearsal for the Mr. Drummer contest at 2 p.m., so we rushed to her apartment. When she flung open the door I couldn't believe my eyes. The place was jam packed floor-to-ceiling with strap-on dildos, stripper Lucite heels and leather pornography.

"Gabriella's still asleep, she was working until 4 a.m. She needs to get her rest because she's having vaginal reduction surgery in a couple of days," Betty offered.

I stared blankly at her in disbelief.

"She had her labia pierced a few years ago but now it's pulled the lips out too much so she's having them reduced."

I turned pale.

"I think I'm going to be late for rehearsal," I said,

trying to change the topic. "And we're finishing learning a song and dance routine to perform on the final night of the contest." Of course, this was just as ridiculous as it might sound. Two dozen leather men doing a show tune in full leather drag. It was as tragic as you'd expect. The song was from *Les Miserables* and nobody could pick up the dance steps naturally. As we paraded around the stage, I suddenly realized that this show was going to be an all out camp fest.

Betty raced me down to the rehearsal studios. Karen, the leather dyke who was running the whole Mr. Drummer event, glared at me.

"You're late again!" she shouted.

"Oh, fuck off," I thought. I couldn't stand her. She was a miserable cow. I had been late every day for rehearsal but only because I was busy wallowing in the pleasures that San Francisco had to offer.

"And where's your leather sash?"

Oops, I had given that to Al Parker in celebration of him fucking me with giant ball sack.

"Oh, never mind, just get into rehearsal and you better remember the routine!" she barked.

The other contestants adored me. They thought I was a total lunatic. Word had spread that when the judges had asked me what the next Mr. Drummer should be, I had replied: "Young." I didn't give a toss. I was feckless and fearless and I was in San Francisco to have a good time, and boy was I.

By the time the night of the final contest rolled by, I was in love with The City. I had settled in for my final days there with Officer Betty and the stunning Gabriella

CHAPTER EIGHT

amidst the bras and thongs and sex toys. Meanwhile Al had moved onto other conquests so I was footloose and fancy-free. I had shot my centerfold spread for *Drummer Magazine* and also a cover and article for a magazine called *Powerplay*. Me, holding a giant Rottweiler on the cover; not-so-subtly suggesting I was into bestiality, which I wasn't.

As it turned out I didn't even place in the Mr. Drummer contest. They only announced the top three but I'm sure I didn't even make the top ten. Then came the moment to present "The Golden Whip Award." This was given to the contestant who every other contestant voted for as his favorite contestant, a sort of Mister Congeniality. The prize was a huge leather golden whip. . . .

"And the winner of this years Golden Whip Award goes to Glenn Marsh, Mr. Drummer United Kingdom. . . ."

ME!!!

I felt happier winning the Golden Whip than I would have felt winning the Mr. Drummer World title. Besides, I was already Mr. Drummer UK. And I always have believed you should spread the wealth. That night after the show, Mr. Drummer Australia came up to me:

"What are you doing now the show's finished?"

Not strangling you, I thought. "Dunno, perhaps going dancing," I replied.

"No, I mean are you going back to England?"

"Probably," I said sadly.

"Why don't you come to Sydney? I have an apartment where you can stay and the leather scene is great."

Fuck the leather scene! Get me in Speedos on Bondi Beach fighting off all the ex-convicts. Bill and I had bro-

OUT OF THE BLUE

ken up so there was no one waiting for me to come home to London.

I bade a tearful farewell to Officer Betty and Gabriella, who was recovering from her vaginal reconstruction and called up Quantas Airlines. Sydney, here I come!

CHAPTER NINE

I ARRIVED IN SYDNEY IN DECEMBER but it was the middle of their summertime. I found a great gym to workout in called City Gym and settled in nicely with Jack, Mr. Drummer Australia, and his boyfriend. The whole city was gearing up for Sydney Mardi Gras, and there was enormous buzz about a gay movie being shot around Sydney called *The Sum of Us* which starred a gorgeous young unknown actor named Russell Crowe.

Australia was enormous fun. As if all the best of the UK and America were combined. I was living in Kings Cross, which was the gay ghetto. I trained each day at City Gym and then hung around on Tanarama Beach. The locals called it "Glamarama" because of the amount of gorgeous people who tanned there. My photo layout came out in the March 1991 issue of *Drummer Magazine*, my first proper porno layout, it read:

"Glenn Marsh Mr. UK Drummer . . . As the first ever Mister United Kingdom Drummer Glenn Marsh has his work cut out for him. The Leather/SM community in his country, along with about everyone else who is overtly sexual, is taking a non-consensual beating of the sort Jesse Helms would like to see happening in the US. Just what a leather titleholder can do under the repressive conditions that exist in England remains to be seen, but

OUT OF THE BLUE

no one doubts that Glenn is the man for the job.

"Glenn is 27 years old, six feet tall and weighs 190 well packed pounds. His eyes are blue and he smiles very, very easily. He has a degree in physical training.

"Mr. UK Drummer's sponsors were *H.I.M* Magazine and "Expectations" (rubber and leather gear) in London and Marathon Films, Los Angeles. Glenn says his goal as a titleholder is 'to promote a healthy sexual image of gay leather men in the 1990s'" . . . what a load of old bollocks.

The article about me in *Drummer Magazine* was accompanied by a rather tasteful layout of me wearing about two hundred pounds of shiny leather harness, jack boots and spiky bicep bands whilst displaying the length of my foreskin and standing on a painter's ladder . . . I was thrilled to the bone.

I became an instant celebrity on the leather scene in Sydney. In fact, the local leather bar was building a float for the Sydney Mardi Gras and they had asked me if I would like to be featured on it wearing my Mr. Drummer outfit . . . of course I shyly accepted the kind offer.

The night of Sydney Mardi Gras rolled around and I nervously climbed aboard the huge truck that had been covered in scaffolding for the leather men to dance on. As the parade made its way through the streets of Sydney I could hardly believe my eyes. There were literally millions of people screaming for us. I knew at that moment I wanted to make Sydney my new home. Years later when I was watching the Russell Crowe film *The Sum of Us* they featured the leather float in the film with me shaking my paps for the entire world to see.

I had no idea how huge Mardi Gras would be. It

CHAPTER NINE

turned out to be gigantic. Sydney gay Mardi Gras brings in millions of dollars to the city every year. There is an enormous parade that stretches for miles, full of amazing floats and it ends at a gargantuan space where three dance halls have been constructed to hold thousands of revelers who are off their heads on various stimulants. The following morning the "recovery parties" begin in all the bars for the hardcore partiers and everybody looks weary-eyed yet content.

I had met a hot bodybuilder in Sydney called Ross Whittaker. He was a doctor from Melbourne. He reminded me of the lead singer from Right Said Fred and everywhere we went cars would pull up and people would lean out of the car windows and sing the hit "I'm Too Sexy" at us. We were stars . . . in our own minds.

"What are you doing after Mardi Gras?" asked Ross.

"I don't know," I said as we lay in each other's arms full of chemical pleasure.

"Move to Melbourne and live with me."

I looked out of my bedroom window and saw the now-empty streets of Darlinghurst, full of litter and drag queens lying in the gutters covered with glitter.

"Melbourne . . . " I gushed. "It sounds like a dream. When do we leave?"

Melbourne wasn't a dream. It was like living back in Nottingham. I felt like a caged beast. Ross was really sweet, however he knew he couldn't hang on to me, and so he set me free. I flew right back to San Francisco. But first I made a little detour via London to pick up Sean. I had big plans for both of us, and I took him along as my willing accomplice. There would be no more Glenn Marsh and Sean Garret. There would be only Blue Blake and Gage Blake . . . the Blake Twins (insert crazed, devilish laughter here).

CHAPTER TEN

PEOPLE ALWAYS ASKED IF SEAN AND I if we were brothers. And why wouldn't they think that? We took the same steroids, did the same workout routines, dressed the same and even got our hair cut in Nottinghill Gate by the same barber, "High and tight please, Giuseppe."

Sean and I had both gotten similar tattoos on a trip to Amsterdam a year before with Harry Giesler and another bodybuilder called Chris Hayler when we ended up so high from eating marijuana-laced space cakes that I couldn't climb up the stairs at the crummy Hells Angels hotel that Sean had booked us into. I never could figure out why he had booked us into there until I noticed the brothel next door specialized in pre-op transsexuals, Sean's favorite guilty pleasure. Sean and I both looked like ex-marines, so that would be our identities in America. The Blake Twins, fresh out of the Royal Marines, was to be our M.O.

Choosing our names was easy. Sean had seen the movie *Pet Cemetery* and liked the little boy's name in it: Gage. Sean had always called me Blue, because of my blue eyes, so I became Blue Blake. I toyed with the name Blue Mason but then remembered at drama school that they had told us that a name with alliteration was always much more memorable. Sean and I found a two-bedroom apartment in

OUT OF THE BLUE

the Castro in a building that had once been a Chinese laundry. We had a local photographer take pictures of the two of us and we put an escort advertisement in the local gay rag saying only "The Blake Twins" and we were on our way.

The phone rang incessantly. Guys would come over for $400 and hour, convinced we were fraternal twins. As soon as I started sucking Gage's dick, they would cum immediately.

We bought bikes and in our spare time rode around the city. Gage got himself a transvestite girlfriend from the local tranny bar, and I slept around a lot, mostly with bodybuilders from the local Gold's Gym or porn stars.

One night I met Jon Vincent in a bar. Jon was my favorite porn star of all time. Italian, bodybuilder, huge dick and in all his films he talked filthy to the guys he fucked. He was supposed to have had a professional baseball career but had blown out his knee. That and his enormous addiction to cocaine had destroyed his baseball dreams so he became a porn star and escort. In bed that night Jon struggled to get hard until I stuck three fingers up his arse.

"Yeah, daddy," he moaned.

Jon Vincent, it turned out, liked being fucked by black men while high as a kite. Sadly, Jon and I weren't meant to be. Mandingo fantasies, yeah, cocaine addiction, nope. Jon died a few years later, penniless and hopelessly addicted to drugs. It was a terrible end for one of the sexiest men in the world.

Every morning Gage and I would work out in one of the gyms in the Castro. One day a guy gave us his business card. It read Jack Fritscher. Jack owned a company

CHAPTER TEN

called Palm Drive Video that made bodybuilder jerk-off films. He thought Gage and I could be huge stars. We went down to the Gold Rush to talk it over. It was Gage's favorite tranny bar and I needed him in a comfort zone so I could persuade him to do the movie with me. Gage didn't remotely think of himself as bisexual, although we both knew the reason we 'escorted' together was so that Gage and I had a reason to have sex with each other. Apart from that he only fucked girls with dicks or real girls that looked like boys. I knew I was madly in love with Gage but I was smart enough to know he would always disappear with a girl . . . and that would ultimately lead to madness for me. It was very *Brokeback Mountain* with me as Jack Twist. In many ways we had the perfect relationship. He wasn't jealous about who I slept with, and I wasn't jealous of who he slept with, because ultimately we both knew our sexual partners wouldn't last but we would be together forever.

I was the smarter of the two of us. While various Korean transvestites were pouring tequila down our throats at the bar, I convinced Gage we should do this softcore movie for Jack Fritscher. We were just to be filmed working out and talking dirty, then jerking off . . . who would ever see it? (Men still come up to me today, eighteen years later and say it's their favorite movie of all time.) It made a fortune for Jack Fritscher. We were to be paid a thousand dollars each, and the thought of cash for having a wank really appealed to Gage. What appealed to me was the thought of doing my first porno movie, nourishment for the "beast" otherwise known as my ego.

We phoned Jack to set up the shoot for the next day.

OUT OF THE BLUE

I learned years later when I started producing porno, if you find hot models shoot them immediately because invariably they will disappear or change their minds if you give them the chance to.

We dressed in combat fatigues, boots and mirrored Ray Bans and off we went. Jack lived on a ranch just outside of San Francisco. Obviously his little homemade films did well because the ranch was huge and very rustic.

We started with a workout, posing and flexing while Jack filmed us. His boyfriend did the lighting and sound. Gage and I were both pretty big at this time, weighing 220 lbs. each at six feet. We cut quite the imposing figures with 54-inch chests and 30-inch waists. We looked like big blow up action men.

Filming began and Gage started slapping my chest and next thing we were kissing passionately. I quickly forgot that all of this was being recorded on camera. Gage began playing with my nipples and I pulled his rock hard cock out of his pants and started sucking it. Remember, Jack thought we were brothers so he carried on filming with a giant hard-on tenting his trousers. Gage shot a huge load, I spunked everywhere, the whole thing had taken sixty minutes and we were $2,000 richer. It had been so easy. Good God, if it was this easy starring in porn I thought, I could shoot a movie a day.

When we got back to Casa Sanchez that night the phone was ringing. It was Gabriella.

"Blue, darling, I need you to do a shoot for *Penthouse Magazine* with me tomorrow. The guy I was supposed to do it with broke his legs falling off a trampoline and I know of nobody else who can do this with me."

CHAPTER TEN

"Sure," I said brightly, "I love doing porn, it's so easy."

In the future those words would come back to haunt me.

The *Penthouse* shoot was actually an amazing experience. We arrived the next day at the studio of Jeff, the *Penthouse* photographer. He was a famous erotic photographer who shot beautiful nudes for various classy sex magazines such as *Penthouse* and *Playboy*. For the photo shoot I was dressed in a tuxedo and Gabriella in a cocktail dress. The layout featured us in sepia tones in various stages of undress. *Penthouse* readers didn't buy *Penthouse* to see cock, so I didn't even have to show my dick.

Over lunch Jeff said to me and Gage, who had come along for the ride, "You know you two should be COLT models. I've got Jim French's number somewhere. Why don't you call him and send him some pictures?" There was no Internet in those days, so everything was sent by snail mail.

The movie I had shot with Gage for Jack was called *The Blake Twins: Raw And Uncut* presumably because we both had foreskins and because Jack, the sly bastard, was selling the footage unedited and calling it the director's cut. He charged $100 a copy, an astronomical amount of money for a porno tape, and made a fortune from it. A lot of bodybuilders in those days were making their own porno jerk-off tapes after the advent of the home video camera. This actually nearly destroyed the industry a few years later because anybody with a few bucks could make their own porno, and they did . . . and the market was flooded with badly produced, ugly model porn. Sold in the back of sex magazines, these backstreet pornographers were raking in the cash.

The one exception to this rule was a guy called Dirk Yates. He lived in San Diego near a marine base, and he would pay young, hot marines $200 to jerk off in front of the camera. They would walk in, drink a beer and jerk off watching a straight porno. Dirk made hundreds of these movies, and with the money from them opened up his own studio called "All Worlds." His is one of the most successful studios in the world, all created by one man's unique vision. Those DVDs are still available today and are still as popular as ever, although All Worlds is now owned by Chi Chi LaRue under his company Channel One Releasing.

Following Jeff's advice I sent a couple of pictures of Gage and I to "COLT Studios" in Los Angeles. A few days later the phone rang.

"Blue Blake, please."

"That's me."

"Are you and your brother Gage available to fly to Los Angeles to shoot for *COLT* Magazine?"

I felt light headed. COLT was calling us . . . they wanted us to be COLT models! I couldn't believe it.

"Anytime," I said.

"Good, I'm putting air tickets in the mail. My name's David, I'll pick you up at the airport."

I was so excited I didn't even ask him what we were to be paid for the shoot.

When Gage came home I was doing the hula round the Christmas tree.

"You're happy," he laughed.

"Guess where we're going,"

CHAPTER TEN

"Dunno . . . do we have any tuna left?"

We lived on tuna, pasta and Gatorade.

"We are going to Los Angeles this week to be . . . COLT MODELS!!!" I squealed

"Nice . . . now take that pineapple off your head and boil us some pasta. *Cops* is about to start." Gage loved anything violent on television. He loved watching cop shows where small town sheriffs would raid crack houses in Bumfuck Texas, and women with no teeth and bruises on their legs would run screaming across the screen. I think it reminded him of Liverpool. He wanted to wallow in his working class roots . . . I was fleeing mine.

I knew Gage wouldn't be excited about being a COLT model. He never got excited about anything like that. This was probably good because I was overexcited about gracing the pages of the esteemed magazine so somebody had to keep my feet firmly planted on the ground.

All we knew about L.A. was that people from San Francisco sneered whenever Los Angeles was mentioned. They said it was full of stuck-up, steroid airheads who were only concerned with how they looked: spending all day working out and tanning. This was music to my ears. San Francisco was having a detrimental effect on how Gage looked. San Francisco was all about body modification, tattoos, piercing, even branding. Gage had gotten more tattoos than I could count, and he had rings in his ears and his dick. I put my foot down when I caught him trying to have his nose pierced with a bone through it.

"Are you crazy?" I ranted, "You're going to look like some Swahili tribesman!"

It was time to get out of San Francisco. We had a lot

of regular clients, but if I got one more call from a guy asking me to shit on him . . . . Perhaps we would like L.A. and L.A. would like us. L.A. *loved* us!

We arrived during a huge rainstorm. Even so, I already noticed a big difference from San Francisco. Everyone was tanned and cheerful.

"I'm glad I didn't put that bone through my nose," said Gage sheepishly.

Jim French's assistant picked us up at the airport and drove us to a motel in the San Fernando Valley. This was the porn capitol of the world, which surprised me because it looked like such a normal town. I don't know what I was expecting, huge neon signs of topless chicks twirling their boobs perhaps. Jim's assistant told us there was a gym a few blocks away.

Gold's Gym of North Hollywood was great. Lots of massive straight bodybuilders and soap opera stars. Even so, we caused quite a stir. We dressed like superheroes: all spandex shorts from Hot Skins and flesh-baring cropped tops from *Flash Dance*. I even wore a do-rag, which was extremely fashionable in those days.

One guy approached us with an interesting offer as we were leaving the gym. He told us that The Tom of Finland Company was going to be making its first XXX-rated film based on the erotic drawings of the famed Tom of Finland. Hugely popular, Tom of Finland was an artist who had indeed been born in Finland in 1920. Tom grew up in a time and place where men were either closeted or flaunted their homosexuality by being outrageously effeminate. Tom's artwork portrayed a different world where super built, super masculine men flirted and had full on hardcore

CHAPTER TEN

sex with each other. Every gay guy I knew who was into bodybuilders had at one time or another been profoundly affected by the work of Tom of Finland. By the time Tom died in 1991, he had greatly challenged gay stereotypes by showing well-built studs who were neither weak nor effeminate. One of the saddest aspects of my life was that I never got to meet this icon who, up until his death, had been living in Los Angeles.

The guy who approached us was a talent scout and said we would make the perfect stars for the film. Of course there was only one problem. Gage had never fucked a bodybuilder before in his life. He certainly hadn't fucked me, and he certainly wasn't ready to do it on film. Details, details, I thought, as my mind whirled around with the possibilities of appearing in the film. I was positive I could convince Gage to star in the film with me. We were about to shoot for COLT, and we had been offered starring roles in Tom of Finland's *The Wild Ones*. Could my head get any bloody bigger? I was going to have to grease it up like a pig to get it out of the door of the gym. I told the talent scout to give us a call when he knew more details about the shoot and slipped him our business card. I loved Los Angeles already!

That night I could hardly sleep from excitement. We had been told there was full wardrobe at the COLT Studio, so we had to bring only ourselves. I couldn't wait! Jim French was a genius, the Leonardo da Vinci of erotic photography. Well, Jim French was also . . . ENORMOUSLY FAT!!! and not incredibly pleasant either. Generally I'm extremely congenial and tend to get on with everybody but I have to admit Jim was a bloody trial. We had arrived at the studio and been led by an assistant through a warehouse full of merchandising—COLT t-shirts, videos, fridge magnets— into a large photo studio. There, under an umbrella, sat Jim French. You know how you can meet people you instinctively don't get on with? That was Jim and I. I was shocked by how he looked, and I don't think that he was crazy about me either. I was a little too Rubenesque for Jim's tastes, whereas Gage was genetically ripped to the bone and covered in veins. Gage was always super vascular but big and healthy looking.

"If only he didn't have those ugly tattoos," was the first thing out of Jim French's mouth as he looked Gage up and down. I grabbed Gage by the arm fearful he would jump on Jim.

I smiled, "It is such an honor and privilege to be working for you Mr. French." I said.

He completely ignored me and shouted, "WARDROBE!"

Regardless of how Jim French looked and acted, he was a genius as a photographer. He photographed us both dressed as leather men and cowboys. His studio had a wardrobe like nothing I had ever seen before. It was packed to the rafters with all kinds of masculine costumes and outfits. Jockstraps hung everywhere and old pairs of sexy boots lined the walls. I recognized so many of the shirts and jackets from the magazines I had seen on the models from the *COLT* magazines when I was growing up. Now I was getting the opportunity to wear the same clothes that had graced the bodies of all the musclemen before me. I felt incredibly flattered.

A CONSUMMATE PROFESSIONAL, Jim made sure that

CHAPTER TEN

each shot he took was meticulously lit and staged. One shot could take an hour to set up and light correctly and I understood quickly why he was a legendary photographer. I learned more in those two days about looking sexy and provocative than I had learned in my entire life.

At the end of the two days, Jim had been swayed by Gage's masculinity and he told Gage he wanted to shoot a whole calendar of him in Hawaii for fifteen days. Gage wanted more than the paltry $300 a day payment. Jim counted on Gage's ego winning out, but Gage was all about the cash. Jim gambled with Gage and lost. As we were leaving the studio, I noticed a magazine with Chris Dickerson in it. Chris had been Mr. Olympia in 1982, at forty-three years old. He was a Nubian god, and he had been one of the bodybuilders I had worshipped in those old bodybuilder magazines such as *Flex* and *Muscle & Fitness*, and here he was stark naked in a *COLT* magazine showing off his engorged, and I do mean ENGORGED, cock.

"Hmmm . . . could I take one of these?" I asked Jim's assistant.

Gage and I returned to San Francisco and Casa Sanchez. Back home we started doing magazine shoots like crazy. A gay TV show about San Francisco had filmed us for their opening credits, and our film *Twincest: The Blake Twins Raw and Uncut* came out. We were mini-celebrities.

After a few months, however, Gage grew restless and homesick for London. Our lease was running out, so I returned to London reluctantly with Gage. London wasn't that bad, it was great to see all our old friends again. I knew I would never return to San Francisco again to live. Instead I had my eye on the bigger prize: Los Angeles . . . Hollywood . . . and I was pretty sure I could become a porn star. I had money in the bank and so at the end of my summer in London, I took the cash and jetted back to Los Angeles.

Gage chose to stay in London. He had fallen in love with a girl named Stephanie who he had met in a hugely popular nightclub called Trade, which was owned by Lawrence Malice, a quasi-celebrity on the London club scene. I first met Lawrence when I was twenty-one and massaging at the Camden Tiger. He was a white Rastafarian with blonde dreadlocks. I thought Lawrence was the dog's bollocks . . . I adored him . . . not sexually, just because he was so much fun to hang around with.

Lawrence used to take me to a fetish club called La Maitresse. He would wear a latex leotard with fake breasts and 6-inch dominatrix stilettos and would suck off straight men in the club toilet. Jackie, the future singer from Bananarama worked in the cloakroom. I loved the place. It was like nothing I'd ever seen before. One night, I saw a woman dressed as a pony with a bit in her mouth pulling around a guy in a horse buggy by leather straps which were attached to her vaginal lips. La Maitresse was full of masters, slaves and dominatrices and you could wear anything. I would always take hooker girlfriends of mine there because they enjoyed getting their chance to beat willing straight men who would kneel in front of them, proffer them riding crops and beg to be lashed. One night I took a South African hooker named Carol, who weighed 200 pounds of plumpy pleasure. She was a favorite of Arab clients because of

CHAPTER TEN

how voluptuous she was. Her boobs were a double FF cup. We made her a mini dress out of safety pins and bin liners and nobody blinked an eye . . . not even when she got drunk on snakebites and ripped it off to gyrate in just her knickers on the dance floor.

So I left Gage in London and returned to L.A. I rented a two-bedroom apartment in West Hollywood, the gay section of Los Angeles. It was a modern building with a rooftop swimming pool. I had never in my life had a swimming pool before so I was incredibly impressed. In San Francisco there had been an old tennis court on the roof of Casa Sanchez so this was immeasurable improvement. The building's supervisor was a hot twenty-five-year-old blonde girl named Stacy who seemed to possess an endless wardrobe of micro mini skirts and high heels. She was a total alcoholic and would come scratching at my apartment door at midnight for some love and affection. Where was Gage when I really needed him?

I began escorting in Los Angeles but the work was slow. L.A. was full of escorts, so it was a buyer's market. Although I had an advert in the local gay magazine *Frontiers*, I needed something to supplement my income. I was used to turning up to ten tricks a day and, apart from the cash, I enjoyed staying occupied. I got a job as a bouncer at a bar called "The Spike" on Santa Monica Boulevard. I worked two nights there; then gave it up. I was too full of steroids and I had a really short temper because of them, so being a doorman definitely wasn't the right profession for me. People would get drunk and rowdy and I would get VERY moody.

While working at The Spike, I was chatted with a

OUT OF THE BLUE

hooker who told me I should go check out a restaurant/bar on Sunset Boulevard called "Numbers." Numbers was an institution in Los Angeles. Full of red velvet booths, it was packed every night with hookers and their clients eating dinner. It had a huge mirrored sweeping staircase you had to walk down as you entered. The minute I walked in the door I loved the place. The boys charged $200 an hour and you could easily turn two tricks a night—$400 a night and your days were free. I was in hog heaven. I met all kinds of interesting people and soon had my own booth where I would eat steak dinners every night before turning a couple of tricks. The food was excellent, and somebody always ended up buying me dinner. In return I was charming and hospitable and pretended not to notice they were older than dust. There was a high preponderance of older men there. On the slow nights the hookers would take each other home, but I rarely did this as I was all about business. This was 1992, and there was still very little Internet, so it was either wait by the phone or go to Numbers. I did both. Years later Numbers closed down and became the famous club now known as Hyde, which is frequented by such quasi celebrities as Nicole Ritchie and Paris Hilton. In fact, it's the club where Britney Spears was photographed flashing her vagina to all and sundry whilst climbing out of her car. That club has definitely seen it all: my pecs *and* Britney Spears' vagina.

Frontiers magazine came out every two weeks and I picked up a copy to make sure my advert was in. It was like a ritual. The back of *Frontiers* was full of ads for escorts and masseurs, a lot of bodybuilders and a smat-

CHAPTER TEN

tering of porn stars. Compared to London or San Francisco, the bodybuilding standard was high, and I quickly decided that if Gage came to Los Angeles, we could increase our visibility greatly with our old "Blake Twins" advert. I called him in London where he was languishing forlornly, having had a series of fights with his girlfriend Stephanie. He jumped at my invitation and literally caught the next plane to Los Angeles. Drunken Stacy accosted him upon arrival. By this time she was so consistently plastered that she kept forgetting to fill the roof top pool with water after it had been drained for cleaning. It was time for a new apartment, preferably furnished, as I was renting all the furniture and it was costing me a fortune. But where would I find one? My prayers were about to be answered.

Unlike San Francisco's gay ghetto, the Castro, West Hollywood was totally rent controlled. I was astonished that you could rent an unfurnished two-bedroom apartment with a pool for twelve hundred dollars a month.

While riding my bike down Kings Road, a particularly attractive street in West Hollywood, I spied a glamorous redheaded female loading suitcases into a truck outside a luxurious apartment building called The Courtyards. On occasion I had seen the actress Bernadette Peters zipping in and out, so I knew the residents were of high caliber.

"Excuse me," I said to the redhead. "I don't suppose you know if there are any apartments to rent here, do you?"
"Well, what a coincidence. I'm looking to rent out my apartment, but there's only one problem."

God, here we go, I thought.

"I'm moving to Aspen with my new husband, and I

OUT OF THE BLUE

have to rent it out furnished and it has two bedrooms." Yet again my fat had been literally pulled out of the proverbial frying pan. I smiled my biggest ingratiating smile and said, "You're the answer to my prayers."

Gage and I moved in the next day. Drunken Stacy begged us to stay because she hadn't yet managed to get Gage to shag her. But I bought her a bottle of Harveys Bristol Cream and the last we saw her she was sitting by the empty pool, crying and sucking the sickly sweet liquor straight from the bottle.

The Courtyards was a glorious apartment building. There was a huge supermarket down the street and a big gay gym nearby. Gage would lounge by the pool of the apartment complex in a thong, which only he could get away with. There is something about thongs that make them extremely unsuitable for most men to wear unless they have buttocks of steel—and Gage, God bless him, looked better in a thong than supermodel Giselle Bundchen. In weeks, everybody in the compound knew us. We became friendly with a porn star who lived in the building named Ted Matthews. I didn't fancy Ted, although he was a good-looking guy. But he gave me some great advice. We were sitting by the pool one day and Ted was admiring Gage's ass. Gage, as usual, was pretending to be oblivious.

A well-known COLT model, who also lived in the building, walked by with his Doberman.

"He's a COLT model," said Ted. Gage looked up. "So are we," Gage shrugged. "Not that it did us any good; I made $600 . . . that Jim French can fuck off."

"Wow . . . COLT models," said Ted. "Have your pic-

CHAPTER TEN

tures come out yet?"

"No," I said, "but if you pick up a copy of *Drummer Magazine* you can see our movie, *The Blake Twins: Twincest Raw and Uncut* advertised in the back."

"Who else have you worked for?" Ted was unimpressed.

"Nobody." I replied.

"Why not?"

"Well, we only just arrived in Los Angeles. I really don't know anybody in the porn business here."

"Look in the back of *Frontiers* magazine. They always have ads looking for porn actors."

I had glanced at these adverts before as they were placed alongside my escort ad.

"Well, I did study drama for three years."

"I thought you were marines."

"Yes . . . marines," I fumbled. "Well, that was after I left drama school."

Ted looked at me strangely then shrugged.

"Anyway . . . check out *Frontiers* in the jobs offered column. Tell them you won't work for less than a thousand dollars a scene. That's the going rate for bodybuilders." Ted stood up, kissed me, winked at Gage (who didn't like being kissed) and left the pool.

I ran upstairs to our apartment and grabbed my copy of *Frontiers*. I brought it back down to the pool. Gage leaned over my shoulder as I thumbed through the want ads.

"Fucking hell!" Gage shouted.

"What?!" I yelled back, jumping out of my skin.

"Look . . . in that personal training ad . . . it's Chris Duffy!" He pointed to a picture of an enormous bodybuilder.

OUT OF THE BLUE

Chris Duffy was a god amongst men. He had won the American bodybuilding championships and was always on the cover of *Flex* magazine and *Muscle and Fitness*. He was married to a female bodybuilder named Joanie. For years I had seen him in magazines and thought he was the hottest guy on the planet. He was hugely famous in the bodybuilding world. What the hell was he doing advertising in *Frontiers*? In the ad he reclined against a wall in a pair of posing trunks, all 300 pounds and 6-foot-3 delicious inches of him.

"I'm going to call him," I told Gage.

"You don't need a personal trainer," Gage scoffed.

"No, but I need Chris Duffy's knob stuffed in my gob."

I had no problem paying for sex. I had never done it before, but I had been in the escort business long enough to know that everybody paid for a shag in one way or another. Whether you were buying your girlfriend a diamond bracelet or taking your boyfriend out for dinner, it was all in hopes of a booty call.

"He's advertising as a personal trainer and he's married," Gage protested.

"He's advertising personal training dressed in a thong."

"I wear a thong," said Gage.

Why did I get involved in these ridiculous conversations with Gage?

"Just shut up and pass me the damn phone," I snapped. "I have a date with destiny."

My sweaty little fingers punched in Chris's number. The phone rang and then picked up almost immediately.

"This is Chris," said a handsome, sexy voice.

"Hello," I started, not even being able to conceive of the

Me at the age of one.

My New Romantic stage, Nottingham.

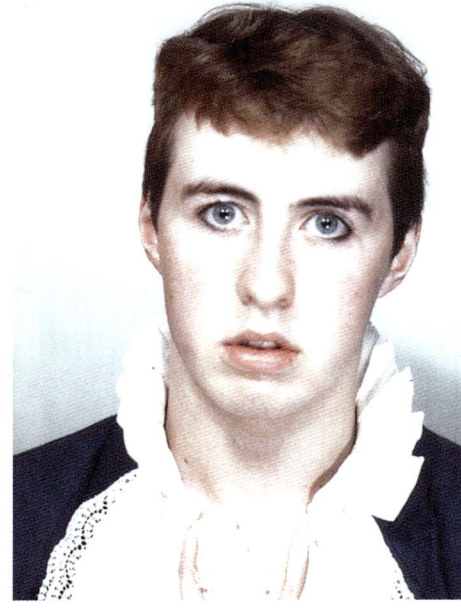

Covent Garden, right in the middle of my punk phase.

Sam and me, roommates at Mountview Theater School.

Gramercy Park, New York, age 20.

Rio de Janeiro.

The night before I left for New Orleans.
Karen begged me not to go; she was right.

Snapshot taken
in London;
I was starting to get
more muscle.

Seriously getting into working out, London.

Winning the Mr. Drummer United Kingdom contest in London.

Me and Officer Betty at the International Mr. Drummer Contest in San Francisco.

At the International Mr. Drummer Contest finals in San Francisco. I was representing the U.K.

Arriving in Los Angeles to embark on my porn career.

Veronica Brazil presenting Best Bi-Sexual Feature during the 1995 Gay Video Guide Awards, Ryan Block standing next to her, and me in mesh and leather. (GREGORY ZABILSKI)

Performing onstage at the Gay Porn Awards in my tighty-whiteys.
(GREGORY ZABILSKI)

Gage and I at Venice Beach with his pimp-mobile; we had been in Los Angeles for just a month.

Me and Ryan Idol in
New York City,
News Years Eve, during
the *Making Porn* run.

Harold and I after our first
year of dating. (TIM PALEN)

Gay Pride Parade in Los Angeles.

Porn star Ken Ryker and me at an awards show.

With Heather Locklear at the opening of *Aida*.

With Joanna Keylock, my costar in *Making Porn*, in Los Angeles.

Me with Barbara Walters at the opening of Disney's *Aida* on Broadway.

Me with porn star Billy Herrington at an awards show.

With porn star TJ Hart at the AVN Porn Awards in Las Vegas.

With Scott Gunz, star of my film *Hard as Rock*.

Coral Smith and Melissa Howard, stars of MTV'S *The Real World*, and me.

With Harvey Fierstein at the opening night of *Hairspray* on Broadway.

Tom Katt, me, and Caesar. Tom and Caesar starred in my film *Cowboy*.

Me with costar Matthew Rush doing *Making Porn* in San Diego.

On the set of
Cowboy Rides Again
with one of my stars,
Frank Shaft.
(Frank has a 12-inch cock.)

Four huge porn legends: Jason Adonis, Matthew Rush,
myself, and Ken Ryker.

CHAPTER TEN

fact that I was talking to Chris Duffy. I was in heaven.

"My name's Blue Blake . . . I saw your ad in *Frontiers*. I was interested in a little . . . personal training."

"Have you worked out before?" asked the handsome voice.

"Hmmm . . . only for a year," I lied. "I thought perhaps you could come round and give me some advice. My glutes are extremely undeveloped and need work." Was I really saying this crap? I had a huge round ass, but I would say anything to lure my straight quarry.

Chris arranged to meet me at my apartment the following Monday night. I was a nervous wreck. I ran out and bought protein drinks, tuna, bananas . . . everything I thought a professional bodybuilder would eat to keep up his 300 pounds of studliness for an hour. I threw Gage out and told him to go bother the transvestites on the corner of the street and changed into an all-in-one wrestling suit. It had blue and white stripes and accentuated my man bosom the way I imagined a straight pro bodybuilder would appreciate.

Chris arrived at 6 p.m. sharp, and we literally fell into each other's arms . . . Well, that's at least how I remember it. I dragged him into the living room and we stripped each other bare. He was everything I imagined. He was absolutely massive with muscles of steel. It was like having sex with Superman. He fucked me with his big cock for hours. Afterwards we lay in each other's arms.

"Have you been with a lot of guys?" I asked.

"You're my first," he said with perfect sincerity. I didn't know if he was lying, and I didn't care.

"What about your wife?" I asked.

"Joanie? It turns her on thinking about me with another guy. Would you like to meet her?"

"Uuuuhhhh . . . sure . . . I guess," I said apprehensively. I didn't want some crazed female bodybuilder attacking me with a bread knife for introducing her husband to homo love.

"She's cool," he laughed, reading my mind.

He got dressed and I handed him $200.

"I feel strange taking it."

"Don't," I said, "I have no problem giving it to you."

"Well, next time it's free."

Next time!!! Did this mean Mr. America, wanted to see me again? No, he was probably being polite.

"Call me," Chris said, as he walked out the door.

Gage stood sulking in the hallway.

"Did you have sex with him?"

"Yes, and it was amazing!"

"Well, there's no way you'll ever see him again then you slag."

I didn't care. Even if I never saw Chris Duffy again, I had still had sex with Mr. America.

"Oh, by the way," continued Gage, "that film company you called, Catalina? They called back, they want you to do a film for them tomorrow."

"What!? A film? For Catalina?" I couldn't believe my luck.

Catalina was a famous porn production company. I had found an advert in the back of *Frontiers* that that read: MODELS WANTED 18-35 FOR ADULT FILMS. There was a P.O. number, and I had sent them some pictures of myself along with my phone number.

CHAPTER TEN

"Yeah, there's a message for you on the answering machine, it rang while you were out buying bananas for Chris Duffy," said Gage snidely.

I hadn't noticed the answer phone had been flashing. I ran over to it and pressed play.

"This is Catalina Video calling Blue Blake. We are shooting a film called *Seeds of Love* directed by Chi Chi LaRue, and we received your photographs and would like to offer you a role in the movie."

I quickly wrote down the number they had left, picked up the phone and dialed it.

"This is Scott."

"Scott . . . this is Blue. . . ."

"Blake," he cut in. "Hi, we received your pictures. Are you free to do a scene tomorrow?"

"Sure," I answered. Remembering what Ted Matthews had told me, I added, "I charge a thousand dollars a scene."

"Well, this only pays five hundred dollars because it's just an oral scene. We like to start newcomers out with just an oral scene before we offer them a full fuck scene."

Five hundred dollars to get my dick sucked sounded OK.

"Well, that should be fine," I said.

"Good, have you made films before?"

"Not really," I said. I didn't think *Twincest: the Blake Twins Raw and Uncut* counted.

"Well, this one is being directed by Chi Chi LaRue. So you're starting at the top."

Chi Chi LaRue was a legend. He started out a drag queen from Minnesota. Once in L.A. he got a job shipping videos for Catalina. Then one day a director fell ill and there was nobody to direct the film that was in production. Chi Chi jumped at the opportunity and in the process made a big name for himself. He now directed constantly for top companies like Falcon and Catalina. Scott filled me in on the rest of the details and told me Chi Chi's address and said to be there at 9 a.m. sharp.

"Be clean," he said ominously. Clean? What the hell did that mean? Wasn't everybody clean on a porn set?

I lay awake all night with excitement. My first proper film role in *Seeds of Love*. Scott had told me I would be working with a guy called Hunter Scott. It was Hunter's second movie, so we were both newcomers.

The next morning I dressed in jeans, muscle vest and a leather bike jacket. Scott had said my costume was to be white underwear that they would provide. Gage drove me to Chi Chi's house in the chop-top cherry red Cadillac he'd bought the minute he arrived in L.A.

Chi Chi lived in a modest two-bedroom cottage on Melrose Avenue.

"This can't be it," Gage laughed. "You told me she was a famous director."

"She's a he."

"Who's named Chi Chi LaRue?" sneered Gage.

"Who's named Blue Blake?" I retorted.

I climbed out of the card and hammered on the front door.

"Just a minute," answered a gruff but sexy voice from inside.

Wow, Chi Chi has a hot voice for a drag queen, I thought. I turned and smiled at Gage who waited dubiously in the car. The door opened and I nearly fell over.

CHAPTER TEN

There stood a stunning guy in white underwear smiling at me. He looked like a young Tom Cruise with muscles.

"Hello," he smiled. "I'm Derek Cruise. Wow, you're huge. Come on in, Chi Chi's expecting you."

I couldn't tear my eyes off Derek Cruise. He was a bit younger than the type I normally went for, but he was breathtaking: thick hair and a smooth, toned body, seemingly straight. I followed him into the gloomy exterior and my eyes drank in the décor—Drab walls and a threadbare couch and a bed in the corner of the living room that Derek had hopped back into. Apparently he had been asleep when I knocked.

"Do you live here?" I asked.

"Yeah, It's Chi Chi's place, and there's only two bedrooms. Zak Spears has the other room."

I had heard of Zak Spears, who was also from Minnesota. He had been working as a construction worker when Chi Chi "discovered" him. You couldn't walk into a porn store without seeing Zak's picture everywhere. Tall, hairy and extremely masculine, he was said to have the sexiest voice in porn. He was a huge star.

"Find somewhere to sit," said Derek. "Move those Barbie dolls."

I suddenly realized the room was full of Barbie dolls in boxes. They were strewn everywhere. There must have been 200 of them.

"Chi Chi collects Barbie dolls," explained Derek.

I moved Wedding Barbie and High School Barbie out of the way and sat on the couch.

"Am I early?" I asked.

"No. Chi Chi's always running late," he said. "He

OUT OF THE BLUE

works late doing drag appearances."

"Does he direct in drag?" I asked nervously.

"Girl . . . are you crazy?" boomed a voice behind me. I turned and there stood a plump, bleached-haired guy with no eyebrows. "It would kill me to direct in drag." This obviously was Chi Chi LaRue.

"Ooh, you're gorgeous," squealed Chi Chi. "Listen, I'm doing a movie called *Posing Strap* in a month. I can offer you two scenes."

"Ummm . . . perhaps we should see how I do in this one first."

"Please yourself," said Chi Chi, as if I were passing up a golden opportunity.

I could tell he wasn't used to being denied.

"Derek is the star of the film we're making, but you don't have a scene with him. You're with Hunter Scott."

"What's the film about?" I asked.

Chi Chi sighed with exasperation. "Girl . . . it's about a scientist that develops a plant and when you eat the seeds of the plant, if you're straight you become gay . . . you play a gardener whom the scientist secretly experiments on. When you and Hunter Scott eat the seeds you suck each other off."

The plot sounded absolutely ludicrous. I was just about to ask Chi Chi, who had written it, when a bedroom door opened and out strolled Zak Spears in a toweling dressing gown. He was very handsome, and I could tell by the way he was looking at me he thought I wasn't bad either.

"Zak," Chi Chi cooed, "Did we wake you?"

"I heard voices."

"This is Blake Blue," said Chi Chi.

CHAPTER TEN

"Blue Blake," I corrected.

"Whatever," she snapped.

"Nice to meet you, Blue," said Zak, shaking my hand and looking deep into my eyes. "Wouldn't Blue be perfect for *Posing Strap?*"

"I already asked him, but he turned me down flat."

"Perhaps I could persuade him," said Zak. "You'd be doing a scene with me."

Now, I wasn't super attracted to Zak, although he had a great body and fabulous looks. My mind was still full of images of Chris Duffy. On the other hand, he *was* Zak Spears and if I was going to make a career in porno it damn well couldn't hurt to do a movie with Zak Spears.

"What does it pay?" I asked Chi Chi.

"Two scenes, sixteen hundred dollars."

"I want a thousand dollars a scene."

"I'm giving you two scenes so the rate is lower," Chi Chi said matter-of-factly. "It's always like that."

This of course was a total lie, but I was new to the industry, so what did I know? Directors were paid X amount of dollars to produce and direct a movie by the production company. Whatever they could cream off the top by underpaying the talent they got to keep. I was about to refuse the offer remembering what Ted Matthews had told me.

"I'd really like to work with you," Zak said.

I realized he was still holding my hand, a fact that hadn't gone unnoticed by Chi Chi, who seemed to have a crush on Zak.

"Why not," I acquiesced.

"Perfect," Chi Chi purred.

"Will Derek be in the movie?" I asked.

"No," snapped Chi Chi, "I have another model for you to work with."

"Is he a bodybuilder? I like bodybuilders."

"And I like breasts, but I don't have them."

"Then I'd rather not do it."

"Of course he's a bodybuilder!" Chi Chi exclaimed. "The movie's called *Posing Strap*; it's about all those 1950s *Bruce of Hollywood* bodybuilding magazines where all the guys wore posing straps, so everybody's a bodybuilder in this film!"

Later, I would discover that Chi Chi and I definitely had different views on what constituted a bodybuilder.

For the moment, I said, "OK, it sounds like it might be fun,"

"Then it's settled."

"Is the film for Catalina?" I asked.

"No," said Zak, "It's for a company called His, they have big budgets."

There was a knock at the door.

"That must be Chris," said Chi Chi. "He'll be working as my production assistant today; we're in a rock band together."

Chi Chi opened the door and in walked Chris Green. He definitely looked like he was in a rock band: black, spiky hair and tattoos. It turned out that Chi Chi was always putting Chris in movies but he never became a big star. He was too off-the-wall looking for the average porn buyer but Chi Chi was a good friend and believed in him. For some reason I liked Chris immediately. I was a little uncertain about my opinion of Chi Chi but I was

CHAPTER TEN

willing to go with the flow.

As Chris loaded up Chi Chi's SUV with various sugary supplies of energy for the day's shoot—boxes of candy, soft drinks, etc.—Zak came up to me.

"You know, I'd really like to buy you dinner after the shoot."

"You mean like a date?" I asked.

"Yeah . . . a date," he grinned.

Why not, I thought, I wasn't seeing anybody, and Zak was a famous, good-looking porn star. I could do much worse.

"Sure. I'd like that."

I gave him my number then turned to find Chi Chi glaring at me. I could tell that he was used to getting his own way. Unfortunately so was I.

We piled into the truck and drove to the location in the hills of Hollywood. Chi Chi had rented a house that had a beautiful private garden, and already the rest of the crew was setting up for the scene we were to shoot. A very slim, mixed race guy approached me.

"Hello. You must be Blue . . . I'm Mocha."

"Like the chocolate," I said.

"Yeah, my real name's Greg, but everybody calls me Mocha. I'm going to be taking all the photos today."

There was something about Mocha that I liked right away. He wasn't good looking but he had a great sense of humor, and I found out that he was one of the most famous photographers in the porn industry. He photographed for every major company and so shot every porn star in existence. He loved to shoot assholes. He had models bend over and spread their cheeks wide. He had a collection of literally thousands of asshole shots.

"Get into makeup and I'll do your glamour shots," he said.

Glamour shots were photographs that weren't necessarily pornographic. They were of models posing and lit extremely well. Glamour shots would be used for the back of the video box cover and for photo layouts in magazines like *Torso* and *Inches*. Mocha made handsome men look like gods. I learned quickly to suck up to the set photographer. These guys could make or break your career.

I wandered into the kitchen of the rented house, and there sat a good-looking guy in his underwear having his face made up.

"Hello, I'm Hunter Scott, we're working together today."

"Hello," I smiled. "I'm Blue Blake."

"I heard about you. You've got a twin brother, haven't you?

"Yes," I lied. "Gage."

As Hunter was getting his make up done I suddenly realized there was somebody else in the makeup room— a tall, skinny blond guy of indeterminate age.

"I'm Crystal. Crystal Crawford," said Skinny. "I'm a good friend of Chi Chi's. I'm actually a director myself."

"And a drag queen too," murmured Hunter under his breath.

Hunter looked Italian with a very athletic, hairy body. He wasn't really my type, but I guessed I wouldn't mind sucking his dick for five hundred bucks.

Hunter climbed out of the makeup chair and I took his place. The make up artist started applying founda-

CHAPTER TEN

tion to my face.

"Listen, I'm doing a movie tomorrow based on *Sliver*, the Sharon Stone movie, and I need somebody to fuck the star in an elevator . . . do you want the part?"

I had seen the film and it was ridiculous. Sharon Stone played a book editor in NYC and William Baldwin was a crazed billionaire who owned the apartment building she moved into. Years later I met Ms. Stone at a party when she was married to her husband the gorgeous hunk of man Phil Bronstein. I was with my boyfriend, who knew her, and my mother, who had absolutely no idea who Sharon Stone was.

"Your husband is gorgeous," I said to Sharon. I had seen Phil at various events with her. He was brawny and a total man.

"Not as gorgeous as yours," said Sharon nodding at my boyfriend Harold.

"This is my mother Jean," I said.

"Jean . . . you must have been a child bride," smiled Sharon.

My mother developed her one and only girl on girl crush on Sharon Stone.

Wow, I thought, this is so easy. Work was being thrown at me. I was going to make a fortune in porn.

"Who do I have to fuck?" I asked.

"A really hot guy called Tanner Reeves; he's really handsome and done hundreds of films."

I had never heard of Tanner Reeves.

"What's your scene rate?" asked Crystal.

"A thousand dollars."

"Hmm . . . that's not in my budget. How about if we

make the scene an oral and I'll give you five hundred?"

I actually thought this was a better idea. I didn't want to agree to fuck somebody I hadn't even met. What if I didn't fancy him and I couldn't get hard?

"OK," I shrugged.

"Great, but don't tell Chi Chi."

With my makeup finished I headed outside to be photographed by Mocha.

"Take off your shirt and lean against the wall," he said.

I did as I was instructed and gave my best porno pout.

"Girl . . . you look hot," said Mocha.

I found out that "girl" was Chi Chi's favorite expression and all the crew had picked up on it. I didn't care. I thought it was funny. I was 220 pounds with a crew cut.

"You're going to be very famous," said Mocha, snapping away. "Who else have you worked for?"

"Hmm . . . really just COLT."

"Wow, you're a COLT model and you're doing hard core? That's really unusual. Normally COLT models don't do hard core."

"Well, I only did one shoot with Jim French."

"One's enough," laughed Mocha. "You'll see yourself for years in those *COLT* magazines." He was right of course.

"Crystal just offered me a film tomorrow," I whispered. Mocha put down the camera and came over to me.

"Make sure you get paid," he whispered back.

I was wondering what he meant by that when I heard Chi Chi shouting, "Hunter Scott and Blue Blake on the set!"

All of a sudden I was nervous. I was very, very, very nervous. This was my first real porn scene for a major

CHAPTER TEN

company and I knew I was going to fuck it up. There were about ten crew members standing around, and I had never felt less horny in my entire life. There was no way I was going to be able to get hard and do this. There was no such thing as Viagra in those days; you had to get hard just by force of will alone. These days on the porn sets there's Viagra and even Cavaject, which is a very common drug used in porn. It is injected directly into the penis to fill it with blood. The effect lasts for about six hours during which time you can even sit and eat lunch and your dick doesn't go down. One side effect is that sometimes Cavaject induces priapism and then the model has to be rushed to the hospital to have his dick deflated with a saltwater wash-through before it literally explodes from the pressure.

"I'm nervous," I said to Mocha.

"Everybody's nervous their first time, but you're gorgeous and you're going to be great."

"OK!" shouted Chi Chi. "Where are my actors?"

We were shooting in a well-lit corner of the garden—Chi Chi sitting behind a TV monitor, the make up artist, Chris Green being a P.A., Mocha clutching his camera, the videographer, another P.A., the guy who owned the house we were shooting in, and the lighting guy—all watching and waiting for me to get hard.

"OK," said Chi Chi. "You're trimming the hedge; you stop, pick up the drink on the table because you take a sip."

This was no problem and went without a hitch.

"Now," he continued, "you're straight but the drugged drinks have made you faaaabulously gay, and Hunter, you pull down Blue's jeans and start sucking his cock."

OUT OF THE BLUE

Wait!!! I wasn't even hard! That was when I learned one of the first illusions of porn. We shot all the footage up to where Hunter pulled my soft dick out of my trousers.

"Cut! OK, let's let Blue get hard."

To my amazement, nobody cared I wasn't hard. It happened all the time apparently. The crew began chatting amongst themselves, and I sat on a lawn chair and played with my dick and thought about Chris Duffy's muscles. That did the trick and I stood up, fully erect. Chi Chi took it from there.

"Stuff it back in your underwear, and then Hunter, pull it out and twang it up and down, then stuff it in your mouth and make sure there's lots of spit."

The moment I put my dick back in my underwear I felt it going soft. Hunter pulled it out, but it wasn't hard enough to "twang."

"OK," said Chi Chi, "let's let Blue get rock hard again."

This carried on for the next two hours until finally Chi Chi had all the footage of my hard dick that he was going to get. My dick felt red and sore from playing with it for two hours.

"Next we're going to get your facial expressions. The cameras are on your face. Now start moaning and talking to Hunter like he's sucking your dick."

This bit was easy.

"Yeah, man, suck my dick," I moaned. "Man, that feels so good, your hot lips on my hard cock." I felt ridiculous, but I had watched enough porno to know what to say. I wanted to make up for not getting hard very easily, so I threw myself into the performance. I realized it was actually very easy to moan and fake being serviced.

CHAPTER TEN

It reminded me of how I used to treat some escort clients.

"Fine, we've got enough of that, now Blue, on your knees and suck Hunter's cock."

And of course, Hunter, being the professional he was, immediately went rock hard. I sucked while the cameraman maneuvered himself around me.

"Spit on it, girl!" screamed Chi Chi.

This had to be the most unsexual moment of my life, being screamed at to suck the dick of a stranger who I didn't even fancy while the whole crew looked on.

Finally, that scene was done, all that was left were the cum shots. A lot of models notoriously have problems cumming at the end of the scene. I was so relieved the scene was over; I came in two seconds. What a relief! My first scene finished, and as I was filling out my model release, I realized perhaps it hadn't been as hard as I thought. I had made five hundred bucks after all.

Hunter gave me a ride home.

"I'm sorry I couldn't get hard."

"No problem. I hear everybody's like that," Hunter laughed.

"But you had no problem."

"I'm always hard," he grinned.

He dropped me off outside my apartment.

"Perhaps we'll work together again!" He waved and drove off.

I ran into the apartment.

"How was it?" Gage asked.

"Not too bad," I said, feeling the five hundred dollars in my pocket.

"Well, good," said Gage, "because some really queer

sounding guy called. He said his name was Crystal Crawford and he left an address for you to be at tomorrow morning. He said wear jeans and don't jerk off tonight. Are you doing another film?"

"It looks like it," I said. "I'm having an early night. I'm exhausted."

And I was. I was absolutely knackered. Making porn was the most tiring thing I had ever done in my life for some reason. I suppose because of the mental and physical pressure of having to look and act sexually alluring when it was the last thing on your mind. I felt like I had run a marathon. I fell dead asleep and didn't wake until I heard the alarm go off at 7 a.m.

As I was brushing my teeth the phone rang. It was Zak Spears.

"What happened to our dinner plans?" he asked.

"Oh, my God, I'm so sorry, it completely slipped my mind," I gasped. Zak laughed.

"Don't worry. I know what it's like to do your first scene. What about this evening?"

"Well, I'm doing a movie today as well. I think it's going to be very big budget. It's based on the Sharon Stone movie *Sliver*.

"Who's directing it?"

"Crystal Crawford."

The line went quiet.

"Hello? Zak? Are you still there?"

"Just make sure you get paid," Zak said, ominously. Him too. After what Mocha had said, I was on guard. I was definitely going to get paid.

Gage had written down an address where the shoot was

CHAPTER TEN

to take place. Amazingly, it was within walking distance of our apartment. I had agreed to have dinner with Zak that night, and he was going to pick me up at 6 p.m. sharp. So I had to be finished with the scene and be home by then.

I looked at the address on the piece of paper: 1200 N. Crescent Heights, just above Santa Monica Boulevard. I arrived at an enormous pink apartment building and rang the bell and was buzzed in. This must be where Crystal lived. We were all probably meeting here to drive to the set I thought. Crystal had told me I would be having sex in an elevator, so the movie must have a big budget to build an elevator on the set.

I knocked on Crystal's apartment door and heard a dog yapping from inside. The door was flung open and there stood Crystal holding a tiny video camera.

"Oh, good, you're on time," he said. "Come on in."

I walked inside the apartment, which was full of pictures of Crystal in drag. He wore huge blonde wigs and, as he was extremely bony, the wigs gave the illusion of eating his head.

"Where's the crew?" I asked. Crystal laughed. "Girl, I'm the crew. I believe in total artistic control, so I shoot the movies myself."

I looked at him incredulously.

"With that tiny camera?"

"Oh, it works fine, you'll see."

I could feel my stomach knotting up. This was going to be a really cheap production, and I would be starring in it.

"What's the film called?"

"I haven't decided yet. Your co-star will be here in a minute and then we can get on the set."

I sat down, and a white fluffy dog leapt on my lap. It had the biggest bow I'd ever seen tied on its head and a diamante collar. I noticed that half the diamantes were missing and the dog needed a bath.

"Who's my co-star again?"

"Fuck, you ask a lot of questions. His name's Tanner Reeves, I told you . . . and he's made hundreds of films."

Yeah, hundreds of cheap budget films, I thought, if he had knowingly agreed to work for Crystal. There was a knock at the door.

"Here he is," Crystal shrieked and flew to the door in a waft of Charlie perfume. The moment Tanner Reeves walked in I didn't fancy him. Oh dear, this was two in a row. Perhaps I wasn't cut out for porn. Tanner had a fake tan and too-white teeth. He reminded me of a lot of the guys I had seen floating around West Hollywood. This was going to be a long, horrible day, I realized.

"OK," said Crystal. "Follow me."

We traipsed out of Crystal's apartment and into an elevator that headed down to the underground car park. As we climbed out of the elevator, Crystal pulled an old stiletto shoe out of a bag he was carrying and jammed it into the elevator door.

"What are you doing?" I gasped.

"Jamming the door so we can shoot the scene here."

"We're shooting the scene HERE?" I asked. "In the elevator? What if people see us?"

"How can they?" said Crystal, "I've jammed the door with my shoe. Now take your cock out and let Tanner suck it."

I was a nervous wreck. There was no way I would be

CHAPTER TEN

able to get hard. What if somebody came into the garage in their car and caught us? We would be arrested for indecent exposure! Crystal stood holding the tiny video camera impatiently, "Hurry up, we don't have all day!"

Tanner sank to his knees in the elevator and began stroking the front of my jeans. I closed my eyes and thought of Gage and Chris Duffy. There was a stirring in my loins. Perhaps I could get hard after all.

Suddenly a piercing siren wail filled the air.

"Damn!" said Crystal. "The elevator alarm's been activated. Quick, up to my apartment before the building manager catches us."

The three of us ran madly up the stairs and dashed into Crystal's apartment.

"We'll shoot the scene here," he said.

"Will it make sense within the movie?" I asked.

"Who cares?" Crystal snapped. "People don't watch these films for the plot. Now get your dick out . . . and it better be hard."

A long two hours later and the scene was finally complete. Crystal had even taken the photos himself of us fellating each other. As I was filling out my model release Crystal said, "Oh no, I've run out of checks, can I pay you tomorrow?"

Warning bells went off in my head, but Crystal's apartment was only a stone's throw from my own. Besides, he wasn't going anywhere, judging by all the crap he would have to move to disappear.

"Sure, I'll be here tomorrow at 1 p.m. sharp to collect it."

When I got home, Gage was waiting.

OUT OF THE BLUE

"You've got messages. One from Zak Spears confirming dinner, one from Chi Chi LaRue . . . and one from Chris Duffy. How was the shoot?"

"Fucking terrible," I said. "What did Chi Chi and Chris want?"

I knew Gage was impressed that Chris Duffy had called, but I tried to act nonchalant.

"He wants you to call him, and Chi Chi left a message asking if we wanted to perform at the gay porn awards."

The Gay Porn Awards?!!! Perform?!!! I snatched up the phone and dialed Chi Chi's number.

"Now, it doesn't pay anything," said Chi Chi, "but it will be great exposure for you and your brother. You'll be carrying Sharon Kane on the stage on a surfboard while she sings one of the nominated songs."

Who knew they nominated songs from porn movies? Who knew they HAD songs in porn movies?

"The awards are being held at The Tomkat Theatre, and Sharon wants to meet you both first." Sharon Kane was a famous female porn star. She was well known on the gay porn scene because she made a lot of the bi movies and she was always dating the straight guys who appeared in gay porn, the gay-for-pay guys. Rumor had it she would fuck them with a strap-on dildo to loosen them up for their screen debuts.

"I'll give you Sharon's number, and you can all arrange to meet up."

"OK," I said. "But Zak is picking me up at 6."

"Zak Spears? My Zak?" Chi Chi gasped.

"Yeah. Didn't he tell you? He's taking me out for dinner tonight."

CHAPTER TEN

"No, he didn't." said Chi Chi, talking through what had to be clenched teeth. "Have a good time."

Sharon Kane came round to our apartment that afternoon. I liked her immediately. She had had a little too much cosmetic surgery on her face so her lips were massive but she was a fun girl. She told us she had a pet pig. Sharon was nominated for a song she had written and would sing it live. There was to be no rehearsal as the show was just two days away.

The Gay Erotic Video Awards were started by a porn reviewer named Sabin, who published a small magazine that reviewed porn movies. The straight film companies had their own annual show in Vegas called the Adult Video News awards (the AVNs), but the gay companies had nothing . . . until now. There were to be various awards: Best Film, Best Actor, etc., but also strange sub-categories such as Best Cocksucker and Best Cum Shot. It was of course going to be a freak show, but there was nothing I liked more than a two-headed monkey boy. Gage seemed indifferent but I knew he loved to flaunt his body so I wasn't worried.

That night I had dinner with Zak Spears. He turned out to be incredibly shy and thoughtful. He told me he had been bullied a lot while growing up because he was gay, and then he had gotten a job on a construction site where his fellow workmen had also made fun of him. This surprised me because on meeting Zak you would never know he was gay. Chi Chi had rescued him from all that and he was grateful for it. He told me he couldn't believe how huge Gage was and asked if he could train with the two of us. I thought it was a great idea. I would get to work out with Gage, who was gargantuan, and Zak Spears, one of the most famous porn stars in the world. Jesus Christ, I was loving L.A.

Gage was really easy going when it came to training partners and I knew he wouldn't mind Zak training with us. Zak and I slept together at his place that night. The sex was unremarkable, and it felt like we were both there because we liked the unreal porn persona of each other. Zak's bedroom was full of vampire memorabilia. He told me he liked vampires; he even had fake fangs lying around and *Dracula* playing on the television.

Gage picked us up the next morning in his "pimpmobile" as I called it, and we went to Gold's Gym Hollywood. Among all the models and actors I spied the model Fabio. I could never figure out if Fabio was gay or straight. I knew he was straight but there was something a little gay about him, his absolute adoration of himself, perhaps. Years later, a friend of mine, Amy, became his roommate. Apparently he was incredibly vain; no shock there. Once during a rainstorm he made her wedge sand bags under the wheels of his car to get it rolling out of the mud so he wouldn't get his own hair wet. I never knew if this story was true because Amy like to exaggerate more than I did, but I laughed every time she told the story. Fabio nearly died during a roller coaster ride when a rogue goose smashed into his face in mid-flight. It was the talk of the gym and the main story on *Entertainment Tonight* that evening.

While we were training, Gage said, "Chris Duffy keeps calling . . . you have to phone him back."

"Do you know Chris Duffy?" asked Zak, "He's one of

CHAPTER TEN

my favorite bodybuilders."

"Blue fucked him . . . on their first date."

"Well, it wasn't exactly a date," I muttered.

I was incredibly flattered that Chris kept calling I but knew he was married so what the hell did he want? I called him as soon as I got back from the gym. I didn't want to get involved with a married man but my flesh was weak.

"Chris, it's Blue."

"Blue, man, I thought you were going to call me."

I didn't remember telling him I would call him but I shrugged it off.

"Sorry, I've been really busy." I had, with Zak Spears.

"Listen, let's get together again. I want you to meet my wife Joanie."

"Sure, how about this Sunday?"

I was performing at the porno awards on Saturday night, but what the hell did Chris mean about his wife? Surely he wouldn't bring her, and if he did, would I have to fuck her??!! I had fucked some beautiful girls, but I just wasn't into it sexually, at all.

"Great," said Chris. "I'll be there at 3 p.m. I'm really horny." So that confirmed we were going to have sex again. I grinned from ear to ear. Who cared if he was going to drag along the old ball and chain? I DEFINITELY loved Los Angeles.

Saturday night rolled around, the night of the Porn Awards. The Tomkatt Theatre was near enough to our apartment that Gage and I walked there. Neither Gage nor I were nominated because we were just starting out in the industry but, being bodybuilders, we knew we would be the biggest guys there, so we dressed accordingly. We wore work boots, rolled down socks, cut-off denim shorts and no shirts, just baby oil (I'm blushing as I write this). We had tans and flattops and were muscle monsters. We arrived at the Tomkatt to a mob scene. Every porn star in America seemed to be outside the Tomkatt Theatre. The place was a dump, but they had laid out the red carpet, and fans had flocked to see their favorite fuck flick stars in the flesh. And there was plenty of flesh.

I spotted my co-star, Hunter Scott, immediately, and the famous porn-star-turned-director/producer, Gino Colbert. Also in attendance were Jon Vincent, who I had fingered in San Francisco; tons of really bad drag queens; Matt Gunther, another famous porn star; Max Grand; Alec Powers; Michael Brawn; Rick Donovan. . . . The list of porn stars was endless, but no matter how famous they were, everyone ogled Gage and me. We were being handed business cards left, right and centre. I stuffed them into my shorts.

Stars were arriving thick and fast. It was like a really, really bad version of the Oscars. Sharon Kane arrived with her boyfriend. She was dressed like the Malibu Barbie I had seen in Chi Chi's apartment, with a huge flower in her hair and tiny miniskirt. David Forest, the infamous porn agent, arrived wearing a white dinner jacket and lots of diamonds; with a whole entourage of boys he represented flocking around him. He introduced himself to me and Gage. Then Chris Dickerson walked in. I couldn't believe it. Mr. Olympia himself. He was just as big, black and incredibly handsome as the bodybuilding magazines had portrayed him. I was drooling like a Saint Bernard.

CHAPTER TEN

"Close your mouth," said Gage.

"I have to have sex with him."

"You might not be his type," laughed Gage.

"I have to!" I shouted, completely unhinged. Chris Dickerson turned and looked at me.

"You're my favorite bodybuilder of all time!" I said. Hadn't I also told Chris Duffy the exact same thing? I was turning into a total pro-bodybuilder muscle whore. I could see myself working my way through the ranks of the World Bodybuilding Federation . . . who would be next? Tom Platz?

"I saw you and your brother in a movie," Chris said. He had a very sexy deep voice, which seemed to rumble through my brain down my spine and into my hard cock.

"*Twincest* . . . did you like it?" I replied in the huskiest voice I could summon.

"Very sexy," said Chris. "Are you going to the after party? . . . I'll be there."

The after party was being held at Rage, a gay club in West Hollywood near our apartment.

"Yes, I'll definitely be there."

"Great . . . I'll meet you there then."

I was blown away. Mr. Fucking Olympia, and he seemed up for some boy love action. Perfect, because I was certainly going to provide it.

"I don't know how you do it," laughed Gage. "Chris Duffy, Chris Dickerson. . . ."

"YOU!!" I thought, but said nothing.

The show was GROTESQUE, unbelievably bad and totally unprofessional. Gage and I were astonished at some of the uglies that were calling themselves porn stars. Very few were larger than life, and the strange moth-eaten venue of the Tomkatt Theater didn't help matters. Award after award was presented and I marveled at how seriously everybody took this, especially when considering how bizarre the categories were: Best Cum Shot, Best Oral, Star with the Loosest Hole. Best Movie that year was *Songs in the Key of Sex,* which I thought was a ridiculous title. Sharon Kane didn't win for her song, but when Gage and I carried her onstage on a surfboard the audience screamed with appreciation. A drunken Jon Vincent finally approached us and hit on Gage who was more interested in all of the transvestites who seemed to gravitate to the porn industry. Gage was in heaven.

Chi Chi came wandering over. I had never seen him in drag before and was surprised at how good he looked. He sort of resembled a cross between the drag queen Divine and the singer Carnie Wilson.

Divine had been a client of mine one rainy Sunday in Earl's Court. He had asked what it would take for me to fuck him and I said, " . . . to be very drunk."

"Let's get you a bottle of gin," he replied. He wasn't in the least bit offended. When I massaged him he was so fat my knees didn't touch the floor on either side of his body. I just floated on an island of blubber. I really liked Divine. I have every single one of his songs on my iPod. He also starred in one of my favorite films of all time, *Lust in the Dust.* Divine had been discovered by the director John Waters, who years later I was lucky enough to meet. John was full of hilarious anecdotes and told one of the funniest stories I have ever heard. John was trying to describe how rough the guys were in Baltimore.

CHAPTER TEN

While driving down the road he had stopped to give a hitchhiker a ride one morning. The hiker pulled out a bag of glue began sniffing it voraciously then offered some to John. Without even batting an eyelid John said "Oh, not for me thanks . . . its only 8 a.m."

That cracked me up.

"Is this the brother I've heard so much about?" whispered Chi Chi.

"I'm Gage."

"Do you want to do a film for me? I've a feeling you'll be a star."

Chi Chi hadn't said that to me. No surprise considering my lousy performance in *Seeds of Love*.

"I only do jerk-off."

"No problem. I'll call Blue for your number."

Things were going swimmingly. Gage and I were having job offers thrown at us by everybody. We were new meat and everybody wanted a slice.

The show lasted a couple of hours and then everybody headed to the after party.

I had to drag Gage to the party because he had no interest. As soon as I walked in, I spotted Chris Dickerson. We wandered over.

"I liked your performance," said Chris.

"Don't lie," I laughed. "It was cheesy."

"No, it was not. You both looked really good on stage," Chris said earnestly.

I bent forward and kissed him. Chris responded by taking hold of my arm and pulling me in tight for a long, hard kiss on the mouth.

"Let's get out of here," he said. "Do you live close by?"

"Five minutes away."

He casually reached over and felt his cock through his tuxedo pants. It was ENORMOUS. To this day, Chris Dickerson has one of the biggest cocks I've ever seen. It was like a baby's arm holding an orange. I practically ran home with him. Gage followed. At the apartment, I ripped off his tuxedo and sure enough, his dick was massive. I didn't see how he would be able to fuck me with that monster. Somehow he managed . . . five times all night. In between fucks he told me he had been living in Palm Springs but was moving back to Manhattan because he was bored with the desert. Although he had been a bodybuilder his whole life, he now intended to study opera and become a singer. He was en route to Manhattan, and I felt a pang of sadness. I could easily have dated Chris. Plus, it turned him on that I was doing porn. I had never had a problem with my boyfriends about being an escort or later being in porn. If they didn't like it, I moved on. I didn't need anybody making moral judgments about my lifestyle. I loved my life. The only person exploiting my body was me.

As I let Chris out of the apartment the next morning Gage popped his head around the bedroom door.

"Sounded like you had quite a night," he grinned.

"Yeah, now I need to go soak my arse in Epsom salts," I winced.

"Well, better make it quick because isn't Chris Duffy arriving at 3 p.m.?"

Aaaaargh!!! That completely slipped my mind. How did I forget that Chris Duffy was arriving for a play date, possibly with his wife, in three hours?

Chris Duffy, Chris Dickerson, Zak Spears . . . man, I

CHAPTER TEN

felt like I was batting a thousand.

The night before, I had spotted Crystal Crawford in drag at the porn awards. I had forgotten to pick up my check from him as I had been so busy sorting out my increasingly complicated sex life.

"Crystal, I'm coming round to get my check for the movie, when's a good time for you?"

He looked nervous. "Well, I'm leaving town day after tomorrow, so how about when I get back in a week."

"I'll be at your place tomorrow at 1 p.m. sharp." I said firmly.

After shooting that retarded movie, even more models let it be known to me that Ms. Crawford was indeed bad at paying. Crystal had obviously never seen me explode in a confined space. I wanted my money, and I wanted it yesterday.

So after Chris Dickerson left, I quickly dressed, jumped on my bike and rode over to Chez Crawford. I banged on the door. No answer. I banged again. No answer. I banged LOUDER. From the other side of the door I heard a dog's muffled bark and a loud sibilant "Ssssshhhh."

"Crystal, I hear you in there!" I shouted through the door.

"I'm here for my fucking money!" I yelled, my anger fueled by my daily intake of testosterone. "Crystal, you better fucking open this door!"

Just as I felt myself approach thermonuclear, a check was pushed under the door. I snatched it up. I wasn't going to wait to deposit the check, so I went straight to one of the check-cashing stores on Santa Monica Boulevard. I had learned a valuable lesson. Never appear in cheap-arse productions, especially those shot in elevators in scrawny drag queens' apartment buildings.

I arrived home, showered, and at 3 on the nose the buzzer rang. It was Chris and his wife Joanie. I realized I was trembling.

Joanie looked like Cleopatra, if Cleopatra had taken steroids. She had long, straight, glossy dark bangs that shone from being expensively conditioned. She was of Italian descent and was super tanned. She had placed second in the Women's American Bodybuilding Championships, beaten only by Lenda Murray. Lenda went on to win the Miss Olympia title five times. Joanie's body was astonishing. She had a very deep voice and, I was told, an enormous clitoris that had been enlarged to the size of a small penis by all the male hormones she had ingested.

The three of us jumped into bed immediately, on the same sheets Chris Dickerson had fucked me on hours earlier . . . I know, it's disgusting, but they didn't notice. They didn't notice because they were as high as kites. It turned out that in his spare time, Chris Duffy made the party drug GHB and stored it by the gallon under his kitchen sink.

Joanie stripped off, lay back and played with her enormous clitoris. "I want to watch you boys," she growled, and I do mean growled. Joanie had the voice of a dockworker who smoked two packs a day. Again, all because of the steroids she had taken.

Whether it was the sound of Joanie's growly voice, the fact that I was with Mr. America, or just the whole perversity of the situation, I got kind of turned on, and with Joanie encouraging me, I fucked Chris's ass. Joanie,

CHAPTER TEN

high on GHB told Chris to suck her cock as she manipulated her giant clitoris. Chris greedily began sucking on her clit while I fucked him from behind. We fucked for hours until we all came.

Afterwards, with Joanie in the shower, Chris said, "I want to date you."

"What about Joanie?" I asked incredulously.

"I want her to be my wife, but I want you to be my boyfriend."

"Does Joanie know about this?"

"I told her how much I like you, and I've never had a boyfriend before . . . " he trailed off.

I would have been crazy to turn him down. I had fancied this guy for years, and here he was asking to date me. So what if he had a drug-crazed wife and I was dating Zak Spears, both suddenly seemed sadly disposable.

Zak called me that night.

"Zak, I have something to tell you,"

"Listen," he interrupted, "Chi Chi is singing at Christina Applegate's birthday party, do you want to go? We're taking a couple of guys from *Posing Strap* as well, a guy called Lance Bronson, who is a bodybuilder from Washington, and some kid . . . I can't remember his name."

Christina Applegate was starring in the hilarious TV show *Married with Children*, and I thought her birthday party would be fun and very Hollywood. I had never been to a Hollywood party. I was excited. I could tell Zak I was breaking up with him another time. I didn't want to ruin his evening.

Chi Chi and Zak picked me up at 8 p.m. I was exhausted. I'd been banging Chris Duffy all day and getting banged by Chris Dickerson all night. I was wiped out. *Posing Strap* was starting production that week, and I had two scenes. One was a three-way with Zak Spears and Jimmy Toro, a guy I'd never heard of. The second scene was a flip-flop scene with David Logan, a British porn actor whom I knew casually from London. A flip-flop scene is where you fuck and get fucked. That would be the first scene I would shoot for the movie. I wasn't looking forward to it as David was blonde and slight and so the antithesis of what I normally fancied.

 We stopped off at Lance Bronson's hotel to pick up him with the other model. When Lance climbed into the back of the car, I nearly died of shock. He was fucking gorgeous; a corn-fed Midwestern bodybuilder. I was in lust. He was doing an oral scene with Zak Spears, having Zak just blow him as he was straight. God, I wanted to be the one blowing Lance.

 Lance and I got on like a house on fire and chatted all night. He told me he was going to move to L.A. to become an action movie star, the next Arnold Schwarzenegger. I listened, enthralled by his gorgeousness. Christina Applegate's party was boring, but we all got drunk, and Chi Chi invited Lance back home for a nightcap. Chi Chi obviously had great taste. I decided to sleep over with Zak. I was still debating whether or not to tell him I wanted to end our very brief fling. Zak and I climbed into bed, and I could hear Chi Chi and Lance in the living room making out. Derek Cruise was sleeping at his girlfriend's for the night.

 Suddenly Zak turned to me and said "Blue, I don't think this relationship is working. I've got too many

CHAPTER TEN

things in my life going on to commit to a relationship. I just think we would make better friends than lovers."

Zak had beaten me to the punch! I wasn't bitter. It had been a quick fling for both of us and I had made a good friend who I enjoy to this very day.

My first day of shooting on *Posing Strap* rolled around. The plot of the film was that Zak Spears—wearing makeup to make him look like an old man—was in an art gallery, looking back to the days when he was a famous erotic art photographer in the Fifties. (Flashback to Zak, photographing the models wearing posing straps. They become hot for each other and start fucking.) Other than this there was no plot whatsoever I don't think. At least none I was involved in.

I didn't fancy my co-star David Logan, and he didn't fancy me, so the scene was agony. It took hours and hours to film. He had to fuck me, and I had to fuck him, and neither of us could stay hard.

The cameraman was incredibly patient, and we somehow got through the scene, and came. I apologized to the cameraman, and he laughed and said not to worry, the scene looked great. When the film came out, astonishingly, it did! This was the first scene where I was filmed fucking somebody, and, much worse I decided, them fucking me. I immediately realized I would rather be the one doing the fucking on film. Getting fucked hurt, you were tense, your arse was tight and it was incredibly un-erotic. You were balanced on crates with a crew underneath you, inches away from your arsehole. If your dick went soft, you had to lift it up and away from the camera so as not to ruin the shot. You shoot the "insertion shot" again and again until you get the perfect shot, and then you need a minimum of twelve good strokes of somebody's dick going in and out of your arse. I used to count them. I hated getting fucked on camera. Even by a straight guy, I hated it.

After I showered and returned to the set, they had set up for the next scene with Zak and my "crush" Lance Bronson. Lance was to lie back and let Zak eat his arse and suck his dick. I was rock hard in my pants. Great, I can't get hard all day, and now I'm pre-cumming in my pants at the sight of Lance Bronson's pink virgin arsehole.

Chi Chi shooed us away. Lance was having real problems getting hard. He wasn't just soft—his dick was concave. When straight boys want to get hard on gay porn sets a monitor is set up off-camera so straight porn can be played to get the boys aroused. Or they look at straight magazines. In very rare cases, a girl is brought on the set. I've only heard of this twice. Once, was when the porn star Billy Brandt was making a movie for the genius director Michael Zen. Billy's girlfriend Sheera lay next to the bed spreading her vagina open. Billy fucked his girlfriend then pulled his dick out of his girlfriend's pussy and stuck it in his co-star's mouth. This carried on until his co-star vomited because he said his mouth tasted of vagina.

Anything would be done on the porn sets to get the actors hard. I carried a little paperback book in my gym bag called *Handjobs* that was full of dirty stories. I would read them until I got hard, then run back to the set and fuck my co-star. Of course, the films were all safe sex, so you not only had to run back to the set, you had to first put on a condom, and the crew had to jump back into position.

CHAPTER TEN

By the time all of this was done, I would be soft again.

To get Lance Bronson hard, Chi Chi, in desperation, called Sharon Kane to come and fluff him on the set. People were always asking me how they could get a job as a fluffer. A fluffer is somebody who sucks the model's dick to get him hard for the filming. The actual job position doesn't exist. It's an urban legend. Although years later I was hanging about on a set of a Gino Colbert straight movie starring superstar Ken Ryker and an actress called Devon Shire. Devon was in a bad mood because she was having her period that day and she kept saying to poor Ken Ryker, "Get over here, faggot, and fuck my pussy before I start bleeding again."

Ken was traumatized and couldn't stay hard, so Gino asked if I would fluff him in the bathroom to help him relax. Ken Ryker had an eleven-inch dick, so I jumped right in. We smoked a little pot, and I started sucking Ken's dick. Unfortunately, we got a little carried away and he shot his load in my mouth. We ran onto the set, and Ken tried to squeeze Mr. Softie into Devon's pussy. The scene was a disaster, but Gino forgave me . . . and after creative editing, the film came out looking great. (Always employ the best editor money can buy; if the raw footage of the movie is a little rough, he will save the film for you.)

So that was my one and only experience as a fluffer, although I would have fluffed Lance Bronson in a second.

With the help of Sharon Kane, Zak and Lance's oral scene was shot successfully. The next day was my big scene, a three-way with Zak and Jimmy Toro.

The day started off extremely badly and only got progressively worse. To economize, somebody had rented extremely cheap lights that exploded the moment they were plugged in. This delayed filming for hours during which I realized that Zak wasn't really talking to me, as I think he was embarrassed that we had broken up and now we were shooting a scene together. I felt as uncomfortable having sex with Zak as he did with me. Who wants to have sex with somebody they have just broken up with? Especially on film.

The third guy in the scene turned out to be a skinny little Mexican kid that neither Zak nor I fancied. So I knew this scene was going to be hell . . . and it was.

"Are you Mexican?" I asked the kid.

"No, I'm Cuban," he corrected. I looked at him doubtfully.

"Yes, yes, I'm Mexican," he wailed, "But I thought you would want a Cuban more."

I don't know why he thought that. I didn't care if the kid was Mexican or Cuban or from Nicaragua, I just wanted to be able to stay hard on camera.

As it turned out none of us could stay hard. I was walking around in a cowboy hat and a dirty, flesh colored posing strap that I had worn for two days. We broke for lunch, which consisted of buckets of delicious Kentucky Fried Chicken, something I enjoyed but tried to avoid. We sat around gorging ourselves on the greasy fast food until it was time to get back to work. Our scene that would eventually run twenty-five minutes in the finished film took twelve hours to shoot. By the end of the day, I was sweaty, filthy, and my dick was sore. I was furious. Chi Chi tried to placate me.

"It isn't nearly as bad as this normally."

CHAPTER TEN

"I will never, NEVER make another porn movie as long as I live," I raged.

"Oh, they all say that," Chi Chi laughed. He was right of course.

I ended up making only one more film with Chi Chi directing. An oral film entitled *Blow Me Down*. Making oral films is a great way for the studios to cut costs. They are made with the excuse that some people only want to see guys give each other blowjobs. The models are paid half their normal rate, which subsequently cuts the budget in half. The best thing about *Blow Me Down* was that I worked with a sexy, humpy, short skinhead model called Max Stone. Catalina, the company I had made *Seeds of Love* for, produced the film. Catalina must have liked my performance because I ended up making ten more films for them.

Although Chi Chi and I never worked together again we would bump into each other at various award shows and parties. Chi Chi LaRue went on to be probably the most influential person in porn history. He ended up starting his own distribution and production company called Channel One and purchasing both All Worlds and Catalina Studios. Over the years I developed an appreciation for Chi Chi that I never thought I would have when I first met him in that small apartment surrounded by plastic dolls on Melrose Avenue. How can you not appreciate someone who starts off as a small town drag queen and goes on to become an icon?

The other films I made for Catalina all became a bit of a blur because none were very memorable. There was *Peep-O-Rama*, in which I had sex with a really hot

OUT OF THE BLUE

straight guy from Canada whose name I forget; *Hidden Instinct* which I can't for the life of me recall even making; *Idol Dreams* starring Tony Idol, who was trying to pass as Ryan Idol's younger brother; and eight more movies. They all seemed to be set in a sex club in Los Angeles called "The Block," which would double as anything from warehouses and garages to docking bays, etc. Josh Elliott, whom I really liked, directed the majority of these films. He was very easygoing, and he had a great crew. We laughed all the time. Josh seemed to know that the films he made were cheap and cheerful and he never seemed to take anything too seriously.

All this time I was in a full-on relationship with Chris Duffy and his wife Joanie. They would both come to my apartment, and we would fuck all day with Joanie high on GHB. Gage, having grown bored with all the local transsexuals, had flown his girlfriend Stephanie in from England and she was living with us. Stephanie had no problem with Gage escorting as she was madly in love with him. Although he was spending money quicker than he could make it, he still refused to do porn films. He had made a jerk off film for Chi Chi but he hated the whole process of being filmed jerking off. Luckily, he was busy as an escort.

I decided I needed to branch out from Catalina, so I started looking for other film companies to work for. Mocha had given my name to Rick Ford, the guy who made all of the straight marine jerk-off films. One day when I was at the gym my beeper went off with a message to phone Mocha.

"Blue, I'm on the set of a film and one of the actors has flaked on us. Rick Ford told me to offer you the lead role.

CHAPTER TEN

It's a day shooting here and a day shooting in San Diego. There's a ton of dialogue and I told Rick Ford you're a really good actor. We are shooting in a garage in West Hollywood . . . can you be here in thirty minutes?"

No-shows on porn sets are a common occurrence because porn stars are notoriously unreliable. Luckily, I hadn't jerked off that morning so I was young, hung and full of cum. I hadn't worked for All Worlds before so I was curious to shoot for a new company, and I had heard that Rick Ford was a really nice guy. I dashed home and threw on a pair of jeans and a lumberjack shirt with the sleeves cut off.

I arrived at the address I had been given to find it was a car repair shop with the crew waiting inside. Mocha greeted me with a hug. "Girl, you're going to be on the cover of this one!"

Getting the box cover of a film was all-important. It raised your status within the porn industry and of course everybody craved that. I had heard I was also going to appear on the cover of *Posing Strap* so I was thrilled.

The movie was a film called *Lube Job* and, believe it or not, it was based on Charles Dickens' *A Christmas Carol*. I played the Scrooge character, an evil boss who owned a garage and abused his underlings by fucking them and then underpaying them. The movie was written and directed by Jeff Kincaid. Although he was only in his fifties, Jeff wore very thick glasses and hearing aids in each ear. He reminded me of a ferret, a very sweet ferret, but a ferret. Jeff and I instantly got on famously. He wrote very exotic dialogue and had done a lot of films for All Worlds. It was all: "Yeah, you fucking male pussy boy slut, take daddy's dick like the man whore you are!"

Of course that just rolled off of my tongue. My co-star was a young blonde kid named Sam Dixon whom I had to fuck on the top of a sports car. Easy.

The scene came off perfectly and, as I liked everybody on the set, I actually managed to stay rock hard and shoot a huge load. I threw myself into the role with wild abandon. Jeff loved my acting and said he wanted me for his films.

The next day I met Rick Ford. He didn't look a day over fifty and I actually quite fancied him. He was very mellow and laughed a lot. He told me he had heard great things about me and looked forward to working together.

The plot of *Lube Job* revolved around my character, an evil garage owner for whom there was no redemption until his ex-boyfriend, who had died in a motorcycle accident: appeared to him as a ghost, showed him the consequences of his actions, and forced him to renounce his evil ways. That meant allowing Sam Dixon to fuck ME to show him what a good guy I had become. I would have preferred to remain evil!!

The porn star playing my dead boyfriend was a really good-looking guy named Dino De Marco—Italian, thick dark hair, very handsome.

After the shoot Rick Ford summoned me to his office.

"Judging by the footage, you are going to be really, really good in the film."

"Thanks," I replied coyly.

"You'll definitely be hearing from us again, I produce a lot of films."

That was an understatement. They were cranking

CHAPTER TEN

out about one a week. Of course, some were of dubious quality, but I knew how to avoid the cheap productions. I was the new kid on the block and word was spreading quickly that I was good.

Jeff Kincaid became one of my favorite directors and All Worlds one of my favorite companies to work for. I starred in a film called *Ramjet* for them where I played an Iraqi terrorist leader who shot down American fighter pilots from the sky with a handheld bazooka. When they crashed I would drag the pilots from the wreckage and fuck them. I even had to rape a young guy named Bryan Kidd, who played the local goat herder. I had the immortal line: "Achmed . . . pass me the young goat herder for his hole is fresh and tight."

Of course this was another Jeff Kincaid flick and I devoured his dialogue with relish. It was pure camp to me.

Ramjet also starred Drew Andrews, Alec Powers, Max Grand and Cutter West. Alec and Cutter were two straight blond beefy jocks who made me swoon. They were both extremely sexy, needless to say. Years later I worked with Cutter, but I never got the chance to work with Alec Powers which was a shame because he was drop dead gorgeous.

Max Grand was an enormous star at the time. He played the pilot who got shot down and was raped. Max looked Persian and had an extremely handsome face. We worked together many times over the following years.

In a film called *Forgive Us Our Trespasses* I played a leather master. Mike Donner directed this movie about a randy priest who prowled leather bars looking for homo action. They had built a leather dungeon on the set and I had to chain a guy between two posts and fuck him. I was in full leather, which was incredibly uncomfortable, and my body harness kept squishing my balls, making me lose my hard-on. The film had more dialogue than I had ever seen in a porn flick but luckily my scene was brief and went quickly. I had kept all my body harnesses and leather accoutrements from my Mr. Drummer days, so they came in handy for anything with a leather flavor. I was slowly building up my resume and becoming more and more comfortable on the sets. I could now even fuck guys I didn't fancy.

One of the most beautiful models of his day was a stunning young bodybuilder named Kyle McKenna from Salt Lake City. He was spectacular looking so when I was offered the opportunity to work with him I jumped at the chance. The movie, *Balls in Play* was produced by All Worlds and directed by Jeff Kincaid. I played an openly gay football player who was harassed by a fellow footballer played by Paul Carrigan. Paul was a total dreamboat. Straight and married, he had roughly hewn features and a stocky build. It was the first time I had played a football player in a film and I was really excited about the idea. Whenever I got the chance to get into a different uniform I would throw myself into the role with utter glee. I never cared if people thought my acting was over the top. All my directors seemed to enjoy it. Probably because unlike most porn models they had to beg to utter a few syllables, I couldn't keep my mouth shut. Once they called "action," I was up and running.

I arrived on the set for my first day of filming and to my astonishment they had built a row of bleachers. Not just that, they had rented full American football uni-

CHAPTER TEN

forms for us to wear. Shoulder pads, football cleats; the whole kit. Being born in England I had never worn an American football uniform, so once I tried it on I couldn't resist parading myself up and down the street. I thought I was the cat's whiskers.

"OK," said Jeff, "Blue, you are fucking Kyle under the bleachers, while everybody is watching the football game . . . action!"

I jumped on Kyle and began ripping at his shorts.

"Hold on a second," said the cameraman "The bleachers don't look real because we can't see anybody's legs through the slats."

"Everybody who isn't on the set climb onto the bleachers and dangle their legs down!" yelled Jeff.

All the crew climbed onto the bleachers and sat there like they were watching a real football game. I loved this about porn. Everything was resolvable. The real film industry could learn a lot about filmmaking from these maverick porn directors. Why hire a hundred extras when you can get the crew to swing their skinny legs around? Why hire Wrigley Field when you can knock together bleachers in someone's back yard?

"Much better," Jeff said, "It looks like we are shooting under the bleachers at the fucking Super Bowl . . . action!"

I again jumped on Kyle and began fucking the hell out of him.

"Cut!" yelled Jeff suddenly, "Kyle isn't hard . . . let Kyle get hard."

Jesus Christ I thought . . . does Kyle have to be hard, I'm the one fucking him. I was definitely going to lose my momentum if we kept starting and stopping like this.

"Sorry," said Kyle shyly, "It's not you . . . it's just . . . " his voice trailed off.

"Hey . . . It's no big deal," I grinned and I meant it. He was so bloody handsome I would have forgiven him anything.

"Is there anything I can do to help?"

"Well, perhaps if you could play with my nipples and talk dirty to me," Kyle whispered.

"Everybody clear the set!" Jeff screamed. Wow, he must have had his hearing aids turned up full blast to hear Kyle's request.

"Let's give Kyle and Blue five minutes of privacy."

The crew climbed off the bleachers and wandered over to the food table and began talking amongst themselves. Kyle sank to his knees and looked up at me imploringly.

"Tell me what a naughty boy I've been, Daddy."

Aah, so this is what he was into. No problem, I could play that role.

"You've been a real naughty boy," I admonished. "Daddy has to punish you for being so bad."

"I'm sorry, Daddy," said Kyle, "Are you angry at me for sucking Fido's cock?"

"Yeah, very angry." I said thinking, who the hell is Fido?

"It's just that I couldn't keep out of Fido's kennel and his pink doggie dick looked so pink and delicious . . . "

Doggie dick??? Pink and delicious??? It suddenly dawned on me that Kyle was talking about sucking a real dog's cock. I had heard that Mormons could be on the

CHAPTER TEN

kinky side when they left the faith but this was INSANE. He was so handsome, who knew he was into bestiality?

"Yeah," I snarled. "Well don't make Daddy have to force you to suck off Mr. Franklin's Doberman next door."

"Would you really make me do that, Daddy?" asked Kyle. I noticed he was rock hard.

"He's hard!" I yelled, "Everybody back on the set!"

The rest of the scene went perfectly. I fucked the hell out of Kyle. So what if he fantasized about sucking a dog's dick? Who was I to judge, as long as he didn't give me mange I didn't give a shit. After the shoot I was chatting with one of the crew about my strange encounter with Kyle.

"I heard he was in a three-way relationship for a while and liked being humiliated," said the makeup artist.

A couple of years later Kyle McKenna killed himself in Salt Lake City, Utah. I suppose he just couldn't deal with his own personal demons. I cried when I heard the news.

The next day I drove to the set with Paul Carrigan. He told me his normal job was working as a Key Grip on mainstream films. He pulled out a joint and we shared it as we watched the crew run around setting up the scene. I had a huge crush on Paul. There was something so inherently masculine about him. He didn't have a perfect body; he was even a little poochie, which excited me even more. I vowed to work with him on as many films as possible. Getting paid a thousand bucks to get fucked or fuck guys like Paul Carrigan was why I had gotten into porn in the first place. My other scene in the film was with a black guy named Jack Simmons, who was to play a rapist who had been hired by Paul Carrigan to rape me before the big game. Jack was a good-looking guy with a big dick.

Meeting me for the first time, he said, "When they asked me to do this film I asked to work with you . . . I've seen you in other films and your talking dirty drives me crazy."

"Well, I'm very flattered," I said, "But did you notice in the script that whilst you're fucking me I'm unconscious because you've drugged me?"

"WHAT!?" he yelled.

It was true, according to the script I was to be unconscious while getting fucked by Jack.

"No . . . no . . . I don't believe it."

Sure enough when we began to shoot the scene I had to lay as motionless as possible. It was impossible for Jack to get hard.

"Please can you just squirm a little bit?" he begged.

I began to wriggle.

"Blue you're unconscious . . . stop moving around!" screamed Jeff, "I want you to look like dead meat."

The scene took hours and hours to film and poor Jack was nearly in tears with frustration. Finally we finished the scene though Jack never got fully hard.

Jeff came up and said afterwards, "Blue you really are remarkably talented. I'm shooting another film tomorrow for All Worlds . . . Its called *Shoot The Chute* . . . would you mind playing a nonsexual role?"

"Sure. What's the role?"

"You'll be a gypsy fortune-teller," Jeff said brightly. I swear to God, I couldn't make this shit up. Who the hell was going to buy a film with me playing a gypsy fortune-teller? Apparently everybody, because I still bump into people who tell me they saw the film.

CHAPTER TEN

When I say gypsy fortune-teller I mean the whole nine yards. Crystal ball, scarf with gold coins wrapped around my head, voodoo dolls everywhere. I found myself swathed in bright colored robes and chocolate pan-stick doing my best impression of Marie Laveau. A gypsy tent had been built for me and I marveled at all the set dressings. Where the hell had the crew found all these shrunken heads? I wondered.

Unfortunately this was the last film I made for Jeff. All Worlds stopped using him. I don't know why. Although we stayed in touch for a while, we eventually lost contact. I will always remember him fondly for the great roles he lavished upon me, even if some of them were more than a little unusual.

When I mentioned to Paul Carrigan that I wanted to work for other studios, he told me about someplace called Nasty Studios. I had never heard of it but Paul told me that they made a lot of films, paid well, and that they were always in need of good looking guys.

"But what kind of films do they make?" I asked Paul.

"All kinds," he winked.

This all sounded very vague but I trusted Paul so I got the address and gave them a call. They seemed to know who I was and asked me to come along for an interview the next day.

Nasty Studios was based in The San Fernando Valley—nothing unusual about that—in a very non-descript grey building. I knocked briskly on the door and walked in. There was an extremely elderly lady sitting at a typewriter with carrot hair and a cigarette hanging out of the corner of her mouth.

OUT OF THE BLUE

"Hello," I said, "I'm. . . ."

"Blue Blake!" she interrupted through a haze of nicotine. "I'm a big fan of yours. In fact, I've gotten off to your films many times . . . nearly wore my vibrator out with that one with you and your brother." Would the Blake Twins' film never die? Now octogenarians were telling me they had seen it. On the wall behind granny fag I noticed a poster of a fat Chinese girl drinking what looked like a pint of cum from a giant martini glass. Following my eyes, she said, "Olivia Ching Ling. One of our biggest 'specialist' stars, said the old lady, gesturing to a poster where a bikini-clad Olivia Ching Ling appeared to be sitting on a circus trapeze . . . WITH NO LEGS. She had huge breast implants and the film was called *Ample Amputees*. The by-line read "No Legs . . . No Problem."

I suddenly realized Nasty Studios was one of those film companies that specialized in extreme fetish films. Gay, straight bi, transsexual, pre-op, a hundred guys on one girl. They did it all. There was a market for these kinds of films but I had always assumed that they didn't sell because how many times can you watch *I Shagged a Granny Trannie*?

"My name's Melinda Delicious," said the old lady.

"Nice to meet you, Mrs. Delicious."

"Oh . . . it's Miss Delicious." I noticed that her blouse was see-through and she was wearing no bra. Her breasts looked like three-day-old squeezed tea bags.

"Perhaps we'll be doing a film together soon," she purred. "I give the best blow jobs. You can see me in *Gums Around Your Plums*."

Saying this, she took her teeth out and threw herself

CHAPTER TEN

back in her chair in a mock glamour pose. The color drained from my face.

"Can I interest you in a cigarella?"

"No, I'm fine thank you. I don't smoke," I stammered, "Well, only sometimes the occasional joint." I realized I was about to start babbling out of fear.

"Miss Delicious . . . is that Blue Blake I hear?" called a voice from the other room. "Send him in please . . . we are waiting."

Miss Delicious jumped to attention.

"You can go in dear, they're expecting you," she said, gesturing towards a conference room. As I walked by her desk she wolf whistled and slapped me on the arse.

"Nice ass," she whispered. I practically ran into the adjoining room.

The room was filthy. Porno magazines and VHS boxes piled high in every corner. Movie posters covered the walls, offering every conceivable fetish you can imagine: enormously fat, extremely thin, really old, and really young. Sitting behind a desk was a hugely obese guy smoking a cigar.

"Blue," he boomed, "Nice to meet you. I'm a big fan, especially of that film you did with your brother." This was getting ridiculous I thought. "My name's Jack Rampant." He stood up to shake my hand and I noticed he had a piss stain on his trousers.

"They call him Jack the Jackal," said a tiny voice from the sofa behind me. I hadn't realized there was anybody else in the room.

"Blue, I would like to introduce to you the very lovely Marla Midget."

OUT OF THE BLUE

I turned and there sitting on the broken-down couch was a female dwarf about two feet tall. She was wearing a lycra mini dress and extremely high heels. All I could think was where the hell did she find those shoes? She had feet the size of a two-year-old child. Did they make stilettos for infants? Her little legs dangled over the side of the couch and she swung them to and fro. She was wearing fake eyelashes and an enormous curly wig.

"Come and sit by me," she invited in a Munchkin voice. I took a seat as far from Marla Midget as possible but she shuffled along the couch until her tiny leg was pressed against mine.

"So here's the deal," said Piss Stain, getting right down to business. "Marla here is becoming a very big star after her last feature *Lolita the Leprachaun,* which we shot on location in Ireland . . . ."

"You flew to Ireland to shoot?" I asked.

"Well . . . actually it was the back yard of O'Reillys Irish pub bar, but it certainly felt like the sweet dells of Belfast." I wasn't sure if war-torn Belfast had any sweet dells but I kept my mouth shut.

"It starred Tony Tiny . . . he's vertically challenged too!" squeaked Marla in my ear . . . she was extremely close by now.

"So we are doing the sequel. . . *Lolita Loves Llandudno,* and as you are Welsh. . . ."

"Uh . . . excuse me Mr. Jackal . . . I mean Jack . . . I'm English," I corrected him. "I've only been to Wales twice, and then I got sick from overindulging in clotted cream and scones and welsh rarebit and threw up in the car and. . . ."

CHAPTER TEN

"ENOUGH!" shouted Jack. "I'm offering you the role of the rugby player who falls for Marla's kittenish charms and fucks her at the end of the film."

"I'll even do anal," Marla whispered.

I felt like I had fallen into some parallel universe. I suddenly realized Marla was running her tiny fingers up and down my inner thighs. I jumped to my feet so quickly Marla fell off the sofa and onto the floor. I picked her up and sat her back on the couch and said, "I'm sorry, Jack, there must have been some mistake . . . thank you so much for the offer but I really have to decline."

"What? You think you're too good for this company?" Jack snarled. I suddenly realized why they called him the Jackal.

"No, of course not!"

"Because I've shit things that were better looking than you!"

"And to think I was going to let you felch me!" shrieked Marla. Felching is a sexual practice where you cum inside of somebody's arse or vagina and then suck it out . . . sometimes with a straw. Like a milkshake, only a thousand times more disgusting.

"Miss Midget, could you leave Jack and me alone for a second?" I asked.

"Sure," said Marla, hopping off the couch, "But don't think the felching offer is still on the table." With this, she strode proudly out of the room.

"So what's your problem?" Jack snapped. "Paul Carrigan told me that you were a good actor."

"Well, the truth is . . . ." All my friends will tell you that any sentence beginning with "well, the truth is" means an enormous lie is about to fall out of my mouth. "When my mother was pregnant with me and went into labor, the midwife delivering me was only three feet tall, and as she started to give birth, my enormous head got stuck, so the midwife panicked and ran out into the street and was hit and killed by an ice cream van."

"Hmmm . . . well you do have an extraordinarily huge head."

Fuck off, I thought, but continued my story. "Anyway, I can't look at a midget or a strawberry sundae without having an anxiety attack." Jack stared at me in disbelief, but I stared right back at him. "In fact," I continued, "The very smell of Ben and Jerry's Chunky Monkey makes me pass out, especially if my twin sister Delilah . . ."

"I thought you had a twin brother," interrupted Jack.

"We're triplets," I lied. "Especially if my triplet sister Daphne . . . ."

"I thought you said her name was Delilah . . . ."

"Especially if Delilah Daphne is eating it while watching anything to do with dwarves . . . due to the fact that she was born with her stomach inside out she can only eat . . . uuuuuuuh . . . ice cream." Of course I realized this story sounded absolutely insane, but once I started lying it was like there was no off-switch in my brain. Amazingly, Jack either believed me or pretended to believe me. He came from behind his desk and gave me a big hug. I thought I could feel his piss stain on my thigh.

"I understand," he said. "Listen, I have a bestiality movie coming up in a month. I need a bodybuilder to get gangbanged by twelve Great Danes . . . ."

"Thanks for being so understanding," I smiled, "And

CHAPTER TEN

please tell Marla that if I wasn't mortally terrified of dwarves I would fuck the arse off of her."

"That's the spirit!"

"And can I let you know about the doggie film?"

"Sure . . . there's no hurry, but make sure you get your rabies shots before the cameras roll." I shook his big meaty hand and walked back into Miss Delicious's office. Neither Marla nor Miss Delicious was there, so I was able to beat a hasty retreat. I never saw Jack the Jackal, Miss Delicious or Marla Midget ever again. In fact, years later I Googled Nasty Studios and it had vanished off the face of the earth.

CHAPTER ELEVEN

I WROTE TO A COMPANY IN SAN FRANCISCO called Hot House. They were fairly new and were producing edgy movies with bodybuilders and hairy guys. They called and said they would like to put me in a film called *Nothin' Nice*. They flew me to San Francisco for the shoot, but hadn't told me who my co-star would be. That immediately set off warning bells in my head. However, it was a job, and I took it.

The trip was a disaster. My co-star arrived looking under nourished and drugged out so I immediately jumped on a plane back to Los Angeles. A big problem with making porn is that some of the models go up and down in size because of their drug intake, both recreational and cosmetic. They cut their hair off at a whim, dye it, bleach it; get tattoos— a whole myriad of things. You always have to see a model the day before the shoot so you know exactly what you're getting. Nobody expects Tarzan to show up looking like Jane. I vowed after this experience never to work with a model unless I'd seen him first. This was a good lesson to learn. I stuck by it throughout my career, and it's served me well.

When I arrived back in Los Angeles, Hot House had already called my apartment to apologize. They told me they would fly me back to San Francisco to work with the model of my choice. I told Chris Duffy about the offer. To my astonishment he said, "I want to do it with you."

"Don't be insane. You're one of the most famous bodybuilders in the world. You don't want to do gay porn, it will destroy your bodybuilding career!"

"I'm sick of being a pro-bodybuilder. I want to make films with you," he said with perfect sincerity. I couldn't believe what he was telling me. Chris was at the top of his game. He would be crazy to give it all up to do porn.

"What does Joanie think about this?"

"Joanie doesn't mind, as long as I don't do it with another woman."

"I absolutely disagree," I said, "I think it's a terrible idea."

However, I could already see in my mind the headlines in the *National Enquirer*: **MR. AMERICA GIVES UP BODYBUILDING TO STAR IN GAY PORN FLICKS WITH MALE LOVER: WIFE SAYS "I WHOLEHEARTEDLY APPROVE."** Maybe it wasn't an entirely insane idea.

I said, "Look, let me think about it. I'll call you after the weekend and we'll talk seriously about it." I kissed Chris goodbye, and as soon as he was gone, I rushed to shower.

Lance Bronson was flying in from D.C. for the weekend. We had stayed in touch since *Posing Strap*. He was coming to town to look for work as an action star, and I offered to let him stay with me. Chris and I didn't have an exclusive relationship, he was married and I wasn't about to let this opportunity slip through my wicked little fingers. I had gotten rid of Gage and Stephanie for the weekend, so

CHAPTER ELEVEN

I had the whole apartment to myself . . . to seduce Lance. He turned out to be easily seducible.

Lance and I never left the bedroom that entire weekend. He even phoned his girlfriend from our bed. He was straight/bi and horny, and I was in total lust with him. Our passion was fueled by the fact that we were both starting our chosen careers, so we thought we would become superstars . . . that and some ecstasy tablets that Chris had left behind on my chest of drawers.

On Sunday afternoon the phone rang. I was screening calls, so I let the machine pick up.

"This is a message for Blue Blake. My name is Dirk Dehner and I own the Tom of Finland Company, We are finally making that film based on the drawings of Tom's work and we would like you and your brother to star in it." This was the film I had been approached to do all that time ago by the casting scout in North Hollywood Gold's Gym.

I flew out of bed and pushed poor Lance onto the floor in my rush to snatch up the phone.

"Mr. Dehner, this is Blue Blake speaking, I would love to be in your film!"

"And I hear you have a sexy brother who would also be good for the film?"

"Hmmmmmmmmm . . . Gage . . . yeah, I'm not quite sure about him doing it but I have a friend here I starred in a film with called Lance who might be interested.

"Well," said Dirk, sounding impressed, "If I could come to your place this afternoon and have a look at you both and discuss the details. . . ."

Dirk arrived a few hours later. Although it was eighty degrees, he was dressed in full leather. He must be boiling,

I thought. Dirk was in his forties; blonde hair and beard, and I found out later he had been insanely attractive when he was younger. Tom of Finland had even drawn him. In fact, he was the man who had brought Tom to America. When Tom died, he left Dirk everything and Dirk had wisely decided to produce a film based on the drawings. He was searching for the sexiest men in the world to star in the film entitled, *The Wild Ones*.

Dirk pointed at Lance, "Is this your boyfriend?"

"No, this is . . . a friend,"

"Well, you're very handsome," said Dirk. He looked us up and down . . . was he wearing Wellingtons?

Lance and I grinned at each other. We were young, hot, and had just been asked to star in the Tom of Finland movie . . . and as Lance was so fucking gorgeous, I definitely wanted to be immortalized forever on film with this piece of straight muscle.

"Are you sure your brother won't do it?" asked Dirk.

"Positive."

Gage had sworn he would never do porn again—all my teachings gone to waste. Talk about casting one's seed on fallow ground!

"Well, the two of you will be great together in my film," said Dirk. He really was quite charming apart from the rubber Wellingtons.

Dirk left promising he would be in touch, and I bade a sad farewell to Lance. Hmmmm, I could fall in love with Lance I thought. The phone rang. It was Chris Duffy.

"What have you been up to?" he asked, sounding high.

"Listen to this, I've been asked to star in the Tom of Finland film, *The Wild Ones*."

CCHAPTER ELEVEN

"What? That's amazing! Who are you working with?"

"A guy called Lance Bronson."

Chris's tone changed from congratulatory to suspicious.

"Isn't he the guy you liked so much?"

"Yes," I said exasperatedly. Why was he asking so many fucking questions, when, still feeling sexy from the ecstasy, I wanted to go and have a wank.

"I don't want you to do it," said Chris matter-of-factly.

"What?"

"Or if you do it, I want you to do it with me." This was getting exhausting.

"All right," I said, calling Chris's bluff, "I have to go back to San Francisco on Thursday to do my scene for Hot House. Do you want to star in that film with me too?"

"Yes, I already told you I did," said Chris emphatically.

Next thing I knew we were on an airplane together flying to shoot the movie for Hot House Studios. Our lives were about to change forever.

When we arrived in San Francisco, the owner of Hot House studios, Steven Scarborough, seemed pretty happy with the two of us. We definitely were completely original looking, being big bodybuilders at a time when porn was full of jocks. Even the guys who looked like bodybuilders in the films were 5 foot 5. Chris was 6´3˝ and I was 6´1˝. He weighed 300 pounds and I weighed 230. We were big and beefy.

"The movie's called *Nothin' Nice*, and you play garage mechanics. Chris comes in—Blue, you're repairing a car. He sees your ass, goes wild with desire and he sticks a speculum up your butt."

EXCUSE ME!! A SPECULUM?!? A speculum is a

metal medical instrument which, when inserted in the vagina or rectum stretches the patient open by the twisting of a screw. It has two prongs that open up a person so the doctor can see inside. The idea that I would agree to let somebody stick a speculum up my arse in a film now seems ridiculous . . . however if anybody was going to do it to me, it might as well be Mr. America.

The set was incredibly cool, an old garage with an antique sports car that I was pretending to repair. I was dressed in greasy coveralls and a jockstrap underneath. When Steven shouted "Action!" I began madly repairing the engine. If you watch the movie closely you'll see me remove the spark plugs and replace them THREE times with the same spark plugs. Chris enters—also wearing overalls—and at the sight of my ass he bends me over the hood of the car, rips off my overalls and eats my arse. The scene was a piece of cake. We were supposed to be mad about each other, and we were. Chris fucked me, stuck the speculum up my ass, ate my arse again . . . I still couldn't quite believe Chris was doing hardcore porn. Amazingly, Joanie had even encouraged him. Without realizing it, I was being drawn into a twisted web that would grow only more twisted over the next year.

The shoot ended quickly and everybody was delighted with the scene. We were paid three thousand dollars. I gave Chris two; I kept one. He was worth two grand; he was Mr. Fucking America for Christ sakes!

I had been a little worried how Chris would handle his first porno shoot but he took to it like a duck to water.

As Chris filled out his model release he turned to me and asked,

CHAPTER ELEVEN

"What should I put where it says stage name?"

Steven Scarborough piped in: "Why don't you call yourself Bull Stanton?"

Great name, I thought and it really suited Chris. Years later when I started producing I named dozens of models . . . Robert Van Damme, Brad Rock, Scott Gunz, Peter Latz, Sal Lombardi, Rhett O'Hara, Ben Campezi, Rico Dulce, Vincenzo Titan. A good strong masculine model name is extremely important in porn and the models for some reason will go crazy with names given the opportunity, especially straight models, e.g. Mason Jarr. I mean, I get the humor of it and it does stick in one's mind but I could never look at Mason Jarr without thinking of, well, a mason jar.

Robert Van Damme has one of the most appropriate names in porn. I first met Robert in a restaurant in West Hollywood. Upon gazing at his god-like beauty I whipped myself over to his table to inform him I could make him one of the most famous porn stars on the planet. Luckily he was with two of his friends who knew who I was so I didn't sound like a totally crazed maniac. He told me he was straight to which I responded, "Perfect."

I immediately cast him in *Muscle Men Moving Company, Inc.*, *Cowboy Rides Again* and *Young Gods* and because of his resemblance to Jean-Claude Van Damme I bestowed him with the moniker Robert Van Damme.

Robert Van Damme is a total enigma because he was once one of the highest ranked ice hockey players in the Czech Republic, in the world in fact. He was married, with three kids, and shagged every hot chick he could get his hands on. Then he began to star in gay porn and

OUT OF THE BLUE

before you could say, "pass me that bowl of borscht" he had become an enormous star and was delighting in man-on-man love action. Of course, for straight men, doing gay porn can often lead to one unfortunate realization: that they actually enjoy having sex with other men. I have seen this happen more times than a millipede has legs. Straight man meets straight girl, falls in love, girl persuades straight man to do gay porn because she thinks its kind of kinky, straight man meets gay boy on set . . . they run off to Aruba together . . . straight girl cries for weeks on Blue Blake's broad shoulders. It's like the gay-for-pay circle of life.

Now that Chris Duffy had embarked on a hardcore porn career, there was no turning back. Dirk cast Chris in the Tom of Finland movie at my suggestion and Chris's insistence. With Lance out of the picture, Chris and I were the stars. I hadn't spoken to Lance since we had fucked and he had returned to D.C. In fact, after *Posing Strap,* Lance never did another porno again. He didn't become a hugely famous action star either although he has appeared on over four hundred fitness magazine covers worldwide.

The miniscule plot of *The Wild Ones* involved Chris and I riding around Los Angeles on our Harley Davidsons, inviting hot guys to join us for an orgy. Chris and I don't appear in the orgy scene, since they couldn't pay me enough. Three-ways were bad enough—I had done a few of those—but orgies were out of the question. I was far too particular about whom I fucked to do a big group sex scene.

The Wild Ones also starred Michael Brawn, Wolf, and Zak Spears, among others. In a weird coincidence, the

CHAPTER ELEVEN

first scene Chris and I shot was set in a garage and we were mechanics just like in *Nothin' Nice*. Dirk directed. A guy called Marcus did the videography. He owned a company based in Brazil called Marco Studios, and he shot a lot of bodybuilders in his films. He was a small, unassuming guy, and I adored him. We just hit it off straight away. In fact, years later I traveled to Sao Paolo and stayed with him for two weeks while we discussed making a film called *Brazilian Blue*. I would star as a British tourist visiting Brazil; fucking my way through the country. The film never got made but Marcus and I have remained great friends.

In our *Wild Ones'* scene, Chris drags me off the street and into a car repair garage. He pulls down my cut-off shorts, eats my arse then fucks me silly.

Although Dirk knew how to spot terrifically hot men, he was a terrible director. A lot of people think they can direct porn just because they watch a lot of it but it's an incredibly complicated jigsaw puzzle that must connect properly. That's why there are so few really talented porn directors. While we were shooting our scene I noticed Dirk was paying way too much attention to the B-roll— this is the acting that sets the scene up— and not enough attention to the hardcore. When Dirk shouted, "It's a wrap" I was astonished. He couldn't possibly have enough hardcore footage for an entire scene. However, I said nothing because I didn't want to cause any hassle on the set. But I noticed Marco looking strangely at Dirk, as if he too couldn't believe we had finished so soon.

After the shoot Chris gave me a ride home. He seemed nervous.

"Can I ask you something?"

"Sure," I replied.

"Joanie and I want to move to San Francisco and we want you to come with us."

San Francisco!!! I never dreamed of moving back to San Francisco . . . still, I had a lot of friends there: Gabriella, Officer Betty and a ton of leather men.

"Let me think about it," I said. "That's a big step for us . . . or me."

I was ambivalent. If it had just been Chris and me, I would have bitten his arm off to move to San Francisco, but with Joanie as well? I wasn't even bisexual for God's sake, and on top of that our sex life was growing stranger by the day. Joanie was really into seeing Chris getting his ass used and she was always trying to "fist" him . . . stick her fist up his ass.

Chris dropped me off at my apartment and I walked in to find Gage watching *Roseanne* while Stephanie was in the kitchen cooking a pot roast. Jesus, my apartment life was turning into an episode of *Leave it to Beaver*! I had to put an end to this.

"I'm moving to San Francisco with Chris Duffy," I announced spontaneously.

I heard "Roseanne" laughing insanely in the corner of the room as if predicting the folly of my decision.

I rented an apartment back at Casa Sanchez and Chris and Joanie rented the apartment above me. Straight away it was a really uncomfortable situation. Joanie sensed that Chris was slipping through her fingers as he became more involved with men. They fought constantly, and when they weren't arguing, they were taking drugs and fucking.

CHAPTER ELEVEN

We had only been in San Francisco a few weeks when I received a call from Dirk Dehner.

"Blue, I have a huge problem." I knew exactly what was coming. "In the footage we have of you, we didn't shoot enough close-up penetration shots."

No shit Sherlock.

"So could you fly back to Los Angeles so we can reshoot just the penetration shots?"

FUCK!!! FUCK!!! FUCK!!!

"I'll talk to Chris about it," I said wearily.

"There's just one more problem," Dirk added, "We don't have it in the budget to pay you."

Now if my career hadn't been just starting I would have told Dirk to fuck off, but truth be told, I liked Dirk and didn't want to mess up his first film. I agreed to indeed fly back to L.A. for the reshoot of the penetration with no pay.

Chris didn't mind. He had left his motorbike in L.A. and wanted to ride it back to San Francisco anyway. Also, I think he wanted a night away from Joanie who was imbibing drugs like a mad woman.

Once we got to Los Angeles we were put up by the Tom of Finland Foundation in Silverlake. The foundation was housed in an old rambling place that was constantly full of pierced and tattooed volunteers. Gage would have been in heaven. Upon announcing that I was moving to San Francisco however, Gage had returned to London with Stephanie, thereby giving up our apartment.

We shot the penetration shots in a cellar dungeon. The walls were full of pictures of guys wearing gas masks and drinking piss. If you watch *The Wild Ones* closely you

OUT OF THE BLUE

can see the lighting and floor beneath me in the fucking shots are completely different in the wide angles than in the close up shots.

The next day, I flew back to San Francisco and found Joanie high on GHB. At that moment something inside me clicked. Looking into her drugged up, pinprick pupils I realized my life in America was over. Just like that. I was sick of this circus that my life had become. I didn't even wait for Chris to arrive back from Los Angeles on his motorbike. I called up British Airways and caught a flight back to London that night.

Chris and I lost touch after San Francisco. I heard about him as the years went by only through the grapevine. He and Joanie moved to Florida but eventually divorced. Joanie became a dog groomer and Chris fell in love with a female impersonator who moved back to San Francisco with him. Chris was a genetic marvel who at a young age was adored by millions of men all over the world. I always thought he seemed to be searching for something that nobody was capable of giving him and that is why he experimented so deeply with drugs. I saw him once more in New Orleans. The last time we spoke he seemed sublimely happy having finally settled down with a guy with no wife around to ruin things for him. Perhaps that's what he needed all along. It definitely wasn't Chris's or my destiny to stay together forever, but for a brief while we were in . . . lust.

The Tom of Finland movie came out and was an enormous hit. It felt like I became an instant star in every porn-buying country on the planet.

A club promoter from Paris called and flew me in to

CHAPTER ELEVEN

make a personal appearance at the King Club, Paris's hottest gay venue. I gave radio interviews, and you couldn't pick up a gay magazine without seeing Chris and I. We were on the cover of *Torso* magazine as "The Dynamic Duo." The cover of *Advocate Men* proclaimed "Tom Boys . . . Tom of Finland Comes to Life." To top it off, we were on the cover of the *Tom of Finland Calendar*. I had achieved in a couple of years what most porn actors never experience in a lifetime . . . infamy.

I languished in London. As autumn drew near and the days grew colder, the siren song of Los Angeles wailed in my ears. As much as I enjoyed my return to England, it wasn't home for me the way it once was. I knew I should be exploiting my newfound porn fame in the U.S. I was wise enough to realize this moment would quickly pass. Even so, I was reticent to move back to Los Angeles because I felt settled in London.

I had also restarted Musclemen Masseurs, my bodybuilding escort agency. It was, as always, a huge success and I had several competition bodybuilders working for me. One of them, Joe, a married forty year old with two kids, had been having an affair with me. He had been the British middleweight champion and was so sexy it took my breath away. Five foot seven and two hundred pounds, he would work from my apartment all day turning tricks and then would return to his wife and kids at night. I fell in love with him. He had a big uncut dick and I was blissfully happy, but something gnawed away inside of me. Joe was never going to leave his wife for me, nor did I want him to. So I rented my apartment to him and decided impulsively to go and live in South Africa of all places.

OUT OF THE BLUE

I had met a really nice client named Ralph who wasn't bad looking, and he told me he owned a diamond mine in Pretoria just outside of Johannesburg. He invited me to stay with him for as long as I wanted so I hopped on a flight and set off for South Africa for six months.

I arrived with a song in my heart and a clear head. Living with a guy who owned a diamond mine was probably going to be super luxurious and who knew—I might fall madly in love with Ralph. He was extremely soft spoken, with thick strawberry blonde hair and blue eyes that, on the three times I had seen him, shone like diamonds.

I knew nothing about South Africa. I wasn't really sure even what the word apartheid meant. On arrival in Johannesburg I searched the airport for Ralph. I saw no one except a priest in long white robes. A strawberry headed priest with sparkling eyes. Was it Halloween? What the hell was Ralph doing dressed as a priest? Was he going to a costume party?

"Blue, it's me Ralph," he waved.

"Yeah . . . I know, great to see you . . . what's with the robes?"

"Well, I didn't know how to tell you in London because I never thought I would have to but . . . well, the truth is I'm a priest." A priest who owned a diamond mine? He must be lavishing money on the sick and impoverished.

"But how do you find time to run the diamond mine?"

"Ah yes, the diamond mine, Well, that actually doesn't exist."

NO DIAMOND MINE. "I took a vow of poverty and now live on the kindness of the township in which I

CHAPTER ELEVEN

preach." My head was spinning—poverty, townships, kindness of strangers. I suddenly realized the plane had crashed and I had died and gone to hell.

"It's not too bad. The nuns and I tend the lepers at the local colony and we all get on wonderfully." He said leper colony like he was pronouncing the words Club Med.

"You live on a leper colony?" I shrieked. I suddenly had visions of my fingers dropping off, followed by my nose. How would I escort with no fingers or nose??

"NO . . . I don't live on the colony, I live at the church on the local army base and offer spiritual comfort to the young Afrikaans soldiers who are far from home."

Now that was more like it. Young soldiers miles from home, good thing I had packed my leopard skin leg warmers. I felt memories of the troops in Northern Ireland wash over me and my dick got hard.

"Why did you lie to me?" I demanded.

Ralph suddenly looked very sad.

"I'm sorry," he said, "I fell in love with you in London and I thought it would shock you to know I was a priest . . . I should have told you before you arrived."

I looked into his big sad eyes and realized how lonely Ralph must have been. Nobody knew he was gay and he had fallen for a bodybuilder escort who had shown him some passion and a bit of slap and tickle.

Once outside the airport I looked around me. The land was dry and arid and the weather was hot but I could suck it up and make the best of it for the next six months. After all the hedonism I almost welcomed this. I wasn't going back to London or the States for the foreseeable future so

OUT OF THE BLUE

I was just going to roll up my sleeves and pitch in. If Ralph could care for lepers and young soldiers so could I. Well I could care for the young soldiers bit . . . or bits.

In South Africa all the young men had to do two years of national service when they reached the age of eighteen. Most were strict Catholics, and Father Ralph's church was a haven to the young homesick troops. Amazingly there was a great gym on the base and I soon realized I was actually as happy as a pig in shit. All Father Ralph's friends drank like fish and they would gather in his house which adjoined the church on the army base and get drunk and sing the Christian pop hits of the day. I didn't bother telling anybody I was gay, as no one I met was "out" and I didn't want Father Ralph being asked unfortunate questions about how we had met in London while he was on his sabbatical.

All the servants were black people, but if they disdained their roles, they knew better than to complain to their employers. Remember, this was the apartheid era and the racism was atrocious.

I had my own room, which contained a bed, a chest of drawers and a crucifix on the wall. Jesus would look down on me disapprovingly every night from his cross as I jerked off thinking about the soldiers I had seen in the gym that day. There was nothing to do but work out so my body grew accordingly. For some reason the only television show that wasn't in Afrikaans was *The Bold and the Beautiful*. I had never watched it in America and I now knew why. The show was ludicrous—all based around some ridiculous family called the Forresters who owned a fashion empire. They could string out a plotline for months on that damn

CHAPTER ELEVEN

show. Brooke Forrester had been pregnant for two years it seemed, but I became hooked as it provided a lifeline to the world I had come from.

In those days there were no computers in South Africa, at least none I knew of in Pretoria. We were actually living in a small area outside of Pretoria called Voortrekkerhoogte. It was a place where the original Dutch settlers had landed and settled. Translated into English Voortrekkerhoogte meant something like "agonizing trek." The Afrikaans church preached fire and brimstone and hell and damnation so the Afrikaan soldiers came to Father Ralph's church instead for prayer.

One day while visiting an old age home with Father Ralph, I listened to an Afrikaan sermon being preached. It was all about growing old and being abandoned by one's loved ones and praying for death to shake off the misery of this mortal coil. Very depressing. When we got back I immediately ransacked the church until I found a bottle of communion wine, which I guzzled until I passed out in a stupor behind the altar.

After spending an uneventful Christmas I decided to hitchhike across South Africa to reach the resort of Cape Town. I had slept with a couple of soldiers but although they were good looking they were terrible in bed. I had heard that Cape Town had a banging gay nightlife so I packed some shorts and t-shirts in an old army bag and set off. Father Ralph thought it extremely foolish and dangerous for me to hitchhike across the continent, but I was so bored a native's spear in my head seemed better than this slow death amongst the religious zealots.

Ralph let me out on the main highway and I bade him

OUT OF THE BLUE

a tearful goodbye. I assured him I would call and he drove off to tend the lepers.

I looked exactly like a young soldier and soon a couple stopped to give me a ride. They were astonished by the fact that I was English and plied me with questions about the Queen and the houses of Parliament and scones and jam. This was how my journey to Cape Town progressed: going from car to car until as the sun went down I was dropped off in the middle of nowhere by my last ride. As the sun sank behind the hills I began to realize that Father Ralph may have been correct and this may have been a very foolish venture for me to embark upon.

So I stood by the side of the road and prayed for a ride as car after car sailed by.

Finally a car stopped and I threw myself inside.

"Man . . . you were lucky we came by," said the driver, "You could have been murdered out there." I nearly wept tears of pure pleasure when he told me he was heading for Cape Town.

A few hours later we arrived in Cape Town. To my surprise it turned out to be like bloody Brighton. It was as boring as hell.

The city is built on the apex of the Atlantic and the Indian Ocean. For some reason, I always imagined the Indian Ocean would be warm and inviting. It was fucking FREEZING. Every day I would hang out on the local gay beach. Well, no beach actually, craggy rocks that one could fall on and smash ones brains out on. All the gays would trek over the rocks like a pilgrimage to bask naked in the South African sun. Every day helicopters would fly over full of tourists and point out the naked gay people. They would

CHAPTER ELEVEN

descend so low that towels would blow into the freezing ocean and people would run screaming into the bushes that bordered the rocks. I would just lie there impassively enjoying the stares and rubbing myself with tanning lotion. That was when I came to an enormous realization. Why was I lying on a rock showing my bits off to gawking South Africans for free when I could be back in Los Angeles enjoying the fruits of my porno labor?

I decided to return to America and pick up my porno career where I had left off.

I hitchhiked back to Voortrekkerhoogte and said a final farewell to Father Ralph. I think he was relieved to see me go as people were starting to ask questions and I think he was afraid his cover was going to be blown. I jumped on the next plane heading to Los Angeles.

Upon arriving back in Los Angeles I moved in with a really good friend of mine, Greg Greene. I had met Greg years before when I had been living in San Francisco with Gage. He and his boyfriend, the porn star Greg Strom, had hired me one night to fuck Greg Strom while Greg Greene watched and called his boyfriend a dirty whore. That was their M.O. I had stayed good friends with Greg Greene, who shared an apartment downtown with a crystal addict named Eddie. I moved in with them, much to Eddie's disgust and began working every night at the hustler bar "Numbers" again.

One night, when I was leaning on the bar at Numbers, a loud drag queen in a tatty nylon dress came running over.

"Blue!" she squealed.

"Hello," I replied looking mystified.

OUT OF THE BLUE

"It's me, bitch, Crystal Crawford!"

"Oh my god . . . Crystal . . . I haven't seen you since . . . ." Well, I hadn't seen her since she had tried to stiff me on my check for that terrible movie I had starred in.

"Listen, I'm seeing your face everywhere, but nobody has known how to get hold of you."

"I've been living in South Africa,"

"Was it fun?"

"Nuns, leprosy, bad sex."

"Well, a great friend of mine, Gino Colbert, is directing a movie called *Night Walk*. It's going to be the most expensive porn movie ever made. I can get you an interview with him."

I could tell that Crystal was trying to make amends for the check debacle so I smiled.

"That would be great."

I gave Crystal my number and left the bar alone. It was a slow night. I hadn't done a film in ages and it was probably time to get back into the business. I had seen Gino Colbert in hundreds of films dating back to the seventies. Gino was a good-looking Italian guy on film with a great smile, and he was a total sex pig. I had heard that he had relocated from his home in NYC to Hollywood and was fast making his name as a popular director. He had just made a film starring Ken Ryker entitled *Matinee Idol*. The film was supposed to star Ryan Idol, hence the title, but Ryan was "indisposed" and so Ken Ryker had taken the role.

The next day I was lying on Greg Greene's balcony tanning when the phone rang. It was Gino Colbert.

"Is this Mister Blake? This is Gino Colbert."

CHAPTER ELEVEN

"Yes," I said, a little flustered. I sort of fancied him from the films.

"Great job in the Tom of Finland film,"

"Thanks."

"I'm making a film called *Nightwalk*, and Crystal Crawford told me you might be interested in appearing in it. Could I come over and interview you for the role?"

"Sure."

I gave him the address and an hour later there was a knock at my door. I opened it and there stood one handsome man, Gino Colbert. He looked exactly as he did in all his films. I smiled and he smiled back. He had beautiful teeth. I love it when people have great teeth.

"You're perfect," he said, without setting foot in the apartment.

Hmmm, I thought, you're not too bad yourself. After spending months in London training with Steve and living in South Africa I was in really good condition—huge pecs, small waist and a golden California tan.

"Can I see you naked?" Gino asked.

We went into the bedroom and I stripped off. Gino whistled.

"Perfect," he said. "You'll be perfect for the role."

"Who will I be working with?"

"Hank Hightower and Ryan Block."

Hank was a stocky handsome hairy Latino and Ryan was a straight, muscled biracial guy with smooth skin. This was a good sign. Obviously Gino knew what he was doing when it came to casting. Both guys were very masculine and I fancied both of them.

"You'll be the one getting fucked," Gino added.

Damn, I thought.

"The movie is also being co-directed by a guy called Michael Ninn."

Michael Ninn was an enormously famous straight director. He had a big hit with a glossy straight movie entitled *Latex*. It turned out that the reason *Night Walk* was getting made was that Michael had shot a straight movie and rather than tear the expensive set down, the production company, VCA, had decided to shoot a gay movie on the same set. The movie was also to star Chad Conners and Dino De Marco, who I had met on the set of *Lube Job*. Dino was to play the role of the devil trying to seduce the young, blond, chaste bodybuilder Chad Conners. I was to play the devil's minion and Will Clark was to play the role of the devil's butler. Will was a cute redheaded boy that I later fucked in a film called *My Bitch,* in which we shared a prison cell.

Gino gave me the role in *Night Walk* and told me that Ryan Block would pick me up the following day to drive me to the set.

I loved that about porn: you were cast one day and the next you were on the set. Sometimes you were on the set within hours of being cast . . . or minutes even!!

The set for *Night Walk* was astonishing. It had been built in a gigantic studio and consisted of futuristic landscapes and vistas further than the eye could see. In my scene a gigantic gong was banged to summon me from a vat of boiling water . . . to be fucked by Ryan and Hank. All the crew was straight and I got some perverse thrill for some reason out of them filming my arsehole. They seemed slightly embarrassed because they were used to

CHAPTER ELEVEN

shooting chicks. Michael Ninn was a genius and he and Gino worked really well together on the set. Unlike so many shoots, it was a totally stress-free environment. I relished the thought of working for Gino again. The sex was hot and I could tell the film was going to be an enormous hit. I felt like I was starring in *Blade Runner* . . . well, apart from all the cock.

I took a real shine to Gino Colbert. We became friends and he was soon introducing me to people high up on the porn ladder who could further my career. One of the most important was Mickey Skee, a hugely famous porn reviewer who with his long blond hair bore more than a passing resemblance to Farrah Fawcett. I met so many people in the industry through Gino, and I owe a lot to his friendship.

One day over lunch, Gino said, "I'm thinking of doing an interracial film. Do you want to star in it?"

"What's the storyline?" I asked. Gino was famous for making films with big plots and that always intrigued me, as I liked the acting part more than I did the sex.

"Well . . . I thought you might like to write it."

Write a film? One thing I liked about Gino was he really believed I was more talented than I actually was. How the hell would I go about writing a porn film?

"Ryan Block will direct it, I'll produce it and you'll write and star in it. Each scene has to contain a white guy and a black guy . . . we can call it *Black and Blue*."

I had absolutely no idea how to sit down and write a porn film but I knew the basic rules. If there were five scenes in a film, as the star, I could appear in the first, third and fifth scene. Four to five scenes were normal for a film. So I sat down and wrote. As I had an English accent I worked that into the script. I would play an English guy visiting his American cousin who I decided would be played by Chad Conners (the hot, blond, straight bodybuilder who I met on the set of *Night Walk* and desperately wanted to fuck in real life). In the film I visit my cousin and regale him with tales of interracial sex in the hopes he will become incredibly turned on and let me fuck him. The rest of the cast was made up of black performers—Gene Lamar, T-spoon, and Ryan Block—and white guys Paul Hanson and Giorgio Falconi.

Chad's apartment was built on a soundstage in the San Fernando Valley and the five-scene film was to be shot on four consecutive days.

On the first day of filming, Milton, the owner of the studio where our set was built, greeted us. He was a stocky middle-aged guy who looked like he could have been captain of the high school football team when he was younger. He used to be a porn star himself and he always had young porn starlets wandering around the studio. The studio was basically a huge warehouse with dozens of different sets that could be erected within days. I never really liked their sets because when they built rooms they always looked sort of thrown together, all shaky walls, no windows and bad furniture. If you knocked on a door the whole fake wall would sway backward and forward.

"Let me show you what I've built for your apartment," Milton said excitedly.

I always got the impression he wanted me to blow him but that was OK because I always imagined EVERY straight guy wanted me to blow them. He flung open a

CHAPTER ELEVEN

door and there was Chad Connners' apartment. It wasn't too bad. It certainly looked like an American college kid could be living there. If the audience spent all their time critiquing the décor we weren't doing our job. This wasn't *Martha Stewart Living*.

Gino arrived with Ryan Block and rubbed his hands with glee. "Perfect, perfect, perfect," Gino smiled.

Gino was always very upbeat on the porn sets. Perhaps because he had been making porn since the seventies, nothing got him down or perhaps because he just really liked working with me as I was so easy going. I wanted the film to look great and so did he. When you have that mutual respect between the star and the director, great films are made.

We sat around waiting for Chad as the rest of the crew arrived. I chatted to the famous straight porn star Mr. Marcus in the makeup room. He had been in another part of the studio filming a scene and I wandered over to watch. He was fucking a really scrawny blonde chick with bruises on her knees and she was screaming her head off because of Mr. Marcus' big black dick. When the scene finished she wiped a tea towel between her legs and said, "That was great . . . I've gotta run because I'm doing another scene down the road, but can I have your number because I know someone we can both do a scene for."

This was definitely how it worked on porn sets. You would meet someone who would offer you work on another film and then you would get more work from people you met on that film. It just spiraled and spiraled.

Mr. Marcus wrote his number down for her and she gave it to a grey-haired guy who had been standing in

OUT OF THE BLUE

the corner watching them fuck.

"This is my husband," she explained, "He's also my business manager."

She pulled up her knickers, slipped a dress over her head and ran out without showering. Mr. Marcus grinned at me and went to use the shower. I realized I was hard from looking at his big dick. He was gorgeous.

I returned to our own set where by now Chad Conners had arrived. He smiled at me indolently. I couldn't wait to fuck him. I had even jerked off thinking about it. The scene where I had to fuck him, however, wouldn't come until the very last day of the shoot. Chad was on the set that day just to shoot the dialogue that would link the scenes together. This went off without a hitch. Chad was a good actor and Ryan Block seemed to know what he was doing as director too. Just in case something went wrong, Gino hovered around making the occasional suggestion. After all, he was the producer.

My first sex scene in the film was with Gene Lamar. He was fifty but didn't look a day over thirty . . . black don't crack. He played a cop who arrested me and fucked me over a garbage can in the back of a nightclub. Gene had a big dick and what with him being dressed as a cop, the scene went swimmingly.

The next scene I had written for myself was probably quite controversial for its time. I was sitting in army gear in a dark room surrounded by glory holes and one by one huge black cocks came through the holes and I began sucking on them. The scene was shot in a sex club in Los Angeles and as I wasn't involved in the casting I had no idea whose dicks I was sucking. Ryan Block who was also

CHAPTER ELEVEN

operating the camera had found the disembodied cocks for me to suck on. Each one was big, and as I worked my way around the room I began to get lockjaw. I could see that Ryan had a massive hard-on in his pants watching me suck all those black dicks one by one. Not knowing who they belonged to sent me into a sexual frenzy. I ran from one to the next and back again cramming all that meat into my gob. It was an extremely sexy scene and one by one they came on my chest and all over my face. After everyone came, I ran for the bathroom to wash off all the strangers' spunk.

Ryan wandered in and took out his dick. "Come on baby . . . give daddy a blowjob too."

Ryan Block and I had always had an intense mutual attraction between us since we had shot *Night Walk*. I knew he was straight with a kid on the way but he just loved me sucking his dick. As it was always fat and hard I sometimes acquiesced if I was feeling horny. This was one of those times. I fell to my knees and gave him the best blowjob of his life. He grunted and in no time shot his load.

"Did you like sucking all that black dick you dirty slut?" he grinned.

"Yes . . . very sexy . . . but who were those guys? Where did you find them?"

Ryan looked sheepish. "Wellllllllll . . . to be honest we didn't have a lot of money in the budget so I found them on the street."

"ON THE STREET?" I yelled.

"Yeah . . . you know . . . like homeless . . . but I made sure they were all clean."

OUT OF THE BLUE

These last words were lost to me as I was swallowing a bottle of Listerine. I ended up not catching gonorrhea but I kept a wary eye on Ryan for the rest of the shoot. Every time I looked at him he would grin and squeeze his fat cock through his pants . . . sexy bastard!!!

My final scene in *Black and Blue* was the one I had really been waiting for. It was the last scene in the film and it was the one where I got to fuck Chad Conners. It involved him being turned on by my tales of interracial sex, going lust-mad, and getting fucked by me and the pizza boy. (Somewhere along the way a pizza boy had delivered pizza in the scene.) Ryan played the pizza boy—not only was he directing and doing the cinematography, but now he was acting. I'd heard of multi-tasking, but this was ridiculous.

Anyway, both Ryan and I would get to fuck Chad, so I was delighted. On the day of the big scene Chad went to Gino and asked him if he could have a quiet word in private with him. My ears immediately pricked up. I must have looked like a fruit bat. I knew Chad hated getting fucked and would do anything to get out of the scene. Of course the film would make no sense because the whole point of the film was that I ENDED UP FUCKING CHAD CONNERS . . . GOD DAMN IT.

"Mr. Blake . . . can I have a word with you?" Gino asked.

He always called me Mr. Blake. Mr. Colbert had extremely good manners.

"We have a little problem."

Here it comes, I thought.

"It seems Chad's ass is bleeding and he won't be able to get fucked in the scene."

CHAPTER ELEVEN

"It's true," Chad said, anticipating my skepticism.

"Show me." Bleeding, he better be having his damn fucking period I thought. "Bend over now." I demanded.

Sure enough, for some obscure reason Chad's ass was bleeding, although now many years older and wiser I realize he must have stuck ketchup up his hole or a bottle of Cherryade or something wet and red to avoid getting fucked.

As Chad couldn't get fucked that left just one alternative or the entire film would collapse: I had to let Chad and Ryan fuck me.

"It isn't fair," I sulked, "I was supposed to be the one doing the fucking. Now I have to douche and I'm not prepared . . . I had devilled eggs for lunch."

This was a complete lie . . . I hated devilled eggs. In fact, a devilled egg has never passed my lips.

"I've got something that will cheer you up," said Gino.

"Nothing will cheer me up," I pouted.

"Well, you did such a great job writing this film, I want you to write two more . . . a trilogy, with the name 'Blue' in the title."

Gino knew what made me happy. I grinned through my misery.

"Really?"

"Really."

"Bring me the enema bottles!" I shouted, "Let's get this show on the road!"

So Ryan and Chad ended up fucking me. The scene was a success despite my moaning and griping. I gritted my teeth and took one for the team . . . well, two for the team actually.

OUT OF THE BLUE

Something most people don't realize is that there is a shortage of super hot guys to star in gay films. That's why when somebody new comes along all the studios fight over him like starved dogs over a pork chop. I'm not talking your average young "twinky" guy. I'm talking about great skin, great hair, great teeth, great dick and great arse. The sort of guy who you see working out at your local gym and would sell your soul for a night of passion with. Jeff Stryker, Ryan Idol, all those old Matt Sterling models who seemed so unobtainable unless you visited your local porn dealer. One such model was a guy called Bo Garrett. He had appeared as if from nowhere at Gold's Gym in Hollywood one day. He was tanned and muscled and had one of the handsomest faces I had ever seen. I asked the girl who worked on the desk who he was.

"I don't know . . . he just joined the gym. I heard he just got out of the marines and he's straight so that means he's mine so hands off!"

Well that definitely sealed the deal. A straight guy new in town with the face of a movie star, surely he must want to do gay porn, I thought. Now as weird as that may sound, surprisingly it would often come true. Handsome guys would flock to Los Angeles to be movie stars, and when they realized it wasn't as easy as it had been back home when they were being cast as the lead in *The Fantasticks*, they would sometimes do a gay film on the sly. Mostly just jerking off, but that could lead to other things sometimes: getting blown, getting rimmed and even perhaps going the whole way as their fame grew. Fame is fame after all and in those days, without the Internet being so pervasive, it was easier to convince guys that nobody they knew would

CHAPTER ELEVEN

see these scenes back on the old homestead.

I peered at Bo over the squat rack, and he looked up at me and started laughing.

"How you doing, man?"

He had one of the deepest, sexiest voices I had ever heard. I think I even blushed.

"Oh . . . I was just admiring your . . . " and then I couldn't think of anything to say. Nothing. I had stalked him all over the gym, and now he was talking to me, and I was speechless.

"Look . . . I may as well just be straight forward with you. My name's Blue Blake . . . " he stared blankly at me, " . . . well, the truth is I star in porn . . . gay porn . . . bodybuilder gay porn . . . and I thought because you are so spectacular looking . . . well, that you might want to do a film with me . . . I mean, you would be the one fucking me of course," I rambled insanely.

"Too fucking right I'd be the one fucking you because I'm not going to get fucked!"

What!! Did my tiny British ears deceive me? Had he just agreed to star in a film with me? I got an instant hard-on. For every hundred guys you ask to star in a film, one will say yes. Figure that in with the fact that those hundred guys are the best looking of thousands of guys you see every day and it's an extremely small percentage.

"Yeah . . . I'll star in a film with you, why not? You can call me Bo Garrett," he grinned.

Wow . . . this was amazing, now there was only one problem. I didn't have a film for him to star in with me, so of course I immediately got on the phone with Gino Colbert.

OUT OF THE BLUE

"Just how hot is he?" Gino asked.

"He's incredible!" I gushed "One of the sexiest men I have ever seen. In fact he was talking to a girl who teaches aerobics, and she got pregnant just by looking at him. I think I'm in love."

Bo really was that sexy. He must have been born with too many pheromones or something because just being in his presence drove me nutty.

"Well," said Gino, "I do have a movie slated called *Just Men*. Does he look like he could have been in prison?"

"Definitely . . . in fact he told me that he had just come out of prison!" I lied wildly.

"PRISON . . . for what?"

There's a difference between employing somebody who looks like they could star on *Oz* and employing somebody who had just *definitely* suffocated their grandmother for the twenty quid in her knickers drawer.

"Hmmm . . . unpaid parking tickets, I think." Did people go to prison in America for unpaid parking tickets? "Gino, believe me when I tell you, this guy is going to make you a fortune, and I feel its my genetic prerogative to share myself getting fucked by him with the rest of the world." I would have said anything at this point to get shagged by Bo Garrett.

Gino agreed to meet Bo and instantly wanted him for a scene with me in *Just Men*. In no time Bo and I began hanging out with each other . . . well, not really hanging out but fucking.

Bo lived in a filthy apartment in the saddest part of Hollywood where he nurtured various vermin he called "critters," from what I could make out, the term "critters"

CHAPTER ELEVEN

seemed to apply to a collection of wild spiders and lizards that hid under the furniture and appliances, waiting for food to be dropped on the floor. Once a morsel was dropped, a giant lizard or spider or creature of unidentifiable nature would dash out from under the sofa and consume the cheese scone, piece of candy or whatever else had fallen on the carpet. The scariest one was called "Stove Critter" and lived under the stove eating bacon bits and old McDonald's french fries, I presume enlarging its reptilian stomach so it would one day be large enough to consume one of my toes as I foolishly wandered by clutching nourishment for it. Stove lizard would drag me under the stove to feed me to its undoubtedly enormous spawn. There were probably ten stove critters living under there, I mean who lives under a stove on their own?

But I could put up with all the creepy critters because I found Bo wildly, sexily eccentric . . . with a HUGE cock. He was indeed straight, so it wasn't just those bitches at Gold's Gym who had been tempting me with false rumors. It was also true that he had been in the marines and afterwards had moved to Hollywood to seek fame and fortune. He told me that when he was a kid growing up on a farm in the Midwest he would "corn hole" his best friend. I never worked out if that meant that he fucked his best friend or stuck a corn cob up his best friend's arse—I found out soon enough when I let him corn hole me and believe me it didn't involve farm produce.

Bo had a big dick and really knew how to use it. I could tell he was going to be a big star. That is until the day we got on the set to shoot *Just Men* and he froze up.

OUT OF THE BLUE

Why is it always like that? You meet a super hot guy, you think he will make a great porn star, you might even fuck him, then you get him on the set and he freezes in front of the cameras.

I had shot so many films by this time that fucking before the cameras had become second nature to me. I loved arriving on the studio to see what sets had been built. There were normally other porn stars hanging around, and we would trade anecdotes and gossip about which films were being made and who was being cast in them. It was all very convivial . . . like a bake sale only with everybody naked and clutching tubes of KY jelly instead of pineapple upside down cake.

The trouble with Bo began in the makeup room. He didn't want to take off his cap to get his hair styled. The make up artist persuaded and cajoled, but there was no way that cap was coming off his damn head. Finally Gino was summoned, and we discovered that for some reason one of Bo's crazy girlfriends had given him a perm or something very similar the night before. He looked fine, he always looked fine to me, but he was mortified and refused to show his head.

"Take clippers and shave the whole fucking mess off!" I hissed at Gino.

"Blue," Gino sternly reprimanded me, "Remember, this is his first time on set." Gino was such a fucking saint.

After an hour of convincing Bo he didn't look like Harpo Marx, we got him onto the set; which was the interior of a prison cell. By this time I was nervous. What if Bo couldn't perform and the scene became one of those

CHAPTER ELEVEN

hellish twelve-hour days? I needn't have worried. It all went swimmingly. However, I could tell that performing on camera wasn't going to be a forte of Bo Garrett's. In fact, he made only a few other films that I'm aware of: *Biker Pigs from Hell, Slick, Saddle Tramps 2, Mavericks* and *Playing with Fire 2*.

We stopped sleeping together, and over the years it seemed each time I saw Bo he became more and more tattooed. Eventually he began dabbling in drugs and then vanished completely for a while. He called me a few years later and told me he had been in intensive rehab for seventeen months for his addictions. We agreed to meet for lunch. Somehow the lunch got cancelled and I ended up never seeing the incredibly sexy Bo Garrett ever again, which was an enormous shame as he was definitely one of the sexiest men I had ever met and one of the sweetest.

CHAPTER TWELVE

GINO CALLED AND ASKED IF I would like to do a "glamour shoot" in leather for a new photographer he was auditioning. I loved glamour shoots. It was my favorite job in porn, along with modeling for the box covers. I think I enjoyed the pampering and the opportunity to meet all the photographers. My favorite was Dean Keefer. He not only shot a lot of layouts for *Playgirl*, but in the day photographed teen queens like Hilary Duff. He would airbrush the pictures like crazy and could make my corpulent waist look almost sylphlike. I would practically choose to do a film if I knew Dean was doing the photography for the box.

During the photo shoot Gino asked me if I had ever heard of Leisure Time Films. I knew Gino shot a lot of scenes for the company, which was owned by straight entrepreneur Mark Carrier.

Leisure Time produced those films you see on the shelves that say "4 HOURS . . . COCK, COCK AND MORE COCK." They made films just consisting of compilation scenes spliced together. Because Gino was directing, the quality was high and the money was good so I agreed to appear in a few. What I didn't realize was that those few scenes would end up in literally *hundreds* of different films. I ended up appearing in *Big Men Eat*

OUT OF THE BLUE

Ass Too, Dirty Boys, Hard Workers, Kinky Gays, Lockdown, Muscle Up—the list is endless. I was naïve, but I had signed the model releases so I couldn't bellyache about it afterwards. That seemed ungracious.

My first scene for Leisure Time was shot on the set of an old alley for a film titled *Dudes*. I was with a model whom I didn't really fancy, but hey, I was getting paid a thousand dollars, and that would go towards getting me a new apartment. My welcome at Greg's was wearing thin due to his moody roommate and I needed my own place. Greg had agreed to move out and get a place with me.

During a break from the fucking, I noticed one of the crew making cow eyes at me. I sauntered over and introduced myself to him.

"Hello . . . I'm Blue Blake." I smiled.

The guy, who was fat and pink with a thick head of hair, grinned. He looked like a giant infant.

"I'm Ronnie Larsen," he said.

Ronnie Larsen . . . I had heard that name somewhere before.

"I wrote the play *Making Porn* that's currently playing on Melrose Avenue."

Of course, I had seen the posters all over the city for the show, a comedy about the gay porn industry. Gino had even been to see it and had told me how good it was.

"You must be an actor because your screaming sounded so realistic when you were getting fucked."

That wasn't acting, that was because I had a nine-inch dick crammed up my arse!

"Would you like to come and see the show? I'll give you and Gino free tickets."

CHAPTER TWELVE

What a nice guy, I thought.

"In fact, I want to write a whole play just for you."

Ronnie was nice but he was also obviously a lunatic. Oh well, I needed a shot of theatre to my "porned out" veins and this would serve nicely.

Gino and I saw the play the next night. There was a crowd milling around when we arrived, no doubt drawn by the erotic posturing of the bodybuilder on the play's billboard. He was a young actor named Eric Jirak and he stood naked on the poster with a clapperboard covering his dick. He was a gorgeous twenty-something and his beauty enticed in the hundreds of gay men who passed the theatre daily.

Inside the box office sat a short chubby woman wearing a man's fedora and an oversized shirt that was unbuttoned practically to her waist . . . was that a hot dog lodged between her breasts? She had beady eyes, which were shielded by small glasses and enough food in her teeth to cure global famine.

"Hi, I'm Blue Blake."

"I'm Caryn," she rasped, "I'm the producer of the show." The producer was selling tickets? I was literally speechless. Gino nudged me in the ribs.

"Hmmmm . . . Ronnie invited us to the show." I said.

"I know . . . he's always giving away free tickets, I hate that." Then, in a dramatic turn, she asked bluntly: "How big's your dick?"

"Uhh . . . about eight inches."

"Cut or . . . uncut?"

"Uncut," I replied cooperatively.

Being in the porn industry I was used to total

strangers asking me totally inappropriate questions, or worse, telling me totally inappropriate things about themselves.

"Perfect," she smiled. "Anyway, here are your seats . . . sit anywhere except on the first row . . . . We charge more for that."

I dragged Gino into the theatre.

"Who the hell was that?" I laughed.

"She's Ronnie Larsen's business partner."

"Well she's certainly a character."

We took two seats at the back of the tiny theatre, and Gino proceeded to point out various porn stars in the audience.

The set consisted of a huge door in the middle of the stage, a bed made out of four wooden crates and two tables on opposite ends of the stage full of dildos of all different shapes and sizes. I realized they were trying to create what looked like a sleazy porn set. It wasn't far off from some of the movies I had starred in, so ten out of ten for realism. The plot revolves around a straight, out-of-work actor called Jack whose wife is forcing him to get a normal job to pay the bills. Rather than give up acting, Jack begins to do gay porn behind his wife's back. When she finds out about his new career she becomes his agent and forces him to do more films. Hilarity ensues.

As it turned out, I LOVED the show. Ronnie, who starred as the jaded porn producer, was a hoot, and all the actors were exceptionally funny as they ran on and off the stage in various states of undress. It was like a Dario Fo farce on crack. I laughed until I cried.

Afterwards Ronnie came up to me.

CHAPTER TWELVE

"You were brilliant," I cried.

"Oh, you liked the show"? Ronnie asked, "Good, because I want you to star in it."

My mouth fell open.

The next day I was in the gym and my mind was still swimming with the idea of appearing in the show *Making Porn*. There was a lot of nudity involved but I didn't care about that. What worried me was that the last time I had acted on stage I was playing a mental in *Marat/Sade* years ago.

I pushed that to the back of my mind. I had more immediate concerns. I was going apartment hunting with Greg Greene that evening.

We found a two-bedroom furnished apartment to share in the middle of West Hollywood, which was perfect as I could walk everywhere. Living at Greg Greene's old apartment, the only place I could walk to was McDonalds. Being able to purchase fresh fruit improved my diet immensely.

A few days after moving in, Gino invited me to lunch with Jeff Stryker. Now who in the world hasn't heard of Jeff Stryker? Porn superstar, probably the best looking guy ever to appear in porn, or certainly among the top three. Discovered by director Matt Sterling, Jeff ushered in a new era of porn in the early nineties: smooth, stunning muscle boys with massive cocks. Years later, when I would produce films, my videographer was Andre Adair, who shot a lot for Matt. As it happened Matt had ended up in a wheelchair but was still directing. It was all very *What Ever Happened to Baby Jane?* Andre hated him. Matt would make the crew carry his wheelchair up and down the stairs on the set —including poor Andre who only weighed 120 pounds.

So when I got the opportunity to have lunch with Jeff Stryker I jumped at the chance. He and Gino were great friends. I was told Jeff would pick me up in his limo, and the three of us would go for lunch. I nervously got ready that morning. I couldn't quite believe Jeff Stryker was picking me up in his private limo. As I applied apricot facial scrub I sang to myself the Julie Andrews song, "For somewhere in my worthless childhood, I must have done something gooooooooooood . . . ." The next-door neighbor's Weimaraner howled in delighted approval.

The doorbell rang and I raced to open it. There stood Jeff Stryker. He was strikingly handsome, even more so than in his films.

"Blue . . . it's nice to meet you."

He talked exactly like he talked in the films, with kind of a super low baritone and all the words coming from the back of his throat.

"It's good to meet you, Mr. Stryker," I gushed.

He threw his head back and laughed, and I could see right down his throat.

"Call me Jeff."

I passed out on the pavement, smashed my head open and had to have twenty stitches. Actually that's not true but I definitely felt like I could have passed out while staring into Jeff's dreamy eyes.

I climbed into the limo next to Gino expecting Jeff to join us. Instead, he climbed into the driver's seat.

"I don't like limo drivers, my last one nearly killed me by driving off a mountain in Laurel Canyon."

CHAPTER TWELVE

As I pondered this unusual remark, Greg came running out.

"Blue you forgot your pager!" Then he stopped outside the car. "My God, your limo driver could be Jeff Stryker's twin!"

"It is Jeff Stryker!" I said, realizing that this sounded ridiculous.

We drove off leaving Greg looking goggle-eyed.

What Gino had neglected to mention was that Jeff was a total speed demon. We pulled away from my apartment with enough acceleration to shoot us to the moon. My face was practically pressed to the leather seat by the centrifugal force.

"I like to drive fast . . . hey, you ok?" yelled Jeff over his shoulder. We arrived in a squeal of brakes and burning rubber, and everybody turned to see who was pulling up in the jet propelled Limo. Mouths fell open when they recognized Jeff Stryker. He opened the door and I fell out on to the pavement.

Lunch was a blast. Jeff was very self-deprecating and funny and I liked him immensely. He asked me if I would like to be in his next film *Underground,* which was being directed by Gino. The role was some guy wandering around a sex club having indiscriminate sex with everybody. I didn't care. It was a Jeff Stryker film, and I was very flattered as the film was packed full of stars. In addition to Jeff Stryker and myself there was Derek Cameron, a sexy blond bottom of the day, Logan Reed who would in later years get mixed up in drugs and do too much meth, Paul Morgan, a straight skater boy who was in every film made for a while, Drew Andrews, who

OUT OF THE BLUE

had starred with me in *Forgive Us Our Trespasses* (I thought his face was horsey), Brent Cross, who I would work with in *Men in Blue*, Edouardo, a sexy Brazillian and many more. It was a huge cast.

I was learning in the industry that unless you were very vocal about whom you wanted to be paired with; they would stick you with all kinds of unsuitable characters. Of course, I loved the men like Bo Garrret and Paul Carrigan and I would always ask to work with them. I didn't care if they had to use copies of *Hustler* to get hard. That turned me on even more. Sometimes they would be fucking me doggie style and I would have a straight porn magazine taped open on my back to keep them hard. Perverted, yet strangely stimulating.

We finished lunch, I gave Jeff my phone number and Gino drove me home.

"Ronnie Larsen wants to make a documentary about the gay porn industry called *Shooting Porn*," Gino turned to me and said, "And he wants to interview you and I for it. Follow us around from set to set . . . there's no money involved but it will be good exposure for you."

Well, I was all about the exposure. In the porn industry you do whatever it takes to keep your name front and center.

"Yeah . . . tell him I'll do it. It sounds like fun."

"He wants to film me directing you in a scene. I'm shooting *Perfect Ten* for Leisure Time . . . who would you like to work with?"

"How about Blade Thompson?" I grinned.

Blade was an extremely sexy straight German bodybuilder with a big dick. I had met him through Crystal,

CHAPTER TWELVE

who shared a place with him. Blade unfortunately went to prison years later for beating and stalking his girlfriend after she ran off with Ryan Idol. Blade served five years then was deported back to Germany. He had a fetish for wearing women's underwear, which came as a complete surprise to me . . . it was like finding out that Arnold Schwarzenegger liked lounging around in teddies from Victoria's Secret.

"Blade would be perfect . . . I'll call him."

When I got home there was a message from Rip Stone on my answering machine. I had met Rip on the set of *Night Walk*. He played a gargoyle that fucked Chad Conners.

"Hey Blue . . . wanna go drinking tonight and pick up chicks to bang? It's Rip . . . call me."

Hmmmm . . . well, I didn't know about banging any chicks but I wasn't averse to a drop of the devil's brew . . . tequila . . . so I called and left Rip a message to pick me up at eight o'clock. I definitely wanted to get my paws on Rip and I had to jerk off before I went out; otherwise I would be lusting after poor Rip all night.

I heard the squeal of brakes at eight o'clock sharp and through the window saw Rip jump out of his brand new Corvette. God knows what my neighbors thought because it was one porn star after another rocking up at my humble abode.

Rip looked spectacular, a tanned Adonis with a head full of curls. Years later he would hit rock bottom and star in bareback films . . . . those dubious, no-condom films where everybody looks hollow-eyed and drugged out. But back then he was still an immaculate god.

OUT OF THE BLUE

We went on a bar crawl, knocking back the "devil's brew." In every bar some chick would hit on Rip. He would spend a few minutes chatting to her before declaring:
"Too thin,"
"Too fat,"
"Too flat-chested,"
"Not busty enough."

I was aghast. Some of these girls were really hot, but Rip just couldn't seem to find the right one. As the end of the night drew near, Rip looked at me and said,

"Well man, no pussy tonight . . . guess I'm gonna be fucking you."

We raced back to the apartment and as Rip poured himself a drink, I zipped into the bathroom to "freshen up." When I returned Rip had left the living room and disappeared into the bedroom. Boy oh boy, was I going to get fucked tonight by that huge hunk of southern . . . BOTTOM!!! There was Rip on his hands and knees with his arse in the air.

"Be gentle with me, Blue . . . I've seen that big uncut dick of yours in action."

He wanted me to fuck HIM?! Oh well. Not wasting a second, I buried my face in his arse. I guessed there would be other times.

Gino approached me with yet another offer, "Would you be interested in appearing at the Second Gay Erotic Video Awards this year?"

"Am I nominated for anything?"

"No,"

"Then there's your answer!" I snapped, recalling the ghoulish memory of years before.

CHAPTER TWELVE

"This year is going to be completely different . . . very classy. A benefit for APLA . . . Aids Project Los Angeles and produced by Harold Huttas, who's on the board of APLA. He's supposed to be loaded, collects art . . . single."

All of a sudden I was feeling incredibly altruistic. I could show myself off on stage—always a very cheap thrill—it was for a good cause, and perhaps I might be interested in meeting Harold Huttas. I had just started dating a guy who owned a company that built department stores all over America but he lived in NYC, the other side of the country and I was hungry for love.

The next day in the gym I was working out next to Ted Matthews.

"Are you going to the porn awards?" Ted asked.

"I'm supposed to be performing at them," I said. "By the way, have you ever met a guy called Harold Huttas?"

"Met him? I used to date him," said Ted.

"Why did you break up?"

Ted shrugged. "Harold was hard to pin down. He's divorced with two kids and everybody's trying to date him. I just couldn't have him to myself."

Well, scratch Harold Huttas, I thought. The last thing I needed was some rich, middle-aged playboy shagging everything that moved behind my back. Behind my back??? I hadn't even met Harold and I was planning his serial cheating already!

When I got home from the gym there was a message from Gino.

"Guess where Jeff Stryker and I went last night? Out for dinner with that guy I was telling you about. Harold Huttas. We told him all about you, and he wants you to

OUT OF THE BLUE

call him, so you can talk about what he'd like you to do onstage at the awards." I knew there was no nudity allowed at the show, so basically I was up for doing anything. "Oh, and he wants you to present the award for Best Bisexual Video, you and Veronica Brazil."

I liked Veronica; I'd met her on the set of Gino Colbert's *Switch-hitters 6*. She had the biggest breasts I'd ever seen. Each one was as big as a bowling ball and she was always taking them out and showing off.

Gino gave me Harold's number but I debated whether to call him. I had no idea why, but for some reason I was completely intrigued by Harold. It was more than the money. I'd been told how philanthropic he was, but I basically knew nothing more about him. I looked down at his number in my hand, picked up the phone and made what turned out to be one of the most important calls of my life.

"Hello, can I speak to Harold Huttas please? This is Blue Blake calling."

"Please hold." A full minute passed.

"Hello . . . this is Harold."

"Harold, my name's Blue Blake. Gino Colbert told me you might have a part for me in your benefit."

"Yes. I had dinner with him last night. It seems he and Jeff Stryker are your biggest fans."

"Harold, you're going to make my head so enormous it won't fit onto your stage," I laughed.

He laughed too, a sexy baritone chuckle. It turned out Harold had one of the sexiest voices I'd ever heard; calm, almost soothing. We spoke for almost half an hour. He told me he had never seen any of my films or for that

CHAPTER TWELVE

matter even heard of me but that other friends of his had and that he hoped I would agree to be in the show. He told me that he had produced tributes honoring stars such as Elizabeth Taylor, Madonna, and Hilary Clinton, all for APLA. He assured me that this year's porn awards were going to be like nothing anybody had ever seen before. Well, that wouldn't be difficult because the awards were always appalling and held in some rat-infested venue.

The best thing about the awards would be running into everybody and laughing about the previous year's adventures in the skin trade. I sometimes got nominated over the years for my scenery-chewing interpretations of various characters, from the homicidal Marine Captain in Michael Zen's *Cockfight*, to the homicidal cop in *Men in Blue*. I never won but that particular year I wasn't even nominated.

Harold was shocked by how badly the awards were run and decided that if organized as an AIDS benefit, with glamour, the event could become a high profile fundraiser. Harold gathered around himself his astonishingly talented team, which included such entertainment luminaries as Bruce Vilanch, who would emcee the event. Bruce was probably one of the most prolific writers of biting humor in the stand-up comedy industry. He wrote constantly for stars such as Whoopi Goldberg, Billy Crystal, and Robin Williams and practically every year wrote the gags for the *Oscars*. Bruce went on to become a star in his own right as a lead in a highly successful Broadway run of the musical *Hairspray*. I was at a benefit a few years later honoring Sidney Poitier where Bruce, who was hosting, announced:

"Both Sidney Poitier and Blue Blake have more in common than they think . . . they both starred in films called *To Sir With Love* . . . ." The mostly gay crowd loved it, but Sidney didn't get the joke.

Hairspray composer Marc Shaiman and lyricist/director Scott Wittman agreed to direct Harold's event. Adam Shankman would do the choreography. Adam later became a director in his own right, directing such campy classics as *Maid in Manhattan*, *The Wedding Planner* and the movie version of *Hairspray*. Incidentally, *Hairspray* the movie starred John Travolta as Edna Turnblad (a role originally played by Divine, my escort client from years before). It amazes me how small the wonderful world of entertainment truly is.

Harold told me he was flying in drag queens Raven O and Joey Arias from NYC to perform. They both went on to star in a Cirque de Soleil show in Vegas.

The awards would take place at the Palladium on Sunset Boulevard and tables were selling for up to $3,500 each. The event was going to be maddeningly glamorous with people like Thierry Mugler, Calvin Klein and Steve Tisch buying tables. Ken Ryker, the biggest porn star in the world at that time was going to be on the poster and a good time was going to be had by all.

Harold told me all this during our phone conversation and I just listened and soaked up the timbre of his voice.

"Can I call you tomorrow and tell you what time rehearsal will be on Sunday?" Harold asked.

"Sure."

The next day the phone rang and it was Harold ask-

CHAPTER TWELVE

ing me if I could come after lunch on Sunday for a rehearsal at the Palladium. We somehow managed to spend an hour talking together on the phone. He told me he was divorced with two children, girls in their twenties. He told me he had just turned fifty and that by trade he was a printer who had gotten his big break printing the posters for smash hits like *Saturday Night Fever*, *Grease* and *Star Wars*. He lived in an area of L.A. called Los Feliz in a house that was built by Cecil B. DeMille for his daughter Catherine when she married Anthony Quinn. Two doors away lived Lily Tomlin in the old W.C. Fields house and opposite was Charlie Chaplin's old residence. Harold lived alone apart from a hyperactive German shepherd named Lizzie whom he had named after one of his best friends, Elizabeth Montgomery. We'd still not met, but I was incredibly attracted to this voice on the phone. I said I would be at rehearsal at one o'clock sharp on Sunday.

The next day over brunch in Santa Monica, my beeper went off. It was a message from the stage manager of the show asking if I could come to rehearsal an hour earlier than planned. I jumped into a cab, my heart beating fast at the anticipation of finally meeting Harold.

I entered the theatre from the back and directly onto the stage, which was fully lit.

"Are you Blue Blake?" called out a guy with a clipboard.

"Yes . . . can you tell me where Harold Huttas is? I just received a message to come in early and rehearse."

"That's him over there in the grey suit," said Clipboard, pointing at a guy with his back to me.

"Harold?" I asked loudly. He turned around, and I fell

instantly, madly, crazily in love. He was GORGEOUS. Short gray hair and a beard with the most beautiful eyes I had ever seen. Very dark brown with eyelashes so long they curled up at the corners. He looked super straight, which was a major plus.

"So this is who I've been hearing so much about," he said, smiling as he walked towards me. I felt like laughing hysterically. I was incredibly attracted to him. He had a great air of command and control about the way he carried himself—not in a leather daddy kind of way but in the way of a man who is self-made and incredibly successful. I introduced myself, but honestly I don't remember what we talked about in those few moments because I was too busy imagining myself in bed with him.

We had only that day to rehearse because the show was the following night.

My segment consisted of a guy lying in his underwear on a huge four-poster bed on the stage, dreaming . . . of me!!! As the music got wilder, the back curtains pulled back and there I stood under a spotlight. I then was to climb on the bed and simulate fucking with a dozen male dancers in their underwear slithering out from under the bed and cavorting around the stage. God knows how they packed a dozen dancers under that damn bed. It was a true spectacle, though. There were to be more porn stars in the show than had ever been on a stage together at one time. Stars were presenting awards, receiving awards, or performing all night. Some of the judges that year included Clive Barker, Greg Gorman, RuPaul and John Waters. So everyone anticipated a classy show.

Harold asked if I would like to sit at one of his tables

CHAPTER TWELVE

with two of his best friends Tim Palen and Abel Villarreal. Tim Palen is a genius who went on to become co-president of marketing worldwide for Lionsgate Films. He created the campaigns for the *Saw* and *Hostel* series and bought about the terminology "gorno" which categorizes the horror genre that permeates our society. He is probably now one of the most sought after people in the entertainment industry.

There was to be a massive party thrown by David Forest after the awards. David was *the* porn agent and had been for many years. He was throwing a party at the famous revolving restaurant in the Hollywood Inn.

Harold's table was at the foot of the stage so I had a good view of the show before I had to perform. That night the Hollywood sky was lit up by klieg lights and limousines were snaking their way past the Palladium and spilling their scantily clad passengers onto the red carpet. Some had opted to dress in tuxedos; others in much more revealing outfits. I was all skintight mesh and leather, and as I climbed out of my limo, the flashbulbs were blinding as they burnt with an intense ferocity.

"Blue . . . I loved you in *My Bitch*."

"You should have won best actor for *Ramjet*."

"You need teeth bleaching . . . " charming!!!

I made my way down the red carpet talking to the porno press.

"Are you still dating Bull Stanton?"

"Is it true you've been seeing Patrick Swayze?" Where did people hear this stuff??

"Did you star in one of the most expensive porn filmsever made?"

OUT OF THE BLUE

"*Night Walk* . . . yes . . . well, I'm one of the stars."

"Didn't Gino Colbert pick you out of a list of 3,000 bodybuilders to play the role of the Devil's minion?"

"Typecasting . . . " I heard someone in the crowd murmur.

"Is it true that Gage Blake isn't really your brother but secretly that you were both brought up in an orphanage together in Liverpool, England?"

Well, they got half of it right, but Orphanage? Liverpool?

I posed for some pictures then beat a hasty retreat inside the Palladium. There was a silent auction of porn memorabilia and I noticed with satisfaction they were auctioning off my outfit from *The Wild Ones*. They even had it on a mannequin. Denim shorts covered in garage oil and matching denim shirt. It looked better on the mannequin than it had on me!

The night was an enormous success and $100,000 was raised for APLA. Considering that only $5,000 was raised the previous year, everybody was ecstatic.

Harold and his team had done an amazing job, and I have to admit my love of his power was a great aphrodisiac. The whole place bowed and scraped to him and for the first time in a long time I thought "hmmm . . . finally, perhaps a worthy partner." Harold was powerful, handsome, rich and very sexy. What wasn't there to be attracted to?

On my way out of the Palladium I bumped into David Forest with his usual porn coterie. That reminded me about David's after party. He had asked me to join his stable of stars, but I felt I didn't need anybody's advice on my career. I knew where I was going, and that was to

CHAPTER TWELVE

the top, baby!! David did represent huge stars though: Ryan Idol, Ken Ryker, Joey Stefano, Jon Vincent . . . . Some of these stars have now unfortunately passed away. Joey died of a Ketamine overdose, while Jon OD'd on heroin. But this was hardly out of the ordinary. Porn stars are always committing suicide, hanging themselves, and throwing themselves off tall buildings. They say that dentists have a high suicide rate but they aren't even in the running when it comes to porn stars. And when they go, boy, they go big time . . . suffocating themselves with plastic bags, drinking rat poison, its almost as though they want to be in the headlines just that one last time as they go out with a bang. Now me, if I were to kill myself, I'm thinking a hundred Ambien and a bottle of Tequila whilst surrounded by my best looking friends who are telling me I'm still gorgeous after all these years. Oh yeah, and I'm ninety-two years old and I'm watching my favorite episode of *Buffy the Vampire Slayer*. Perhaps everybody thinks once of committing suicide, but ultimately life is way too short as it is.

Rip Stone and I arrived at the after party. I was still encased in leather and mesh and immediately circled the revolving restaurant searching for Harold. I couldn't find him so I sent Rip off to get me a tahitian punch. David Forest was wearing a Hawaiian shirt so I guessed the party was tropically themed. Years later, having met David millions of times I realize he ALWAYS wears a Hawaiian shirt. No wonder Rip came back clutching two beers. Damn, and there is nothing I like better than something fruity and exotic with an umbrella mixed in a pineapple husk. I grabbed a seat next to two good-looking guys, Barry Krost, and his lover John DeShane. I didn't know them personally, but was aware Barry was a big time manager to stars like Liza Minnelli and Angela Bassett. I struck up a conversation and they told me how much they had enjoyed my stage performance.

I asked Barry "I don't suppose you know where Harold Huttas is, do you? I saw you onstage with him tonight presenting an award to Ken Ryker."

"Yes, he's right behind you," I turned around and sure enough, there he was dressed in a black leather suit and looking as handsome as ever.

"Does he have a boyfriend?" I whispered.

I didn't stay to hear Barry answer. I zipped myself over to Harold's side like a shark heading for chub before some other porn trollop moved in. From the corner of my eye I noticed Ted Matthews gnashing his teeth.

"You did a great job," Harold said.

"Thanks," I laughed.

We both stared at each other.

"So I was wondering if you would like to give me a ride home," I asked. Harold looked uncomfortable.

"Well, I'm not here alone."

I had heard that Harold fancied the Falcon porn star Kevin Williams and, in fact, had invited him to sit at his table that night for the award ceremony. I looked around but Kevin was nowhere in sight. Good job, I would have wrestled him to the ground and yanked every bleached hair out of his all-American head . . . why was Harold having this strange effect on me?

"Are you with Kevin Williams?" I asked nonchalantly.

"No," laughed Harold, "Although I wouldn't mind

CHAPTER TWELVE

being with him. I'm here with my boyfriend."

"Boyfriend," I said through gritted teeth.

"Well, kind of ex-boyfriend really,"

This was all too much for me.

"Well I better go," I said. "Rex Chandler offered to give me a ride home in his limo, so I better split before he leaves."

This was true; Rex had offered to give me a ride home. Perhaps I might get the chance to gnaw on his huge cock in the backseat. I turned and left Harold behind, already pushing him out of my mind, and went to find Rex's limo. I found it all right—with him inside, doing coke with his girlfriend!!! I was having no luck. Rex drove me home and I fell into bed alone. How the hell did I manage to go to the porn awards and end up in bed alone? As I pondered that sad mystery I fell asleep.

I awoke at 7:30 a.m. to the sound of my phone ringing. I picked it up.

"Hello . . . can I speak to Blue please?"

I recognized the voice immediately.

"Hey, Harold," I said sleepily.

"Listen . . . I was wondering if I could buy you dinner tonight?"

"Sorry, I don't go for dinner with guys who are in relationships," I replied coolly.

"I'm not in a relationship . . . I mean . . . well, we broke up last night."

I sat up quickly. He could be a lying bastard but perhaps it was true.

"OK, dinner," I acquiesced.

"Excellent, I'll pick you up at 7 p.m. sharp. We'll go

OUT OF THE BLUE

to Cicada on Melrose. Its owned by a friend of mine, Stephanie Taupin."

Stephanie was married to Bernie Taupin who was Elton John's writing partner. He wrote all the lyrics for Elton's music. Cicada was the place to see and be seen. Years later when Stephanie divorced Bernie the place was bought by Robert De Niro, who renamed it Ago.

Harold arrived outside my apartment at 7 p.m. sharp just as he'd said. I loved people who were punctual. He sat outside patiently in a black Range Rover. Greg spied Harold through the window.

"I don't know Blue, he seems kind of old."

"Greg, I'm sick of dating porn stars and straight bodybuilders, and I really fancy him."

"Please yourself," sulked Greg.

I had a great night with Harold. We got the best table in the house and made out for two hours. We sucked face like teenagers much to the dismay of the straight crowd. After a fabulous night Harold drove me home.

"Can I come in?" Harold asked.

"Not tonight." I'd decided to proceed with caution.

"Can I see you tomorrow night?"

"I have a shoot all day for my new movie. It's being directed by a really famous director, Michael Zen."

"Well, I've just opened a new restaurant on Melrose called The Shed. Will you come and celebrate with me there?"

"Sure," I smiled.

"Then let's say tomorrow at seven again."

We kissed and I floated off to bed on a cloud of Harold lust.

CHAPTER TWELVE

As mentioned, Michael Zen is one of the most amazingly talented directors in porn. He is a true genius. Probably in his late fifties, he has a stunningly attractive young wife. I had first met Michael weeks before when he had come to audition me at my apartment for *Cockfight* for the role of the crazed, sadistic drill sergeant who is driven slowly insane by the denial of his own homosexuality and his lust for a young nubile recruit. Michael was very serious about his auditions and he wanted porn stars who could actually act. The scripts he directed were very intricate and precise and had pages of dialogue.

The script was perfect for me. I got to chew not just the scenery but the carpet and curtains too. I stomped around my apartment and ranted and raved and Michael sat there with his mouth hanging open. When I had finished auditioning, he clapped his hands and shouted, "Bravo . . . you are perfect, you have the role!"

All Worlds paid me five thousand dollars for the film. FIVE THOUSAND DOLLARS!!! It felt like a fortune and probably was in those days. I was also delighted to find out that Rip Stone had been cast in the film and I would be doing a scene with him. Rip Stone, Max Grand, Paul Carrigan, Logan Reed, it was a veritable smorgasbord of macho delight . . . a cornucopia of testosterone.

Set on an army base my character causes the death of one of his recruits because of his unrequited love for him. Bryan Kidd would play the recruit. This was the second time I had worked with Bryan, he had also played the young goat boy in *Ramjet*. He was short, blond and looked fourteen years old. He must have been a pedophile's dream. He should have been starring in a film entitled *Tasty Tots* or *Get There Before the Hair*, not *Cockfight*. Bryan's character died at the end of the movie then comes back as a ghost to drive my character to the brink of insanity. At the end of the movie I howl at the moon completely naked. It was midnight and I was freezing my bollocks off. In a review months later *Manshots Magazine* compared my performance to Jack Nicholson's in *The Shining*. All Worlds definitely got their five grand's worth. I was rewarded that year with a Best Actor nomination for the role.

After shooting the first scene the next day, I joined Harold and two of his friends at The Shed. The restaurant was already becoming incredibly popular. It was situated on Melrose next door to Cicada and had leather banquettes, handsome brickwork and a roaring fireplace.

I hadn't had time to change as I was already late, so I strolled in wearing my army fatigue costume.

"Sorry about the outfit," I apologized, "I'm shooting a movie."

"Oooh . . . Who is the director?" asked Hugh, one of the guests.

"Michael Zen."

"Is he similar to Spielberg?"

"Only if Spielberg has you whip your cock out at the drop of a hat," I joked. I looked over to Harold to make sure I hadn't overstepped my boundaries, but he just smiled. Hugh's boyfriend Michael jumped in: "Hugh, Blue is a huge porn star."

Hugh blushed very sweetly. "I'm sorry, I had no idea."

"No big," I laughed. "Shall we have the potato tacos

CHAPTER TWELVE

to start, somebody told me they really are quite delicious and the only thing I've had in my mouth all day is Bryan Kidd's arsehole." Hugh choked on his Campari and soda. I looked at Harold, who rolled his eyes. I was in love.

After two weeks I still hadn't slept with Harold. I was in no hurry but Harold was. One evening he came by as if he'd had enough.

"You're just a prick tease," he accused.

Well, that was certainly a first.

"Harold, are you drunk?"

"No," he slurred belligerently as he stepped into the room and almost tripped over the cat.

"Listen, go home and call me in the morning when you're sober. I'll get you a cab."

"I'm not drunk and I'm never calling you again!" Harold shouted, searching the wall for the door. He sailed out the door in a cloud of scotch.

The next morning the phone rang. It was Harold.

"Blue, I'm so ashamed. I . . . ."

"Harold, you don't need to apologize."

That night for the first time we made wonderful sweet love and thirteen years later we still are making the same sweet love. Harold is my inspiration, a rare man of wonderful compassion and caring who I would trust with my life. In thirteen years we have argued only a handful of times and I am still astounded by his levels of deep empathy. He is my reward in life.

After two weeks together, Harold wanted me to give up porn. He was traveling to Paris for a month over Christmas and had rented an apartment overlooking the Arc de Triomphe. He asked me to go with him but I was

OUT OF THE BLUE

finally about to open in the play *Making Porn* as Ronnie Larson had promised. I couldn't let them down.

We had been rehearsing the play in Ronnie's horrible living room amongst the dog bones and sugary treats that were scattered on the carpets. Gino had persuaded Ronnie and Caryn to put real porn stars in the lead roles and so they had cast a young blond Canadian called J.T. Sloan and myself. I really liked J.T. but he was renowned for not being able to open his mouth without a big old lie dropping out.

"Oh, I make three thousand dollars a scene." Lie.

"I was just flown on a private jet to Dubai." Lie.

"I love huge cock." True.

As Caryn was only paying the rest of the cast five dollars a show they refused to rehearse with me in their spare time, so as the first evening of my performance in the show rolled around, I had never rehearsed my role with any of them. Plus I had never even set foot on the stage. Caryn made me sit in the audience and watch the show every night, but that's not the same as actually rehearsing onstage with a cast. For the first time in my life I was an absolute nervous wreck. I was as nervous as I was on the set of my first porn film *Seeds of Love*. I mean I was a Valium popping wreck. Ronnie and Caryn kept telling me my performance was amazing but what the hell did they know. They were hardly my barometer for success.

Harold left for Paris and the next thing I knew it was opening night. As I packed my costumes to leave for the theatre I was overcome by a wave of nausea. There was no way in hell I would be able to set foot on that stage. Was I crazy? What was I thinking? I hadn't had any

CHAPTER TWELVE

proper rehearsal and I would become a joke around Los Angeles. I decided I just wouldn't do the show. I would lock myself in my apartment and refuse to come out. I picked up the phone.

"Caryn," I said affecting a weak croak, "You won't believe this, I've just come back from the doctor's and he says I have food poisoning, and it would be absolutely impossible for me to appear onstage tonight, in fact, not just tonight but for the entire run."

Caryn wailed like a wounded animal. I was scared.

"In fact, he said I might even have rubella and would have to be quarantined!"

"Blue Blake," she always called me Blue Blake, "Listen to me, you just have stage fright."

Too bloody right I did. I was petrified. I was going to be onstage in a show I thought I didn't even know the lines to . . . NAKED!!!

"No, Caryn, I'm incredibly sick . . . I'm convinced I might even have cholera!"

"I'm coming over to get you!" yelled Caryn, slamming the phone down.

I looked around for somewhere to hide before I remembered she couldn't get into the apartment complex as it was locked up tighter than a nun's asshole, and the only way she could get in would be for me to buzz her through the security door . . . or if somebody else opened the door for her. Within minutes I turned to see Caryn hammering on my living room window. Some traitor to my cause had given her access.

"BLUE, OPEN THE DOOR! YOU'RE NOT SICK, I JUST SAW YOU MIXING A MARTINI!" she screamed.

OUT OF THE BLUE

I flung the door open.

"I'm not going on that stage, I've had no rehearsal!" Doors opened all over the complex, and people stepped out to listen, which for some bizarre reason encouraged me to be horribly dramatic. I fell to my knees.

"Please, please, I'm terrified!" I cried, wrapping my arms around Caryn's trotters.

"Blue," Caryn said in a coaxing, soothing voice. "You're brilliant in the play, you're one of the best actors I've ever seen!"

She was really going overboard on the compliments, and like a fool I sucked it in; her words were syrup poured on the French toast of my ego.

"I'll stand in the wings, and if there is a moment when you feel you can't continue we'll send on your understudy."

"Do you promise?" I wept.

"Would I lie to the most brilliant actor that has ever appeared in *Making Porn*?"

Caryn crammed me into her car that was full of dog hair and cigarette butts and whisked me off to the theatre. As soon as I got onstage and the lights went up; my fright dissipated. Just like that, I was off and running. I loved every moment of being back on stage in a play. I remembered all my lines and when the curtain came down to hoots and hollers and wild applause I was elated.

Harold called from Paris and I babbled excitedly about how I had once again been bitten by the theatre bug. I could feel him smiling at the other end of the phone.

Caryn and Ronnie were taking *Making Porn* to Off Broadway starring Rex Chandler. They didn't offer me a

CHAPTER TWELVE

part in the show as they told me it wasn't in their budget but even so I was happy for them. I knew the lightweight, campy comedy would be a huge hit in NYC.

Harold returned home and we began seriously dating: dinners every night and lost weekends spent in bed with each other. Months passed when one night I received a call from Caryn.

"Blue, it's Caryn . . . we need you in the show, can you catch the next flight to New York?"

CHAPTER THIRTEEN

UPON MY ARRIVAL IN NYC, I learned that Rex Chandler had been a disaster in the show. He fought constantly and bitterly with his fellow actors, particularly the actress Joanna Keylock who was playing his wife. Rex wasn't a trained actor, and the stress of performing eight shows a week Off Broadway had been more than he could bear. There had been a huge fight amongst everybody, and Rex stormed off. That left Ronnie and Caryn without a porn star in the play and that was their main "hook."

Of course I jumped at the opportunity . . . OFF BROADWAY . . . was she kidding? I would do it in a heartbeat! I called Gino who told me I could stay in his NYC apartment just off Central Park. I packed a suitcase and bid a tearful farewell to Harold. The play had had a long run in L.A., so who knew how long I'd be in New York? He promised to fly in every other weekend and said he would send me care packages to get me through the NYC winter. It was October and had just starting to get cold on the East Coast.

I arrived in Manhattan feeling like anything was possible. No longer Glenn Marsh from Nottingham selling my blood to pay the bills, now I was Blue Blake from London starring in an Off Broadway show. I pinched myself because none of it seemed real.

OUT OF THE BLUE

Gino's apartment was a cozy one-bedroom. I settled right in and was met the first night by Vince Lambert, a journalist from the gay magazine *Next*. He was friends with Ronnie and Caryn and filled me in on all the drama that had occurred with Rex. I listened spellbound as I ate raspberry sorbet. All that eating out with Harold had made me plump and if I was going to be on stage naked I had better be looking sharp. Vince told me that there were rumors that Ryan Idol was also going to join the cast, replacing Rex, so there would be two porn stars in the show, me and Ryan. At the moment there was another actor playing the role but he wasn't as big a draw as Ryan would be. I had never met Ryan Idol properly but he was a serious superstar. We would sell a ton of seats with his star wattage.

Once again I was afflicted with terrible stage fright due to lack of rehearsal time. I realized this was Ronnie and Caryn's modus oporandi. They expected you to just climb off the plane and onto the stage and give a brilliant performance. Luckily I had been prepared for this and had been sleeping with my script to remind me of my part.

Even so, I had opening night jitters. We were performing in the West Village at the Actors' Playhouse. Ronnie was again playing the role of the evil porn director and the show, under his eagle eye, went zipping along full of peppy one-liners and brief nudity. The audience ate it up. We were sold out every performance and the cash came rolling in.

Caryn placed an ad in the *New York Times* theatre page and they shot me for the poster and for the playbill. I walked home every night after the show to Fifty-sev-

CHAPTER THIRTEEN

enth Street because it would take me the fifty blocks to decompress, heady from the audience applause. I became enormously close with Joanna, the one girl in the show. I had a total gay boy crush on her. She had blonde hair down to her waist and porcelain skin and reminded me of a mermaid. She was obscenely talented and I worshipped her. Years later she named one of her sons Liam Blue to my absolute delight. After each performance Joanna and I would run out of the stage door and walk arm in arm through the crowd outside the theatre. People would stop us to sign their playbills and tell us how hysterical we had been in the show. We were shallow but loving it. Life was immaculate it seemed.

Then Ryan joined the cast.

Ryan Idol is one of the most spectacular looking people to ever work in the adult industry. He really should have been playing a dashing doctor in *General Hospital* but he missed his calling and ended up in porn. Ryan had originally been a marine stationed in Hawaii but after a big fight with one of his commanding officers he was thrown out of the service with no way to return to his hometown on the Mainland. Of course that wasn't going to stop a resourceful guy like him, so before he knew it he was turning tricks and coining it in. This of course led to porn films and in no time he was a mega star.

Thick brown hair, amazing body, great teeth but as mad as a box of frogs, Ryan arrived in NYC looking a little the worse for wear. Since he had partially retired from starring in porn he had hit the bottle hard but he was still a handsome bastard. So despite the fact that he liked his liquor, he still had a great face and girls (and boys) would always swoon around him. My relationship with Ryan was always unusual; we were incredibly ambivalent about each other. He could be as sweet as pie or, if he was drunk, a raging lunatic. What kept his ego in check when he first arrived Off Broadway was that the cast was all trained actors who had been doing the show for a while so he was constantly playing catch up.

My name and image were removed off the playbills and poster and replaced by Ryan's. I didn't mind, since he was a much bigger star, and I liked the fact that his name guaranteed we played to sold-out audiences.

Ryan and Caryn became very friendly . . . a match made in hell, if ever there was one. They bonded over their love of cash and, boy was Ryan a cash cow waiting to be milked. He got a percentage of the box office. I was being paid a thousand dollars a week to flaunt my bits on stage nightly, so I was happy with that, and the situation was rosy. Until the night of the big fight.

A few days previously the Gay Erotic Video Award Nominations had been announced. I was nominated as Best Actor for my role in *Cockfight* and Ryan was nominated for Best Actor for his role in *Idol in the Sky*. So there we were, doing eight shows a week together and competing for the most prestigious porn award in the world. Something had to give. Starring in a successful Off Broadway show became a disaster waiting to happen when mixed with Ryan's love of booze.

One night he arrived drunk half an hour before curtain. Ronnie told him he couldn't perform that night and Ryan grew belligerent and refused to leave the theatre. Knowing that Ryan didn't have an understudy and he

CHAPTER THIRTEEN

couldn't perform sloshed; I collected my belongings and began to leave the theatre.

"Look," said Ronnie, "Blue is leaving, so there definitely will be no shows."

"Get back on this stage!" Ryan screamed at me, "I'm the fucking star, and what I say goes!"

Man . . . I flew onto the stage like I had a Pershing missile up my arse. Ryan took a swing at me, but I deftly dodged it. I grabbed him and began beating his head against the stage.

"You're killing each other," Ronnie shrieked. Meanwhile, the other cast members fled to lock themselves in the dressing rooms. As I shook Ryan by the neck, I suddenly came to my senses, dropped him and rose to my feet. I left the theatre fuming. That night's two shows were cancelled.

The next night, before the show, Ryan apologized to me. I forgave him for two reasons: [1] I had to do eight shows a week with him and [2] it was Christmas and on New Year's Eve Ryan and I were booked to make a personal appearance at the Palladium in front of three thousand gay men and their girlfriends to promote the show.

Two days before Christmas Harold flew in. I had been feeling lousy. Being naked eight shows a week in a freezing cold theatre was taking its toll on me. I caught double pneumonia. My doctor ordered me to stay in bed for a week. Caryn went crazy. The show was completely sold out. There was no understudy for me and she insisted I do the show. She told me I could lie down on the filthy backstage couch to rest between scenes. I refused; telling her the only place I was going to lie down was in my own bed. At her wit's end, Caryn summoned another actor, David Thompson, and begged him to perform my role. David had been learning the lines anyway because he was heading to D.C. to play my part in the touring company Ronnie and Caryn were forming. Even so, David was weeks away from being ready to play the role. But that didn't stop Caryn. She had once had the stage manager play Ryan's role, script in hand throughout the night, when Ryan was sick. Anything rather than cancel a performance. The poor guy had walked through the curtains at the beginning of the show and begged the audience to suspend all disbelief as he was a positive TWIG and he had to strut around naked. It was all about the cash for Ronnie and Caryn. It was total lunacy.

David faired as well as could be expected under these circumstances and then fled back to Los Angeles a week later when I was ready to resume my role of Ray Tanner.

On New Year's Eve, Harold and I, along with Ryan and his beautiful Persian girlfriend Ellie gathered in my apartment. Ryan always had stunning girlfriends. I liked Ellie a lot, as did the entire cast. We did a couple of lines of coke; more to keep us awake than anything, and set off to the club. It was freezing but the glow of fame was keeping me warm. The club was packed with New Year's Eve revelers who were more than a little "partied up." The ecstasy was flying and the general atmosphere was one of unrestrained euphoria.

Ryan and I didn't take the stage until 3 a.m., but when we did, the crowd screamed so loudly our hair was blown back as if in a wind tunnel. We introduced ourselves, invited everybody to see the play and then we told

CHAPTER THIRTEEN

the audience we had a surprise for them. We introduced . . . Madonna!!!

Actually it was a skinny drag queen in a bleached wig and coned bra corset, more like McDonna really. But the blissed-out crowd of partiers was oblivious to the fake-out. Some started crying as if having an epiphany. We fled the stage and wended our weary way home. Life was good; life was great in fact. Years later I came to realize why there was always such madness around Ryan. He was gorgeous, and great beauty attracts great chaos. Having worked with some of the most spectacular looking men in the world, sadly very few have had spectacular lives to match. But Ryan hung in there and was cast in a Broadway revival of the hilarious sex romp *The Ritz* starring Rosie Perez. I was delighted. Ryan had beaten me to Broadway by a mile and I was actually elated for him. For some reason I felt like a proud father . . . now there's madness for you.

The documentary Ronnie and Cary produced, *Shooting Porn*, was finally released and was an enormous hit. It overflowed with colorful characters from the industry but the three personalities around which the documentary was structured were Chi Chi LaRue, Gino Colbert and myself. Even better, the poster for *Shooting Porn* pictured me sitting naked in a director's chair holding a megaphone to my mouth!

Shooting Porn was incredibly explicit. There is a scene where Blade Thompson is fucking me on a bed and the shooting had to stop because his dick was so big it made my stomach ache. You see me crawling off the bed rubbing my stomach while Gino begs for just a few more strokes of insertion. Ronnie and Caryn had spent months trailing around porn sets and had created a superb expose of the industry. There were models holding pet lizards, chatting about dildo scenes and douching, confessing they'd be selling shoes if it weren't for porn. All in all it was an extremely entertaining piece of porn pop culture.

Shooting Porn was screened at gay film festivals all over the world, so when Caryn asked me if I would like to travel to The London Gay Film Festival and discuss the film in front of a live audience I said yes in a second. The film was showing on the South Bank, a very chic art district. When we arrived at the theatre, we were told that the film was sold out. In fact, it had been the quickest selling ticket ever in the history of the festival. We were incredibly flattered. After the screening we fielded answers from the audience. Caryn was actually very good on the stage. She was incredibly insightful regarding the industry, which was strange as she wasn't actually involved in the porn industry, but she had been so deeply immersed in the lives of porn stars for the past couple of years that she obviously had a good sense of the business. All the London muscle boys were out in force, and they asked me questions regarding their favorite porn stars. It was truly an exhilarating experience and it made me so pleased that I had agreed to appear in the documentary.

The movie opened in limited release around NYC and soon I was being approached on the street regularly to be complimented on the film. Everywhere I went, people had either seen the documentary or the play or both. I was finally feeling fulfilled as a performer. I was starring in a hit play and had a film in movie theatres. I was lit-

CHAPTER THIRTEEN

erally giddy . . . all of a sudden I had a greater appreciation for Ronnie and Caryn. In hindsight I don't think I would have become as well known without them.

Around this time I had begun work on the final film of Gino's trilogy *Men in Blue*. I flew back to Los Angeles to shoot the final two scenes to complete the film. The plot I had written ran like this: I played a rogue homophobic cop being investigated by Internal Affairs after my new partner commits suicide on the first day of the job. Also my character had shot and killed five Latino crack dealers in suspicious circumstances after having been sodomized by them in a crack den. Internal Affairs was out to prove I was a bad cop and the film took place in a police station over a series of flashbacks. The guy playing my police partner who commits suicide was Brent Cross.

Brent was a straight jock with thick dark hair and a bubble butt. In the film he comes round to my apartment on his first day of work and I answer the door in my underwear. I tell him I'm running late and make him a cup of coffee, which I then fill up with some unnamed substance that renders him semi-conscious. Then I put him in girls' panties and rape him. After the rape, my character takes Polaroids of him and says if he breathes a word of what has happened, I would show his young wife the pictures. This leads to him killing himself and my character being investigated by Internal Affairs. What a potboiler.

Ron Jeremy, who is probably the most recognized male face in the entire adult industry, played the Internal Affairs investigating officer. He has parlayed his

OUT OF THE BLUE

fame into several reality shows and is a genuine superstar in porn. Years later I was at a *Playboy* party with Ron and guys would literally freak out around him:

"HEY RON . . . YOU'RE THE MAN!"

"FUCK, RON . . . I WANNA BE YOU WHEN I GROW UP!"

It was insane. I knew exactly what this reaction to Ron was all about. He represented Joe Schmo . . . an everyman who got to spend his days fucking nubile chicks for cash. As the adult industry grew exponentially, so did Ron's fame and belly. He was recognized everywhere. At the time he did *Men in Blue*, however, his star hadn't yet risen, so appearing in a gay porn film was just a job to him.

Men in Blue opens with my character in uniform getting drunk on raw bourbon in a squad car. I pull over two cousins, played by Gino and Paul and force them to suck each other off. Then Paul comes in Gino's mouth. The scene mixed abuse of liquor and authority with just a smatter of incest thrown in for good measure. Gino had rented an authentic squad car, and clad in my police uniform, I threw myself into the role with all the realism I could muster.

In another scene I break down the door of a crack den to find four Latinos smoking crack. Ryan Block, Andreas Bergane, Rod Garetto and Juan Antonio played the Latinos. Juan didn't speak English and mistook all the fake drugs on the set for real crack. He told his agent he would never make another porn film again. After my character is raped by the Latinos, he pulls out his gun and shoots them all to death. In the final scene when Ron Jeremy is

CHAPTER THIRTEEN

exhausted from trying to force a confession from me, he leaves the room and eats the pussy of policewoman Sharon Kane. As he's doing this, Sharon watches me get fucked by Cutter West on a table through a two-way mirror in the police interrogation room.

The film caused an uproar. Some magazines refused to review it, saying it promoted homophobia and illicit drug use; that it glorified rape and was just generally completely amoral. And some magazines loved it, calling the movie the best piece of erotic film making in years. *Men in Blue* earned a four and a half star rating out of five from *Gayvn Magazine*. I was extremely proud.

Every year in Chicago during the International Mr. Leather Contest there is an award show called the Grabby Awards. The show is presented by *Gay Chicago Magazine* and honors the best in porn. Over the years it has grown immensely and is now one of the major events on the porn calendar. Ten years ago the show wasn't as enormous as it has since become. Back then, it was held in a bathhouse. I was nominated for Best Dramatic Actor for my role in *Men in Blue*. By this time I was so used to being nominated for awards and not winning, that I had lost all sense of anticipation. I flew to Chicago because I was curious to attend the International Mr. Leather event, having once been a leather title-holder myself. Also I wanted to see Chicago, which I had never visited. The city was packed with leather guys. At the host hotel there was a huge leather fair where people sold everything from inflatable butt plugs to pissing videos.

The night of the Grabby Awards rolled around and I trotted off to the bathhouse to attend. I had also been

OUT OF THE BLUE

asked to present an award so I was done up in tight leather pants and jacket. Chi Chi LaRue was hosting the event. As I listened to the nominees for Best Dramatic Actor being read I noticed a stunning bodybuilder at the back of the room. He was a knockout. I wandered over to him and introduced myself.

"I'm Blue Blake."

"I know," he grinned. "They call me Caesar . . . and they've just announced your name on stage . . . you've won Best Actor, congratulations."

I couldn't fucking believe it. I spun around and ran to the stage. I was handed a perspex statuette with somebody's arse engraved on it along with the words:

GAY CHICAGO MAGAZINE
"BEHIND CLOSED DOORS"
1998
GRABBY AWARDS
BEST ACTOR
DRAMATIC
BLUE BLAKE
MEN IN BLUE—NEW AGE PICTURES.

I'd finally won! I went on to win many more awards but this was my first. Although it's a Perspex plaque with somebody's arse on it, I still treasure it. The most tasteless looking award of all time was a Probie Award, which was a giant gold paper mache cock. I never won one of those.

CHAPTER FOURTEEN

LAST YEAR I WAS IN SAN FRANCISCO to receive an award for a film I had produced and directed called *Musclemen Moving Company, Inc.* It was named one of the top ten best selling on-demand films of the year on the Internet. The award was presented to me by the video on demand site Maleflixxx. These days porn has moved from VHS to DVD to, finally, video on demand. We are living in the technological future and, as in years before, pornography is once again spearheading the technological advances.

Chicago Gay Magazine asked if I would attend their upcoming Grabby ceremony in Chicago. The ceremony coincided with the International Mr. Leather event so Chicago would be full of fags, and I thought to myself, why not? I decided I could go and slake up some worship at the very least. I told them I definitely would be there. By this time I was enjoying my film infamy and there were a lot of the people in the industry that I genuinely liked and hoped to run into. It was always interesting meeting the latest models who worked for the other studios and I figured at the very least it would be fun to see how big the Grabby's had become.

I hopped a flight to Chicago and the night I landed went straight to the International Mister Leather opening night party. It was just like being back at the Mr. Drummer contest, albeit seventeen years had passed, and I was a little more jaded. Make that a lot more jaded. Nothing could shock me now.

"You're Blue Blake, aren't you?"

I turned to face a guy about sixty years old. Balding and kind of starved-looking, he stood in front of me absolutely naked apart from a yellow jock strap and little leather ankle boots. He had the palest skin I had ever seen with clumps of hair growing from different parts of his body, mostly his ears and nose.

"I love the films that you make . . . I want to star in them."

"Well," I began rather smugly, "It's a tough road into porn and I'm not quite sure if that's a road you should be thinking of traveling. It's long hours and before you can really become a star. . . ."

"Oh, I am a porn star," he interrupted, "I just starred in *Piss Pigs 4* for Treasure Island Media."

"Isn't that a bareback company?" I asked with considerable disdain.

"Yes . . . I think you should have a little more piss and barebacking in your films, and I'm certainly the man to provide those things."

And the night just spiraled downwards from that moment onward, one more bizarre conversation after the other. I learned something that night. There were still plenty of things that could shock me.

The Grabby Awards took place the next night. The show was now held in an enormous auditorium and the evening began with Chi Chi LaRue and two drag queens

CHAPTER FOURTEEN

performing the entire score of *Dream Girls*. First on film, then continuing live on stage. I hadn't been asked to present an award so I just sat back and enjoyed the show. Halfway through the evening they presented their Wall of Fame Awards—the Grabbys' version of the Hall of Fame Award. Chi Chi appeared on the stage.

"Our next recipient was born in England."

Oooooh, an English winner . . . I began craning my neck around the theater looking for possible honorees.

"He started his career as a COLT model."

Oooooh . . . just like me. I must have been lost in thought, because all of a sudden everybody was staring at me. I realized suddenly that Chi Chi was announcing my name as one of the Wall of Fame recipients for that year! I climbed on the stage in a daze and I don't even remember the speech I gave. As I walked offstage I realized I was clutching the award that Chi Chi had presented me with. And guess what? It was STILL a perspex arse . . . and I'm glad it was!!!

I didn't win Best Actor the year Ryan and I were competing against each other, but neither did Ryan. He eventually left *Making Porn* and was replaced by Sonny Markham, a young straight bodybuilder who really was a terrible actor. The show began to suffer and fall apart. Although Ronnie and Caryn had both made great money from the show, Ronnie wanted to move on and work on other projects. He would write a handful of other shows but none of them would be as successful as *Making Porn*. One day when I felt I could no longer stand to do the show, which by now had become a hollow shell of its original incarnation, I told Caryn that I was returning to Los

OUT OF THE BLUE

Angeles. She begged me not to leave but she knew my mind was made up. I wanted to get on with my life with Harold. I was deeply in love. Harold had flown in every other weekend for months and had been nothing but supportive and a tower of strength amidst all the craziness that had surrounded me. I had gotten into the industry to make money, and as this no longer was an issue, at Harold's suggestion I agreed to retire from the porn industry. I was famous, and I could have carried on performing for years, but my heart was no longer in it. So I figured it was good to go out on top.

Caryn asked me as one last favor, to fly to Washington and join the D.C. road company. I didn't want to, but I acquiesced for two reasons: I had never been to Washington so the idea of living there for three weeks appealed to me immensely, and I also wanted to leave the show on good terms in case I ever wanted to come back.

What Caryn had neglected to tell me was that the reason David Thompson had left the play was that Ronnie had flown into D.C., seen the appalling state of the show and had promptly fired the entire cast. Then, realizing that there were no understudies to fill the roles, he demanded that the cast perform for the rest of the run. David told Ronnie to stuff it and caught the next plane to Los Angeles. This left a hole in the show—my part incidentally—and so I stepped into my old role and joined the disgruntled cast.

Playing the ingénue role of Ricky was Kurt Young. Kurt was David's boyfriend and had won more porn awards than any performer in history. He would later break up with David and go on to date the mayor of West

CHAPTER FOURTEEN

Hollywood. But for now he was a shy, slim kid clutching a Chihuahua—his and David's love child I presumed. The show was indeed an absolute wreck, full of barely adequate actors of the extremely mediocre variety. Bad word of mouth was destroying the sold-out D.C. show, but I had no intention of performing in a lousy production. I called together the actors for extra rehearsals and began to piece together the play until it resembled the Off Broadway version. We pumped up the humor and threw out all the lugubrious parts. After a week we were zooming along and everybody was much happier.

We performed the show in an old church that had been converted into a theatre in the middle of the gay district, Dupont Circle, affectionately known as "The Fruit Loop" or "Bouffant Circle." We sold out every night, and once the cast had relaxed into the now hilarious show we tore the town up. Every night we went dancing and drinking and hung out with sexually ambiguous politicians.

At the end of three weeks I was sad to leave D.C. but happy to be returning to my life in Los Angeles with Harold. I had been gone for six months and despite the trials and tribulations of living apart, Harold and I had weathered it all and in fact became closer because of it. Once home, I moved in with Harold. I figured there was no point in running from my destiny.

That year the Gayvn Awards nominated me for my lead role in *Men in Blue* as well as for Best Screenplay. Although I didn't win—the award went to Vince Rockland for his role in *Three Brothers* in which he had co-starred with his two real life brothers Shane and Hal Rockland—I didn't mind. Considering the thousands of performances given each year, it was an honor, as they say, just to be nominated. The show was much more upscale now, with even a bad three course dinner served to the audience. All the studios now bought tables and everybody schmoozed and hugged and kissed and secretly longed for their names to be called so they could climb on the stage and collect an award for having the biggest hole, or slurping more cum or . . . hold on . . . "Bitter, table for one."

    The day after the awards, Gino called and told me he had a surprise for me . . . what? That I hadn't been beaten out of two awards for a film that I had written and starred in for him? I loved Vince Rockland. He was attractive and had a huge cock, but I always thought his eyes were too wide apart, and for some reason they always gave his face the appearance of a mountain goat. There was something almost devilish about his face. However, he had a tremendous body and was super friendly. So how had a goat-faced, brother-fucking model beat me for best actor considering he couldn't act? I knew this for a fact because he had appeared in the play *Making Porn* in Canada with my girlfriend Jennifer whom I had met starring in *Making Porn* in Boston. She said Vince wandered listlessly around the stage searching not only for his lines but his character. But why should Vince Rockland make a great stage actor? He was a porn star and, like most porn stars, Vince just couldn't grasp the technicalities of being on stage in a play. I am always astonished when producers cast porn stars in mainstream projects and then complain they can't act. If half of the actors in Hollywood can't get under a proscenium

CHAPTER FOURTEEN

arch and successfully play Montague, why the hell should a porn star be expected to? Porn stars, unless they have had training, belong as delightful trifles in salacious romps. Everybody likes to see their favorite porn star live and in the flesh but nobody wants to be sitting squirming in the audience while he searches for his next line. It's cringe inducing.

One year Jeff Stryker took his one-man show to Provincetown for the summer. Provincetown is a famously gay haunt in the warm summer months, but Jeff's show sold out not just to gay people, but straight people too. I had seen the show in Los Angeles and although Jeff had struggled with the concept a little, it hadn't really mattered because at the end of the show he got naked, came down into the audience and let them all feel his cock . . . and that's what three quarters of the audience were there for in the first place. Jeff Stryker has true star quality that emanates from every pore of his being.

A few years after Vince Rockland beat me for the Best Actor award at the Gayvn Awards he went to live in a commune in India. While out buying a spicy chicken vindaloo from a street-side vendor, he was run over by a cart carrying piles of brightly colored saris. It broke both his legs. I heard the cart was being pulled by a wild herd of Peruvian mountain goats. I felt so terrible I made a huge donation that year to the "Homeless Goat Foundation of America." (The address can be found in the back of this book.)

I was excited to hear Gino had a surprise for me, but what on earth could it be? Gino picked me up with a big grin on his Italian face.

OUT OF THE BLUE

"Where are we going?" I asked eagerly.

I'm taking you to lunch with one of the biggest distribution companies in the world . . . Cal Vista . . . . They loved *Men in Blue* . . . when you finally decide to produce and direct your own line of films this is who will take you on."

Cal Vista was an enormous distribution company, and in those days without great distribution you were screwed. You could produce the greatest films on the planet, but if they never make it into stores what good are they? At one time all the major studios had distributors; then some broke away and started handling their own distribution. You not only need a good domestic distributor, but you also need good foreign distribution. Cal Vista was a major player second only to Paladin.

Although Italian, Gino was like a Jewish father who believed he had an incredibly talented son. He was always trying to get me to start up my own line of movies. He believed I was incredibly creative and that I would make a great producer and director and that this is where my future lay. But I just wasn't interested. It was his passion, not mine. Although I was incredibly flattered, I knew I would make a total disaster of such a venture because I don't have an organizational bone in my body. I must have been dropped on my head as a baby and that part of my brain was wiped clean or I was just born without that organizational gene. He persisted in pushing me to get behind the camera but I thought he was mad. As it turned out, he wasn't mad at all. In fact, he was actually better at predicting the future than Madame Lila and her all-seeing crystal ball.

We sailed off in his car over Laurel Canyon into the

CHAPTER FOURTEEN

San Fernando Valley where all the major porn studios were based and arrived outside an enormous building with the words CAL VISTA ENTERTAINMENT spelled out elegantly in ten-foot letters. It all reeked of class and wealth. Gino had told me on our drive over that the company was owned by the famous pornographer Sidney Niekerk. Sidney was old school. He had been in the business forever and his word was his bond. We walked into the reception area and were immediately ushered into Sidney's private sanctum, an opulent office full of trophies he had won all over the world for his contributions to the adult industry. The awards were mingled among what looked like the finest pieces of objets d'art money could buy. Sidney himself was a robust handsome grey-haired man of indeterminate age. He had eyes that twinkled and I immediately liked him enormously.

"Bluuuuuuuuuuuuuuuuue," he bellowed in a strong European accent. "Wooooooooonderful to meet you." He had one of the biggest grins I had ever seen. "Dani loves your films," he continued.

"Dani Duran runs foreign sales," Gino replied to the confused look on my face.

"Dani's joining us for lunch."

I was glad Dani liked the films. At least that way he could sell them with conviction. Dani was probably an older gay jock type who likes bodybuilders, I thought. The door opened.

"Here's Dani now," Sidney said.

I turned and nearly fell out of my chair . . . Dani Duran was a SHE—and one of the hottest blond vixens on the planet! She reminded me of Ann-Margret in *Kitten with a*

OUT OF THE BLUE

Whip and I was tore up from the floor up. She was a bombshell. There are just some women who can totally work it, and Dani Duran was one of those chicks. I fell in love with her instantaneously.

"BLUE BLAAAAAAAAAKE!" she purred. Dani had a sexy, husky voice, a cross between Demi Moore and a bottle of scotch. One day I will go into therapy to see what it is about hot blonde straight girls and myself. Thank God I wasn't straight because the planet would be littered with little Blue Blakes demanding expensive toys.

We all climbed into Sidney's chauffeured town car and zipped off to lunch together. I was squeezed next to Dani, and I couldn't help noticing her small waist and her ample bosom. As if those attributes weren't enough, her long blonde hair fell almost down to her waist. We arrived at an Italian restaurant that was closed but when Sidney's car pulled up, the doors were flung open and we were escorted inside. No one else was in the entire place.

The waiters ran around as Sidney ordered dish after dish of the best tasting Italian cuisine.

Helping himself to a dish of linguine, Sidney said to Dani,

"I told Blue that you loved his films."

"I looooove them," cooed Dani, "Especially *Men in Blue*."

"Thank you," I blushed.

"Gino told me you wrote it," she said.

"Yeah . . . its true."

"Well, I'm sure Gino told you it has sold really, really well."

"I was telling Blue that if ever he starts up his own

CHAPTER FOURTEEN

company he has to come to you for distribution," said Gino.

"OOOOOOOOOOOH definitely!" exclaimed Dani, "I would LOVE to distribute your films for you!"

"Well, that's very kind of you," I replied modestly, "But as I keep telling Gino, I'm happy working for other companies but I definitely won't be opening my own studio . . . definitely not."

A year later I opened my own studio Big Blue Productions and I signed with Dani and Cal Vista International for my foreign distribution. When Dani opened up a domestic distribution company, Arena, I immediately signed with them too. In 2003, Arena presented me with their Producer of the Year Award. I was incredibly honored. Dani is to this day one of my closest friends and confidantes. She is a great inspiration and advisor to me, steering me through the storm-tossed waters of porn when I thought I would sometimes lose my mind. To this day Arena and Paladin distribute my entire line of films, and it honors me that they do so.

There had been no closure in my relationship with Caryn Horwitz, but that was all about to change. One day I got a call from Caryn. I hadn't seen her in a few years but she had an interesting business proposition for me. She asked me if I would like to once again star in *Making Porn* but this time co-produce the show with her. I had heard through the grapevine that Ronnie and she were running out of money, so I knew they needed my financial input to get the play up and running again. I was ready to get back into the show, and the idea of producing a play really appealed to me. I agreed with two provisos:

OUT OF THE BLUE

[1] I got to cast the role of the major porn star and [2] If I found a suitable star, Caryn could not produce the show without me using that star.

Caryn told me this sounded very reasonable. Although both Ronnie and Caryn were hardly reliable business people, I knew Caryn wouldn't fuck me over. I was a naïve, trusting soul.

Shortly after Caryn's call, I flew to New Orleans for Southern Decadence, an almost pagan ritual that occurs during the height of summer, when the French Quarter is full of gay people and drag queens celebrating . . . well, I suppose celebrating being gay. I was staying at the Four Seasons Hotel when I heard my ex-boyfriend Chris Duffy was also in town. I hadn't seen Chris in years. Not since I had fled San Francisco without so much as a proper goodbye. I had even thought he might be dead from the copious amounts of drugs he took. Turns out he was very much alive. He was in town with a client of his, a plastic surgeon from the Deep South.

I tracked him down and arranged for the three of us to meet at a local gay restaurant. Chris was as crazy as ever, only now that I wasn't dating him, the madness seemed almost endearing. He told me that he was meeting up with Jake Gianelli, a famous escort, and Jake's new boyfriend Matthew Rush, a Falcon lifetime exclusive model who by then was probably the most famous porn star out there. It seemed almost serendipitous that Matthew was in New Orleans and I figured judging by how he looked he would be ideal for the role of Jack in *Making Porn*.

The next day Chris and I met with Jake and Matthew at their hotel. I had bumped into Matthew over the years

CHAPTER FOURTEEN

at various award shows and liked him immensely. I didn't know if he could act, but I knew he had to be better than Rex Chandler or Vince Rockland. Caryn wouldn't care because Matthew looked great and would be an enormous draw. He happily agreed to star in the show, and I told him we would be opening in San Diego at the St. Cecilia's Playhouse. The show would be running for five weeks beginning right after Christmas.

Matthew, it turned out, was great in the role and we took the show to Boston. It turned a tidy profit. I suggested to Caryn we should open the show in Fort Lauderdale, which had replaced Miami as the gay Mecca of the South. Caryn agreed and we began to pack. That's when the bomb dropped. Caryn told me she no longer needed me as co-producer. Furthermore, she asked me to perform in the show for half my previous salary. And, in order to cut back on the costs of the play further, I was to share a hotel room with Matthew. Having co-produced the play in two cities, I knew how much the show was making, and I knew she was just trying to elbow me out of the production. I had no contract with Caryn as I felt for whatever reason I could trust her. We had developed a wary friendship over the years the way that two people do who are bound together from moments of extreme drama and adversity. I chose instead to gracefully leave *Making Porn*, never to return. Everybody who had told me that Caryn would ultimately fuck me over had been right. It was a harsh lesson in the ways of the world and how some people value money over friendship.

Years later I sometimes think of Caryn and even miss her in a strange way—especially her exposed décolletage that was always stuffed with the remains of calorie-laden snacks.

The hours spent with the play were some of the happiest times of my life. I think perhaps I still miss the camaraderie. If nothing else, I took from the experience three great friendships: Joanna Keylock, my beautiful, beautiful mermaid; Jennifer Leach whom I would have married if I had been straight and if she would have had me; and wonderful Keith who played the role of my best friend in the show and quickly became one of my best friends in real life. Just the blessing of these three make up for all the screaming, crying and drama that went on performing in that damn show. Sometimes out of madness comes great joy.

I stayed true to my word and never performed in a gay porno movie again. There's nothing worse than porn stars who retire then announce their comeback a few months later. I was satisfied with my body of work in a profession that I had never intended upon making my own. I can look back at my time spent being a "porn star" with humor and fascination that my life ever went down that road.

A life in porn had been good to me. Unlike so many of my peers, I emerged pretty much unscathed. I met some of the most unusual, interesting people who helped shape my views on life and sexuality. I made friends for life with some, and discarded others because of the insanity they surrounded themselves with. Would I recommend a life in porn to anybody? Nope. Would I recommend it to a not bad looking guy from Nottingham who was born in a house without a toilet?

ABSO-FUCKING-LUTELY.

EPILOGUE

IN 2005 BLUE BLAKE was inducted into the Gayvn "Porn Legend" Hall of Fame.